P h i

philosophy
in focus

Gerald Jones
Daniel Cardinal
Jeremy Hayward

Academic consultant
Michael Hand

D0495488

Authors

Gerald Jones is Head of Humanities at the Mary Ward Centre, London; **Daniel Cardinal** is Head of Philosophy at Orpington College; **Jeremy Hayward** is Programme Manager of the Citizenship PGCE at the Institute of Education.

The academic consultant Michael Hand is a lecturer at the Institute of Education, University of London, and writes on a range of topics in philosophy of education and philosophy of religion.

Photos

Cover Marc Chagall, *The Memorial East Window, All Saints Church, Kent,* 1963 (detail) © ADAGP, Paris and DACS, London 2004 (photo: John Townson/ Creation); **p.198** *Calvin and Hobbes* © Watterson. Reprinted with permission of Universal Press Syndicate. All rights reserved. Published in *The Essential Calvin and Hobbes* by Bill Watterson, 1995, Time Warner (ISBN 0 751 51274 5).

For Helly and Anya

Although every effort has been made to ensure that website addresses are correct at time of going to press, Hodder Education cannot be held responsible for the content of any website mentioned in this book.

Orders: please contact Bookpoint Ltd, 130 Milton Park, Abingdon, Oxon OX14 4SB. Telephone: +44 (0)1235 827720. Fax: +44 (0)1235 400454. Lines are open from 9.00a.m. to 5.00p.m., Monday to Saturday, with a 24-hour message answering service. You can also visit our websites www.hoddereducation.co.uk and www.hoddersamplepages.co.uk

First published in 2005
by Hodder Education
an Hachette UK company
338 Euston Road
London NW1 3BH

Impression 8

Year 2014

Typeset in 11/13pt Galliard by Dorchester Typesetting Group Ltd, Dorchester, Dorset
Artwork by Tony Jones/Art Construction, Tony Randell
Cover design by John Townson/Creation
Printed and bound by CPI Group (UK) Ltd, Croydon CR0 4YY

A CIP catalogue record for this book is available from the British Library.

ISBN: 978 0 7195 7968 4

Contents

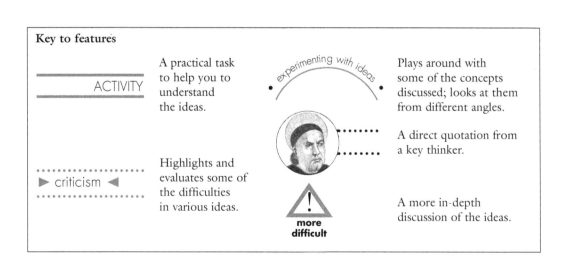

Key to features

ACTIVITY — A practical task to help you to understand the ideas.

▶ criticism ◀ — Highlights and evaluates some of the difficulties in various ideas.

experimenting with ideas — Plays around with some of the concepts discussed; looks at them from different angles.

A direct quotation from a key thinker.

more difficult — A more in-depth discussion of the ideas.

The series

This series is for students who are beginning to study philosophy. The books fill the middle ground between introductory texts, which do not always provide enough detail to help students with their essays and examinations, and more advanced academic texts, which are often too complex for students new to philosophy to understand.

All of the study guides are written around the themes and texts for the AQA AS Level philosophy specification; this book is also suitable for students studying AS and A Level Religious Studies (see page 17). In addition to the *Philosophy of Religion* there are five other guides:

- Plato's *Republic*
- Descartes' *Meditations*
- Sartre's *Existentialism and Humanism*
- *Epistemology: the Theory of Knowledge*
- *Moral Philosophy*.

The authors have substantial experience of teaching philosophy at A Level. They are also committed to making philosophy as accessible and engaging as possible. The study guides contain exercises to help students to grasp in a meaningful way the philosophical theories and ideas that they will face.

Feedback and comments on these study guides would be welcome.

Words in SMALL CAPITALS are explained in the Glossary on page 221.

1

God and philosophy

Introduction

He hadn't been gone two minutes when there was an explosion in the street . . . I knew that he was at the front of the house when the bomb fell. I went down the stairs . . . I didn't see Maurice at first, and then I saw his arm coming out from under a door . . . Maurice was dead. Extinct . . . He would never have the chance to be happy again . . . I knelt and put my head on the bed and wished I could believe. Dear God, I said . . . make me believe. I can't believe. Make me . . . Make me believe. I shut my eyes tight, and I pressed my nails into the palms of my hand until I could feel nothing but the pain, and I said, I will believe. Let him be alive, and I will believe. Give him a chance . . . Do this and I'll believe. But that wasn't enough. It doesn't hurt to believe. So I said, I love him . . . I'll give him up for ever, only let him be alive with a chance, and I pressed and pressed and I could feel the skin break and I said, People can love without seeing each other, can't they, they love You all their lives without seeing You, and then he came in at the door, and he was alive, and I thought now the agony of being without him starts, and I wished he was safely back dead again under the door.[1]

Graham Greene

ACTIVITY   In the extract from Graham Greene's novel *The End of the Affair*, Sarah Miles sees her lover, Maurice, apparently killed in a bomb-blast, and in despair she turns to God. Although she doesn't believe in God, she prays for a miracle, the resurrection of Maurice. In return for this miracle she offers a sacrifice: if God gives Maurice his life back then she will give up her relationship with him and will devote herself to God. The miracle appears to take place, Sarah cuts off all contact with her lover and starts to believe in God.

1 What reasons do you think Sarah has for believing in God?
2 Do you think these are good reasons?
3 What are the main reasons people around the world have for believing in God?
4 Do you think these are good reasons?
5 List all the things that would have to happen for you to believe in God.
6 What would be the strongest reason for believing in God?

Why do people believe in God? Is it because of some intense mystical experience, like the one Sarah Miles has? Is it through some more tangible presence, such as a voice in the night, or a vision or visitation? In the absence of a personal encounter with God, many people have found evidence of God's existence through hints and clues in the world around them. Or perhaps people can become believers through a sheer act of will, by deciding that it's best to believe in God. Over the centuries possibly the most common reason for belief in God has been people's trust in the authority of the Church: the Church teaches that God exists, so God must exist. Worryingly this tends to discourage personal investigation and reflection on belief; as Dostoyevsky commented, the Church is now founded 'on miracle, mystery and authority . . . And men rejoice at being led like cattle'.[2]

Philosophers tend to dislike being led like cattle towards a particular belief. They are curious meddlers, poking their noses into all aspects of human life, and trying to find out for themselves what they should or shouldn't believe. What particularly excites philosophers is investigating the beliefs that people have about the world, and the way we think we ought to live. Because religion deals with both these issues it is no surprise that philosophers have had much to say about religion over the past 2,000 years. A rich body of philosophical work has built up in Western philosophy around the religious traditions of Europe and the Middle East. This 'philosophy of religion' has dealt with questions like: Who is God? Can his existence be proved? How can God let innocent people suffer so much pain? What place does faith have in our belief in God? Can we even meaningfully talk about God?

In this book we look at all these questions and more. A summary of the topics we cover can be found below on page 17. In this chapter we begin by looking at the relationship between philosophy and religious belief, and then at what philosophers have had to say about the nature of God, about who God is.

Philosophy and religious belief

1 For each of the following beliefs, decide which are reasonable to believe, and which are unreasonable to believe.
   a) Many allergies are caused by dust mites.
   b) Unicorns have one horn.
   c) I've seen the Houses of Parliament.
   d) History tends to repeat itself.
   e) The Eiffel Tower is in Paris.
   f) Lobsters dislike being boiled.

g) Every time you deny the existence of fairies one dies.
h) $E = mc^2$
i) D-Day was an important event in 1945.
j) There are nine planets in the solar system.
k) Brazil scores at least one goal in every soccer match.
l) If Napoleon had played for Brazil he would not have headed many goals.
m) Looking into the sun makes you sneeze.
n) Ghosts can pass through walls.

2 For those that you think are reasonable beliefs, what makes them reasonable? Try to place them into one of the following categories, according to how you came to believe it: through common knowledge; personal experience; testimony or authority; true by definition.

Is philosophy a threat to religion?

In relation to religious truth, philosophy is ambiguous. It is at once a menace and an ally.[3]

Ninian Smart

When you ask yourself *why* you believe this or that truth or what *reasons* you have for believing it, then you'll probably find that the answers fall into one of the categories given in the activity above. You may believe something because it is common knowledge, or because someone told you, perhaps because you have experienced it yourself or because it is obviously true by definition. However, philosophers question our common sense assumptions and beliefs. Rather than simply accept what is common knowledge, what someone told us, or what our own experience suggests, or even what appears self-evidently true, philosophers will ask whether any of these grounds is ultimately secure. If we can come to question and doubt the reasons for believing what we do, does this mean we need to give up our beliefs? While in our philosophical moods we may often think so, but in ordinary life it is surprisingly hard to give up the familiar beliefs that govern the way we live. Our system of beliefs forms a cosy nest within which we are comfortable and which we are reluctant to leave. We tend to cling obstinately to our beliefs in the face of sceptical questioning.

Nevertheless, philosophy poses a serious threat to a whole range of our beliefs, including, of course, religious beliefs, and if we are to take such beliefs seriously we do need to meet the challenge posed by sceptical philosophers. Religious beliefs are often based on authority, or on certain feelings about the world that can't quite be put into words. Under the scrutiny of philosophers, the authority of the Church, or of charismatic leaders, or of scripture, all appear shaky grounds for belief. Basing religious belief on intense and mystical personal experiences fares no better in philosophy: after all why should we trust one-off, unrepeatable experiences to be good guides to truth? Philosophy, then, is a menace to religion where, through critical investigation, it questions the foundations of religious belief.

If we submit everything to reason our religion will be left with nothing mysterious or supernatural. If we offend the principles of reason our religion will be absurd and ridiculous.[4]

Pascal

Philosophy is also a menace because it competes with religion in our search for answers to those ultimate questions that humans ask about the universe: Why are we here? How should we live? What is the meaning of life? What happens to us when we die? Philosophers from Plato onwards have sought to answer these questions with thorough, coherent, satisfying and reasoned theories that need no reference to religion or to God. So St Paul writes to the Colossians warning them that they should not be misled by the useless teachings of the Ancient Greeks. To the evangelical Paul the philosophers have got it wrong, and their theories can only distract us from the truths of religious teachings about God and the world.

Take care that no one leads you astray by philosophy and useless misleading teaching.

Colossians 2:8

At the same time, however, theologians have from the beginning of Christianity used philosophy as an ally to support religious belief. Philosophy can be used as a tool to explore religious belief, to investigate the nature of God, to unravel some of the mysteries of scripture, and to arrive at a deeper understanding of faith. Even those who are most opposed to philosophy would admit that there are *reasons* for believing in God, and where there are reasons there is the potential for philosophy. Even St Paul acknowledged that philosophy could offer some insight into the nature of God and the universe, when he addressed a group of Athenian philosophers:

It is in [God] that we live and move and have our being, as some of your own writers have said.

Acts 17:28

The opening section of John's gospel, in the New Testament of the Bible, also owes a debt to Greek philosophy. 'In the beginning was the Word [*logos*], and the Word was with God, and the Word was God.' (John 1:1) John deliberately uses the concept of *logos*, usually translated in this context as 'word', but which has the broader philosophical meaning of 'rational account' or 'explanatory principle' or 'source of order'. So what John may be saying in these mysterious lines is that God is that which gives rise to and explains the existence of the universe.

Since these beginnings philosophers down the centuries have used philosophy as an ally of their belief. St Augustine drew on the Greek philosopher Plotinus (c. 205–270) in order to throw light onto Christian beliefs, and St Thomas Aquinas made it his life's work to show how the theories of the pagan philosopher Aristotle could be reconciled with, and enrich, Christian teachings. There have been periodic reactions against the presence of philosophy in religious thinking, and there is generally a grass-roots animosity towards philosophy for the hostile reasons outlined above, but philosophy has never quite departed from religion. It may be the case that, as Francis Bacon (1561–1626) said, 'a little philosophy makes men atheists; but a great deal reconciles them to religion'.[5] In other words it is only a superficial understanding of philosophy that threatens religion, but a deeper understanding brings philosophers to religion.

So philosophy and religion have a fragile marriage, the former emphasising reason, the latter emphasising faith. But by relying on a combination of these it may be possible for believers to have their philosophical cake and eat it: they can put their trust in reason to prove that God exists, and if this fails then faith can step in and provide an even better (more religious) reason for belief in God. As Ninian Smart says: 'It is as though the Christian were saying: "There are two good grounds for Christian faith – first, that God's existence can be demonstrated rationally, and second that there is no hope whatsoever of demonstrating God's existence rationally." '[6]

The contexts of religious philosophy

Philosophers and theologians sometimes seem to think they have a vantage point that is far removed from the world, and from which they are able to pronounce eternal truths about the world. But we should consider that all the philosophers and theologians who have thought deeply about God did so from within their own specific cultural context and philosophical tradition. In this section we look at some of the ways in which thinkers may be influenced by their context.

Philosophers are influenced by their historical context, by the events of the world they live in. So, for example, Aquinas was influenced by Aristotle in a way that his predecessors were not. It's not that Aquinas' predecessors weren't interested in Aristotle; it's just that there were only a few works by Aristotle in circulation at that time. It was only in the twelfth century that the (mostly violent) interaction of Christian Europe with Islamic Spain and the Middle East led to the translations of Aristotle from Arabic into Latin. Aquinas happened to live in the right place at the right time in order to merge Aristotle's philosophy with Christianity to create a particular, and influential, understanding of the nature of God.

Philosophers are also influenced by the philosophical tradition they are a part of. So, for example, during the nineteenth and twentieth centuries there developed a great divide in the approaches of Continental European and Anglo-American philosophy of religion. This reflects a division in many other areas of philosophy, with French and German THEOLOGIANS focusing on the experience of religion, whilst British philosophers tended to take a more analytical approach, focusing on language and the meanings of key religious terms.

We also need to consider the religious context of philosophers. There were three distinct religious cousins that grew out of the Eastern Mediterranean and came to dominate Western THEOLOGY: Judaism, Christianity and Islam. Each of these religions shares some core beliefs about the nature of God; they are all THEISTIC religions believing that God is the supremely powerful creator of the universe, who has a personal relationship with humans. But there are enough differences between these religions to prevent us from lumping all religious philosophers together. Christian (e.g. St Anselm), Jewish (e.g. Maimonides) and Islamic (e.g. Avicenna and Al-Ghazali) philosophers have all been influenced by their respective religions. Moreover, even within these religions we should note that there are different sects and branches, for example Catholicism and Protestantism within Christianity, and these shape the thoughts of those philosophers brought up within these branches. So we should avoid confusing 'religion' with one particular branch of a religion, or defining it as Thwackum does in *Tom Jones*: 'When I mention religion, I mean the Christian religion; and not only the Christian religion, but the Protestant religion; and not only the Protestant religion, but the Church of England.'[7]

However, this particular book focuses on the work that Western philosophers have done within the context of Christianity: either for or against it. There are equally rich traditions of Jewish and Islamic philosophies, but we feel that they are distinct enough to deserve their own textbooks, and that conflating them within a single book would not be appropriate and would not do justice to them. Consequently when we talk about 'philosophers' in this book we are primarily referring to philosophers brought up within a Christian tradition (even if they reject that tradition); when we talk about 'believers' we are referring to those who believe in a Christian God; and when we talk about God we are talking about God as defined by Christianity, which means referring, when necessary, to God as 'he'.

Finally we should note that the religious context is not just determined by the teachings of a particular sacred text. Religions such as Christianity are based in part on these texts, but also in part on the teachings of those who have interpreted the texts. For example, the early Christian Church was structured by the 'Church Fathers': individuals like St Augustine, St Ambrose and St Jerome, who interpreted the Bible and developed a unity in Christian thinking. Various Church Councils (such as the Council of Nicea in AD 325) also hammered out differences so far as they could, deciding which were orthodox and permitted beliefs, and which were heretical. The set of beliefs that a medieval Christian was 'signing up to' was known as the creed, and the Nicene Creed, for example, stated that Jesus was of the same substance as God. This religious tradition and creed, which were additions to the Bible, in turn determined and limited the types of philosophical questions that medieval scholars asked about their religion.[8] But the tradition and creed also gave Protestant thinkers in the seventeenth century, with their new 'back to basics' approach, something to react against and reject.

Investigating the nature of God

Many debates in the philosophy of religion revolve around proving the existence of God, and we have chosen to look at these in Chapter 2. But before trying to prove *that* something exists it seems sensible to know *what* it is that you are trying to prove. After all, if you don't know what you're looking for then how will you know when you've found it? As David Hume puts it: 'The question is not concerning the *being* but the *nature* of God.'[9]

Understanding the nature of the thing you're looking for can also help you determine the best method for finding it. For example, if you want to find a Heffalump, and thus prove their existence, then knowing where Heffalumps hang out, what their probable movements are and what sorts of things they enjoy doing should make catching one easier. Similarly it seems that a useful starting point for anyone wishing to prove the existence of God would be first to establish what sort of thing God is, what characteristics God has, in other words what God's nature is.

For each of the following determine what would be the best method of working out whether such a thing existed. The first one has been completed as a guide for you.

Things to be proved	Method of discovery
Life on Mars	Define life as DNA. Send robot to Mars, collect samples and analyse for signs of DNA.
The invisible rabbit that only your little sister can see	
The ghosts of Hampton Court	
A living dinosaur in Loch Ness	
A tenth planet circling the sun	
Elvis Presley	
God	

Two approaches: Revealed theology and natural theology

A promising place to start our investigation into the nature of God is the sacred texts on which religions are based, for example the Torah, the Bible or the Qur'an. These books record the foundations of the religion through the REVELATIONS of certain individuals. These individuals, it is claimed, had some direct or indirect contact with God, and may be best positioned to reveal something of God's nature. However, it could be argued that, as philosophers, we should be sceptical of religious texts because they tend to assume that the revelations they record are genuine and that their interpretation of God is the only true one. Yet it is precisely these assumptions that we are trying to investigate.

An alternative starting point for our investigation into the nature of God would be to look around us at the universe he is said to have created. By analysing the various features of this universe (the types of things that exist, the laws that govern it, human behaviour, etc.) we might hope to establish what God must be like. If we start here we might at least avoid the charge of bias when we make our first report on the nature of God, since we wouldn't be looking at the text of any particular religion.

Religious philosophers and theologians have taken both these approaches: the first is called REVEALED THEOLOGY, because it trusts sacred texts to reveal religious truths and an understanding of God; the second approach is called NATURAL THEOLOGY, because it stresses the possibility of understanding God via human reason and observation alone. Throughout this book we encounter a tension between these two methods or approaches: the first stresses faith (which we examine in Chapter 4), the second stresses reason (which we assess in Chapter 2). As potential philosophers we are naturally drawn to reason, but as potential believers we cannot put aside faith, and the goal of many religious philosophers down the ages has been to resolve the tension between these two.

There is a third approach that involves finding out what God is *not* in order to understand what God is. This is attractive to those who take the view that God is so mysterious, so different from us and from anything we can experience, that we can't begin to imagine what he is like. The medieval Jewish philosopher Maimonides (c. 1135–1204) suggests that the only route to knowledge of God is this 'negative path', or VIA NEGATIVA.[10] So, for example, we can only know the simplicity of God by knowing what it means *not* to be simple: to be divisible, or changeable, or complex in the way that everything we see around us is complex. St Thomas Aquinas had some sympathy for this approach[11] and we touch on this further in Chapter 5 when we look at how it is possible to apply specific attributes meaningfully to a being as mysterious as God.

Most religious philosophers have not been content to let God's nature remain a mystery. They have attempted to draw out some of the features that God must have if he is to be the creator of the world around us and if he is to be the source of the revelations of the sacred texts. So let us now look at what philosophers have to say about the nature of God.

1 Write down as many words that you can think of associated with the idea of 'God'.
2 Now see whether you can place them into groups of related concepts. What labels would you give to these groups or categories?

Revealed theology: The God of Abraham, Isaac and Jacob

I am . . . the God of Abraham, the God of Isaac and the God of Jacob.

Exodus 3:6

Have you not read in the book of Moses . . . how God said to him 'I am the God of Abraham, and the God of Isaac, and the God of Jacob'? He is not God of the dead, but of the living.

Mark 12:26

God of Abraham, God of Isaac, God of Jacob, not the God of the philosophers and scholars.

Pascal, unpublished note

In a note found after his death, the seventeenth-century mathematician and writer Blaise Pascal distinguishes between 'the God of the philosophers' and the God as revealed in the Bible. The implication of Pascal's words is that if we seek to know and experience God then we should turn to the Bible, and not to those religious philosophers who go far beyond the Bible in their quest to understand God. We shall see in the pages that follow how different the 'God of the philosophers' is from the 'God of Abraham'; and a question that believers might need to ask is 'is the God of the philosophers the God whom I actually worship?' Pascal thought not, but plenty of other philosophers have disagreed. In the rest of the book we focus almost exclusively on the words and thoughts of philosophers on God. However, in this section we shall abide by Pascal and see what we can glean about the nature of God from the Bible.

The God of the Bible is a God whose character varies in its description according to the changing fortunes of his people. Various periods can be found within the Bible, and the personality and attributes of God develop over these periods. The pre-prophetic period (before 900 BC) was a time of optimism when Moses and his descendants established their roots in Canaan, and their God was placed above all the many competing gods of the region. During the prophetic period (900–500 BC) prophets such as Isaiah responded to the religious and political threats of their neighbours by describing their God, who is called Yahweh, as the only true God. Finally in the post-exilic period (following the release of the Jews from captivity in 500 BC) the Jewish concept of God was refined further, perhaps influenced by the philosophical beliefs of the Persian and Greek occupiers of Canaan. What remains fundamental throughout these different periods is that the God of the Bible is the object of worship, and is the only being worthy of worship. Below are some of the main characteristics of God that emerge from the descriptions of him given in the Bible.

The only God

For much of the opening books of the Bible, Yaweh is thought of only as the God of Israel, with other nations and tribes having their own gods. The first commandment states: 'You shall have no other gods besides me' (Exodus 20:3) but it does *not* say 'I am the only God.' It is several hundred years later (around the prophetic period in the eighth century BC) that the existence of other gods is ruled out altogether: 'I am the Lord and there is none else. Besides me there is no God' (Isaiah 45:5). By the time of the New Testament, God has become universal. Now he is the only god, and one to be worshipped by all people, not just by the people of Israel.

The creator

God is described throughout the Bible as the creator. The opening lines are 'In the beginning God created the heavens and the earth' (Genesis 1:1). This is reiterated in the opening verses of the last gospel: 'All things were made through him' (John 1:3). As the creator, in the Old Testament God is described as intervening in the world regularly: for example, he walked with Adam (Genesis 3:8); he caused the sun to stand still to help Joshua win a battle (Joshua 10:13); he created floods (Genesis 6:13) and destroyed cities (Genesis 19:24) when he was displeased with his creation. However, God becomes increasingly absent from his creation, and many Psalms are laments about this absence and pleas for God to reveal himself (e.g. Psalm 102). An interesting consequence of God being the creator of the universe – and hence of space and time – is that God seems to have to be outside of space and time. This is the kind of corollary (logical consequence) that philosophers have fun drawing out, and we shall see more of these below.

A personal God

'God created man in his own image' (Genesis 1:27). The God of the Old Testament is full of emotion and action that is recognisably human. He has his favourites, the Hebrews, and he encourages them to wage war against the other tribes of Canaan; for example, Moses calls God 'a man of war' (Exodus 15:3). Although his military disposition fades through the Old Testament other personal qualities remain, but these are guided by his righteousness rather than his favouritism for Israel (see the book of Amos). God is vengeful; he is jealous; he is a law-maker who watches over and protects all people so long as they are faithful to him and his laws; he is a judge who punishes those who break his laws; but he is also 'merciful and gracious, slow to anger and abounding in steadfast love' (Psalms 103:8). God's positive and compassionate qualities are emphasised in the New Testament, with God portrayed more often as a father or a shepherd than a law-maker and judge. It is only at the very end of the Bible, in the letters of John, that we find all God's attributes summed up by the single word: 'love' (1 John 4:16ff).

A holy God

The term HOLY captures all that is felt about the special nature of God and his relationship with humans. It is used throughout the Old and New Testaments, it is what sets God apart from everything else and it indicates God's uniqueness not just as a creator or as a supreme power, but as a being who should be worshipped (and feared): 'Be holy, for I am holy' (Leviticus 11:44); 'Holy, holy, holy is Yahweh' (Isaiah 6:3); 'The Lord of hosts you shall regard as holy, let him be your fear, let him be your dread' (Isaiah 8:13). God's holiness is bound up with his spiritual and moral perfection (Isaiah 5:16), and to believers it thus has the power to overcome their sins. The effect of God's holiness on those who experience it is analysed in some detail by Rudolf Otto in his article 'The Numinous'.[12] Otto invented the word NUMINOUS to describe the 'shudder' of awe and dread that people feel when they encounter God (see page 87).

The God as described above will be familiar to many believers. However, these features of God have not usually taken a central position in the writings of philosophers. Instead philosophers have chosen to focus on certain technical attributes of God, which are perhaps a consequence of his status as a perfect, unique and holy creator. The analysis of these technical characteristics makes up the 'God of the philosophers', in Pascal's term, and it is this God who remains the focus of the rest of this book.

Natural theology: The God of the philosophers

One God, who is the author of this whole universe . . . immaterial . . . incorruptible . . . who is, in fact, our source, our light, our good. [13]

St Augustine

God is that, than which nothing greater can be conceived.[14]

St Anselm

By the word 'God' I mean a substance that is infinite, independent, supremely intelligent, supremely powerful, and the Creator of myself and anything else that may exist.[15]

René Descartes

A person without a body, present everywhere, the creator and sustainer of the universe, able to do everything, knowing all things, perfectly good . . . immutable, eternal, a necessary being, and worthy of worship.[16]

Richard Swinburne

Pascal thought that God was infinitely beyond our comprehension, and he wondered who would dare to think they could know what he was or whether he existed.[17] Despite this, philosophers down the centuries have dared to imagine they could tell us something specific about the nature of God, and the quotations above, which span over 1500 years of religious philosophy, are representative of the theistic philosophical tradition. What all these quotes emphasise is God's greatness and perfection. God is the most perfect and greatest of beings and hence he is supremely good, knowing and powerful, he cannot change and is eternal. At the same time he is the source of all other beings: the creator of the universe.

In this section we shall look at four of the main characteristics that philosophers have consistently ascribed to God, many of them stemming from the Bible's claim that God is perfect (Matthew 5:48).

Omnipotent

The God of Abraham was able to do anything; this was the message behind the countless examples in the Bible of what God could and did do: 'He will not grow tired or weary, and his understanding no one can fathom. He gives strength to the weary and increases the power of the weak' (Isaiah 40:28–30); 'With God all things are possible' (Matthew 19:26); 'For with God nothing is impossible' (Luke 1:37). The power of God to do anything was termed OMNIPOTENCE by philosophers (from the Latin *omni* = 'all' and *potens* = 'power') and it takes a central position in God's perfection. There has long been a question mark over the meaning of omnipotence; can God literally do anything?

Some philosophers, such as J.L. Mackie,[18] have been eager to point out the incoherence of the concept of 'omnipotence', and hence the incoherence of the idea of 'God', and we will be examining his argument in Chapter 3. In defence of omnipotence religious philosophers have been prepared to offer limits to God's power. In *Summa Contra*

Gentiles 2:25 Aquinas lists twenty types of things that God can't do, for example he can't do what is logically impossible such as create a married bachelor. Similarly he cannot alter what has already happened; or force us to choose something freely. Many have felt God cannot change the laws of mathematics (he cannot, for example, make $2 + 3$ equal to 6) or act in a way that goes against his fundamental nature (e.g. do something EVIL).

■ Omniscient

By the nature of their profession, philosophers place a high value on knowledge, and we shouldn't be surprised to find that religious philosophers consider perfect knowledge to be an aspect of God's perfection. As with omnipotence, God's OMNISCIENCE (Latin *omni* = 'all', *scientia* = 'knowing') is illustrated in the Bible by examples, rather than stated explicitly. Psalm 139:4 tells us that 'even before a word is on my tongue, O Lord, thou knowest it altogether', although in the first book God's knowledge does not seem to extend so far: 'But the Lord God called to the Man [Adam] and said to him "Where are you"?' (Genesis 3:9). Again, as with omnipotence, philosophers are interested in how far God's omniscience extends. Is God's knowledge only *propositional*, meaning it involves 'knowing that . . . ' something is true, such as knowing that the world will come to an end on 26 May 2010, or that Adam has eaten forbidden fruit? Does it involve having *practical* knowledge of how to do things, such as how to ride a bike or create human beings out of clay? Other questions we might wish to ask are 'does God know what I'm freely about to do?' and 'can God know what it is logically impossible to know, for example the area of a round square?'

■ Benevolent

'O give thanks to the Lord, for he is good, for his steadfast love endures for ever' (Psalm 106:1, and 107, 117, 118, 136, etc.). In the Bible, God's BENEVOLENCE (*bene* = 'good', *volens* = 'will') is recognisable and familiar to humans. It is a goodness full of passion and love, based on righteousness; and it carries the consequence of angry retribution to those who disobey him. The account of God's goodness provided by religious philosophers is more abstract and less personal, and influenced by the two giants of ancient Greek philosophy, Plato and Aristotle. In its widest sense, God's goodness is seen as the source of all goodness, and so according to philosophers like St Augustine God's goodness filters down through all of his creation. In its narrower sense God's goodness refers to God's own moral character, and is exemplified in his love, his justice and his wisdom. Even the writers of the Old Testament recognised that God's benevolence had to be reconciled in some way with the horrific pain and suffering that exists in this world. We shall look at this, the so-called PROBLEM OF EVIL, below on pages 114–132.

Immutable

If something never changes, and cannot change, then it is termed IMMUTABLE. As with the previous three properties, the idea of God's enduring (immutable) nature has its origins in the Bible. 'They will perish, but you will endure; they will all wear out like a garment . . . but you will remain the same and your years will never end' (Psalm 102:26–27); 'For I, the Lord, do not change' (Malachi 3:6). Immutability is more difficult to understand than God's goodness, power or knowledge, because there is nothing analogous to it in our usual understanding of a person. The concept may make more sense when we consider that change only occurs in things that can be divided up into 'parts'. So, for example, people are made up of many different parts both mentally and physically, and these parts change (e.g. through getting older, or through injury). But God does not have any parts either in space (God does not have a body; he is INCORPOREAL) or in time (God does not exist over different periods of time, he is eternal); in other words God is said to be 'simple'. Because God is not made up of parts, and because he is perfect, he cannot change and does not need to change. This also suggests that his attributes cannot be separated from one another. So it's not the case that God is omniscient *and* omnipotent *and* benevolent etc. Instead we should think of these as just different aspects of the same thing, namely God's essential nature (his 'Godness' if you like).

The presumption of atheism

We now have a better idea of the subject at the centre of theistic philosophy: an all-loving, all-knowing, all-powerful God, who is unchanging, eternal, incorporeal, who created the world and who has a personal involvement in his creation.

To many people the existence of such a being is not in question: God created the world and he created us – end of story. However, philosophers, particularly those with sceptical or critical tendencies, do not accept this story's conclusion so easily. Even philosophers who are devout believers, such as Aquinas and Descartes, have felt the need to go beyond what was obvious to them, namely the existence of God, and have tried to demonstrate the truth of their belief.

Antony Flew has recently argued that such demonstrations of God's existence are not an optional extra in the philosophy of religion, but are essential.[19] He claims that it is up to believers to prove that God exists, and that in the absence of any such proof, ATHEISM (belief in God's non-existence) is the only reasonable default position. Flew draws an analogy with the British legal system, whereby we presume the accused person is innocent and it is up to the prosecution to show beyond reasonable doubt that the defendant is guilty. In the same way, Flew argues, atheism should be presumed to be true, with the burden of proof resting with religious believers to demonstrate that there are rational grounds for believing in God. We shall look at some of the most important demonstrations of God's existence in Chapter 2.

experimenting with ideas

An atheist and a believer stand before the Supreme Court of Philosophy. The issue at stake is whether God exists. The atheist insists that he has nothing to prove, that there is no God, and that it's up to the believer to persuade him that there is a God. The ball is in the believer's court. However, the believer says that she has nothing to prove: it's obvious that there is a God, and it's up to the atheist to show that there isn't.

As the Supreme Philosophical Judge you will have to make the decision about where you think the burden of proof lies. Do you think it is up to the atheist to prove there is no God (or at least no God with the attributes outlined above), or up to the believer to prove that there is a God?

At the end of this chapter we are now better positioned to grasp the nature of the God that religious philosophers are trying to prove exists. This puts us in a better position to judge whether such proofs can be successful. Such proofs are clearly a task for natural theology, since in revealed theology knowledge of a supreme being is received directly through revelation. It may well turn out that any proof of God's existence is never going to be conclusive and there will always remain room for doubt, and for faith.

How this book matches AS/A2 Level Exam Specifications

This book was conceived as a general introduction to the main ideas and arguments within the philosophy of religion. However, as a textbook it covers topics within a number of A Level exam specifications, including Religious Studies, as outlined below.

Chapter	Topic	AQA Philosophy	AQA Religious Studies	Edexcel Religious Studies	OCR Religious Studies
Chapter 1 God and philosophy	➤ Philosophy and religious belief	Yes			
	➤ Natural and revealed theology	Yes			
	➤ The God of Abraham	Yes			
	➤ The God of the philosophers	Yes			
Chapter 2 Arguments for the existence of God	➤ The structure of arguments	Yes	Yes	Yes	Yes
	➤ Ontological arguments	Yes	Yes	Yes	Yes
	➤ Cosmological arguments	Yes	Yes	Yes	Yes
	➤ Teleological arguments	Yes	Yes	Yes	Yes
	➤ Arguments from experience	Yes	Yes	Yes	Yes
Chapter 3 The challenges to believing in God	➤ The conception of God	Yes	Yes	Yes	Yes
	➤ The problem of miracles	Yes	Yes	Yes	Yes
	➤ The problem of evil	Yes	Yes	Yes	Yes
	➤ Christian ethics	Yes		Yes	
	➤ Arguments from morality	Yes		Yes	Yes
Chapter 4 Faith and belief in God	➤ Evidentialism and fideism	Yes			
	➤ Faith as acceptance of revealed truths	Yes			
	➤ Faith as a basic belief	Yes			
	➤ Faith as an act of will	Yes			
	➤ Faith as an attitude	Yes			
Chapter 5 Talking about God	➤ The peculiarities of religious language	Yes		Yes	Yes
	➤ Verificationism and falsificationism	Yes		Yes	Yes
	➤ Wittgenstein's theory of meaning	Yes		Yes	Yes
	➤ Myth, symbol and analogy	Yes		Yes	Yes

Key points: Chapter 1

What you need to know about **the philosophical perspective on God**:

1   Philosophy can be both a threat and an ally to religion. Philosophy questions the foundations for our beliefs; it is highly critical of beliefs based on authority or revelation; and philosophers have consistently offered non-religious answers to questions about the meaning of life, about how we should live and what happens when we die. However, philosophy has also been used by believers to investigate and enhance their beliefs, through the construction of proofs for the existence of God, through analysing religious concepts and language, and through responding to the challenges of atheistic philosophers.

2   Philosophy is not done in a vacuum: there is always a historical context to the questions philosophers ask, and the answers they give. Philosophers of religion are also part of a philosophical and religious tradition, and their work is going to be influenced by this tradition.

3   There are two broad approaches that can be taken by believers who wish to investigate their belief in God. The first is revealed theology, which points towards the revelations of religious texts and prophets or mystics as a source of understanding God. The second is natural theology, which uses human reason and observation as a method of understanding God.

4   As given in the Bible, revealed theology tells us that God is the one and only God; is the creator of the universe; is a person who has a close relationship with his creation; is holy, and some people have encountered this holiness through their experience of the numinous.

5   As determined by reason and observation, natural theology tells us that God is: omnipotent, with the power to do anything; omniscient, knowing everything; benevolent, in that goodness is part of his essence; immutable and simple, in that all his perfections are actually one essence, he is unchanging, he is not a part of space or time.

6   The presumption of the atheist, according to Antony Flew, is that belief in God needs to be demonstrated. For Flew the burden of proof rests with the believer in attempting to prove that there is a God.

Arguments for the existence of God

Introduction

We have seen how philosophers have attempted to analyse *who* God is, now we turn to look at their attempts to prove *that* God is. In Woody Allen's short story 'Mr Big', a private detective is hired to find God and his first lead is a religious leader:

'You ever see Him?'
'Me? Are you kidding? I'm lucky I get to see my grandchildren.'
'Then how do you know He exists?'
'How do I know? What kind of question is that? Could I get a suit like this for fourteen dollars if there was no one up there? Here, feel [the cloth] – how can you doubt?'[20]

Careful reasoning in support of a belief or theory is a fundamental part of the tradition of Western philosophy. It is not surprising then that when philosophers turn their attention to religion they often wish to supplement sacred texts and revelation with their own arguments in support of their beliefs. The use of human reason and arguments to determine truths about God is central to natural theology, and Christian philosophers have sought to demonstrate that God exists by a process of reasoning since at least the time of St Augustine (354–430). The Vatican Council of the Catholic Church has declared that God can be known with certainty, and through the natural power of human reason.[21] This declaration was made in part on the basis of a passage in the New Testament which claims that if we attend properly to the nature of the world around us we'll notice that it must have been created by God.

Ever since God created the world, his invisible qualities, both his eternal power and his divine nature, have been clearly seen; they are perceived in the things that God has made.

Romans 1:20

Rational demonstrations of God's existence reached their zenith with the medieval philosopher St Thomas Aquinas, who offered five ways to prove God's existence. During the eighteenth century, proofs of God's existence began to fall from favour with religious thinkers and philosophers alike. David Hume (1711–1776) and Immanuel Kant (1724–1804) are often credited with doing permanent damage to the classical arguments for the existence of God. However, religious philosophers have continued to reason for the existence of God, and the past century has witnessed resurgence in this area.

As we're going to be looking in detail at some arguments for God's existence, it is worth making a few points about arguments in general.

How are arguments structured?

When we talk about arguments we are not referring to a quarrel, or some kind of personal battle of words involving a denial of everything the other person says combined with gentle sarcasm and incisive put-downs. An argument, in the sense we're interested in, consists of one or more statements offered in support of a further concluding statement. The supporting statements, the ones that provide the justification, are referred to as the PREMISES of the argument, and the concluding statement is obviously referred to as the CONCLUSION. If a passage contains the words 'and so', 'therefore' or 'hence' then this is a good indication that a conclusion is being drawn and that an argument has been made to support this conclusion. The premises may need to be combined in order to support the conclusion, or they may support the conclusion individually.

The goal of most arguments is to convince us of the truth of the conclusion, and so to persuade us to believe it. As a conclusion rests on its supporting premises it is essential that every premise in an argument be true. This means that when constructing, or evaluating, arguments we must pay careful attention to each premise. There are various types of premises which can combine to provide grounds to support the conclusion:

- general observations (e.g. 'politicians do whatever it takes to keep themselves in power')
- statements of fact (e.g. 'there were only enough lifeboats on the *Titanic* to save half the passengers')
- theoretical assumptions (e.g. 'every event must have a cause')
- definitions (e.g. 'God is a perfect being')
- hypotheses (e.g. 'if you eat carrots then you'll be able to see in the dark).

It is helpful to make the premises explicit when evaluating or constructing an argument, so that each one can then be weighed up and considered. As arguments usually take the form of densely written prose, you may have to tease out each premise, and many philosophers do this by assigning the premises numbers, and presenting them as a list. We have tried to do this in this chapter with each of the major arguments for God's existence, and it is hoped this will make the arguments easier to understand and evaluate.

As well as paying attention to the truth of each premise, we also need to consider the overall structure of the argument. You might like to think of the list of premises as a sum that 'adds up' to the conclusion. If the premises correctly add up to the conclusion, that is, if by accepting them we are forced to accept the conclusion, then the argument is termed 'valid'. However, as with any human calculation, there is always the chance that mistakes have been made. An invalid argument is one where the premises do not add up to the conclusion, in other words the argument falls short of fully justifying the conclusion. This may be because the argument is flawed or because the argument is an inductive one (see below).

Deductive and inductive arguments

Aquinas

Demonstration [of God's existence] can be made in two ways: One is through the cause, and is called a priori *. . . The other is through the effect, and is called a demonstration* a posteriori.

Summa Theologica 1:2:2

Valid arguments are known as 'deductive' or 'deductively valid'. In a deductive argument the truth of the premises guarantees the truth of the conclusion, so long as no errors have been made. The key word here is 'guarantee'. With a deductive argument (or argument from DEDUCTION), if we accept the premises to be true then we absolutely must accept the conclusion to be true. If, as we've claimed, the goal of an argument is to persuade people to believe its conclusion, then deductive arguments must be a powerful tool: after all, if we can guarantee the truth of a conclusion, we have good reason to believe it. However, this great strength can also appear as a weakness. For deductive arguments can't establish anything new with their conclusions: they simply reveal what is already contained in the premises. For this reason, they don't really get us beyond what we already know. Another weakness is that while we can know that the conclusion must follow *if* the premises are true, we still can't guarantee that the premises actually are true. Knowing that the conclusion has to follow from the premises is all very well, but it simply passes the buck and we still have find a way to establish the truth of the premises. To make clearer the strengths and weakness of such arguments, take the following standard example of a deductively valid argument:

1 All men are mortal.
2 Socrates is a man.
3 (Conclusion) Therefore Socrates is mortal.

Here if we accept the two premises, then the conclusion follows necessarily. The great strength of the argument is that it appears to be impossible to deny the conclusion once we've accepted that the premises are true. We might say that so long as we accept the premises to be true then we can work out the truth of this conclusion in an A PRIORI manner, in other words prior to any further experience or fact-finding, simply by teasing out what is already given in the premises. Everything can be done in our heads. However, this also means that we haven't really learned anything new here. The conclusion, as mentioned, says nothing more than was already contained in the premises. Moreover, while we know that Socrates must be mortal *if* he is a man, and *if* all men are mortal, we have still to find a way of establishing that these other facts are actually true. So deductive arguments appear to leave us with further questions to address, namely how to establish the truth of the premises.

Inductive arguments (arguments from INDUCTION) are often contrasted with deductive ones because they strive to reveal something new in their conclusion. This is one of the strengths of such arguments. However, because this means they have to go beyond the information contained in their premises, they lose the power to guarantee the truth of their conclusions. This means that no inductive argument can be fully valid, and their conclusions are only ever probably true, even if the premises are certainly true. Typically, induction occurs where an argument moves from what is known (e.g. facts about the past, or particular observations) to what is unknown (e.g. speculations about the future, or generalisations). Induction is frequently used in the sciences and social sciences, whenever we move from empirical data to theories about the data. A typical inductive argument might be:

1 Every raven I've ever seen has been black.
2 There are 100 ravens kept at the Tower of London.
3 (Conclusion) Therefore it is likely that all 100 ravens in the Tower are black.

Even if we accept the premises as definitely true, this conclusion doesn't necessarily follow. This is because there might be whole families of London-born albino ravens, which

I don't know about, or it might be that for every 100 black ravens in a population two of them will be albino. Just because I have only ever seen black ravens doesn't establish the likelihood that they are all black. Note that, just as with deductive arguments, we still have to accept the premises as true before the argument can be at all convincing.

Another example of an inductive argument is one where we draw a conclusion from a finite set of instances:

1 John 'Stumpy' Pepys used to play drums for rock 'n' roll legends Spinal Tap but he died in mysterious circumstances.
2 Eric 'Stumpy Joe' Childs used to play drums for Spinal Tap but he too died in mysterious circumstances.
3. Peter 'James' Bond used to play drums for Spinal Tap but he eventually died in mysterious circumstances.
4 Mick Shrimpton now plays drums for Spinal Tap.
5 (Conclusion) So it is likely that Mick Shrimpton will one day die in mysterious circumstances.

Here we have observed that these drummers are all similar to each other in one respect (they were members of Spinal Tap), and concluded that the new drummer must be similar to the others in some further respect (he will die in mysterious circumstances). Of course, the conclusion does not follow necessarily from the premises. Mick Shrimpton may be different from the others, he may evade the Grim Reaper of Rock and live to a ripe old age. So, like other inductive arguments, this one cannot establish its conclusion with absolute certainty. Here the strength of the argument will depend on how strong the similarities are between each case of drumming tragedy. We will be looking at the strengths and weaknesses of a particular type of inductive argument (one based on analogy) when we come to the TELEOLOGICAL ARGUMENT below.

ACTIVITY Read through the following arguments, asking yourself

a) what is the conclusion of each one?
b) which are inductive arguments, and which are deductive?
c) which arguments do you think work, and which don't?

1 I've split up with every person I've ever been out with, so the relationship I'm in at the moment is bound to end too.
2 Men are incapable of driving safely, because they are prone to uncontrollable hormonal changes that can lead to road rage.
3 If you don't believe in God you will go to hell. Stuart doesn't believe in God. So Stuart will go to hell.
4 Philosophers spend much of their time sitting around and thinking, which means their muscles weaken and so none of them are any good at strenuous exercise such as lifting weights.

5 Paul says he had a vision of the Virgin Mary in his bedroom last night. Paul is known to be a trustworthy person and so it likely that the Virgin really did appear to him.

6 It's wrong to kill innocent people. But babies are people too, even when they're in the womb. So it's wrong to have an abortion.

7 Saddam Hussein denied he had any weapons of mass destruction. But we knew from his denials in the past that he's a liar. So he must have them somewhere, and we should keep looking until we find them.

8 My little sister is three and she loves adverts for toys, so your three-year-old sister should enjoy them too.

9 If God exists then he would have created a world without suffering and evil. However, examples abound of terrible suffering and evil in the world. So God cannot exist.

10 No England football team for the last 30 years has got through to the finals of a major competition. So they will obviously fail in the next World Cup.

A priori and *a posteriori* knowledge

We saw that the strength of both deductive and inductive arguments will ultimately depend on the plausibility of their premises. If the premises are obviously false, then the arguments cannot be any good. So how do we establish the truth of the premises of an argument? One obvious answer is through experience. To return to the examples above: the claim that all the ravens I've observed are black is based on my own experience. Such knowledge seems fairly straightforward and unassailable. I should know, after all, what I have experienced. Similarly, knowing that Socrates was a man comes from experience, albeit indirect experience via the testimony of others. I may have read about him in a book, or heard about him from a teacher. Knowledge that is acquired in this kind of a way is known as A POSTERIORI, meaning that it depends on or comes *after* experience. To know such things I have to have experience of them.

But philosophers have also been very interested in another way of establishing their premises that does not require reference to anyone's experiences of the world around them. Such knowledge is known as *a priori*, meaning it does not depend on experience. Examples of such knowledge come from mathematics, e.g. '2 + 3 = 5' can be known just by working it out in your head. Its truth doesn't depend on doing any experiment counting real-life objects. Of course, I do need to learn the meanings of the terms involved in the expression of this sum, but that is the sole extent of the role of experience here. Other examples of *a priori* knowledge are statements that have to be true because of the definitions of the words they use, such as 'You can't steal your own property' or 'Abel's brother was male'. So long as I understand the meanings of the words in such a sentence I can be sure that it is true. In other words, I can work it out in my head, just by thinking about it, and I don't need to go out into the world to check that this is true.

Arguments for God's existence

When we come to examine the arguments for the existence of God we need to bear in mind what has just been said about arguments in general. This means thinking about the following questions.

- What are the premises?
- Are there any hidden premises (or assumptions)?
- Are the premises true?
- Are there any flaws in the reasoning?
- Do the premises support the conclusion?
- Does the conclusion go beyond the premises?
- With inductive arguments, is the probability of the conclusion high, or are there other, more probable conclusions which account for the evidence?

In his *Critique of Pure Reason* Immanuel Kant grouped all the arguments for God's existence into three categories:[22]

- PHYSICO-THEOLOGICAL arguments, which are based on specific experiences of the world. These may be TELEOLOGICAL arguments, that is arguments from design, or arguments from personal experience.
- COSMOLOGICAL arguments, which are based on the existence of the world in general.
- ONTOLOGICAL arguments, which are arguments made independently of any experiences.

It is important to remember that there isn't just one type of each argument, but many different versions, hence our use of the plural 'arguments' throughout. In this chapter we shall look at four types of argument that aim to prove the existence of God:

- ontological arguments
- cosmological arguments
- teleological arguments
- arguments from experience.

In addition we shall look at the arguments from morality in Chapter 3.

Ontological arguments

Introduction

In this section we look at ontological arguments and the criticisms made of them as they developed from the time of St Anselm through to Descartes. We shall also briefly look at modern perspectives on the arguments.

Ontological arguments for God's existence are supposed to be deductively valid. In other words, if we accept their premises as true, the conclusion is said to follow necessarily. Such arguments, if successful, would clearly represent an incredible achievement for human reason, for they promise to establish God's existence with absolute certainty! However, as we saw above, before we can be certain that they succeed we need to be sure that the premises used in such arguments are true. But ontological arguments also claim that their premises are unassailable since they concern only definitions and the analysis of concepts, and specifically the analysis of 'God'. Because we can examine the concept of God in a purely *a priori* manner it represents a firm starting point for our argument. Thus an ontological argument should establish the existence of God with the same degree of certainty as is to be found in mathematics.

But how can we begin from premises that are knowable purely *a priori*? Surely, we would need to begin with some experience of the world before we could establish the existence of anything. If we want to know whether the Black Panther of Bodmin Moor exists then we examine eye-witness accounts, assess the video footage, carry out autopsies on the savaged lambs, and perhaps even recruit thousands of foolhardy students to trawl across the barren hills searching for panther droppings and paw prints.[23] On the basis of the empirical data (the experiences) that we have gathered we then build up a case for, or against, the existence of the beast. So here the proof of the existence of the Black Panther begins with evidence obtained *a posteriori*. However, an ontological argument claims to establish the existence of something (namely God) without drawing on any observation, evidence or experience. How is this possible?

Unpacking concepts

The ontological argument works by analysing the concept of God. This process of analysing a concept can be thought of metaphorically, as 'unpacking' the concept. In other words we must discover all the ideas that are bundled together within the concept. For example, Figure 2.1 illustrates how we might 'unpack' the concept of 'triangle'. We find it contains the following ideas: it is a shape with three sides, the sides are straight lines connecting to form angles, and those internal angles add up to 180 degrees.

Figure 2.1
Unpacking the concept of 'triangle'

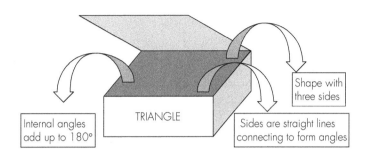

Figure 2.1
Unpacking the concept of 'triangle'

Unpack each of the following concepts into their component parts (the characteristics or ideas that make up each concept).

  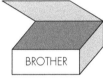 

Let us now look at how we might unpack a statement about the world in order to reveal an *a priori* truth. Take the claim that *Elvis' mother was female*. Without knowing anything about Elvis, his mother, or their stormy relationship, we can safely conclude that the claim is true. We do this through a simple unpacking of a key term 'Elvis' mother', as shown in Figure 2.2.

Figure 2.2
Unpacking the concept of Elvis' mother

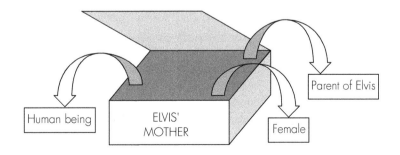

Our analysis, or unpacking, reveals that 'Elvis' mother' is the human, female parent of Elvis. So we can now see the obvious truth that *Elvis' female parent was female*.

There are many claims made that have a similar sentence structure to this, for example that 'freedom fighters are really terrorists', or that 'love of money is the root of all evil', and to assist our analysis it is useful to identify two distinct parts of a statement (or PROPOSITION):

1 the SUBJECT (the thing the statement is about, e.g. 'love of money')
2 the PREDICATE (the properties we're claiming that the subject has, e.g. 'is the root of all evil').

ACTIVITY   For each of the following propositions identify which part is the subject and which the predicate.

  1 A beast is terrorising the people of Bodmin.
  2 Britney loves Prince William.
  3 Tabloid newspapers aim to educate rather than titillate.
  4 Noah counted the animals two by two.
  5 The cow jumped over the moon.
  6 Humans could fly too if only they could flap their arms fast enough.
  7 God exists.
  8 The Earth is about to enter another Ice Age.
  9 Cain's brother was male.
  10 This triangle's internal angles add up to 180 degrees.

Once we have identified the subject and the predicate we can then ask whether the claim is true. This usually means gathering empirical evidence, for example that Britney really does love the Prince and is not just in it for his mother's fabulous jewellery. However, the final two propositions are special cases, as they are both true by definition. With a little analysis the predicate (e.g. 'was male') can be shown to be already contained in the subject (e.g. Cain's male sibling). And saying 'this triangle's internal angles add up to 180 degrees' is very uninformative to people who know what a triangle is: they know it is true by definition. This means that it is possible to know that some propositions are true *a priori* and these do not need any further empirical investigation.

So, to return to the question, one way of justifying a claim *a priori* is to show it is true by definition through analysing the concepts used in the proposition; in other words to show that the subject already contains within its meaning the property we're claiming that it possesses. With an ontological proof of God's existence a similar process takes place: by analysing, and fully understanding, what 'God' means, we shall see that the proposition 'God exists' is true by definition and hence that God must exist.

St Anselm's first version of an ontological argument

Anselm

> *Why then has the fool said in his heart, There is no God (Psalm xiv.1), since it is so evident, to a rational mind, that thou dost exist in the highest degree of all? Why, except that he is dull and a fool?*
>
> *Proslogion*, Ch. 3

St Anselm (1033–1109) is widely credited with inventing ontological arguments in his book the *Proslogion* (meaning 'the discourse'). He writes in the preface that he was searching for a single proof of God's existence, one that would not only demonstrate that God existed, but also reveal his existence as the supreme good, depending on nothing else. In the *Proslogion* St Anselm offered at least two versions of this proof, later dubbed the 'ontological' argument by Immanuel Kant. Both proofs rely on the analysis of a particular definition of God; by fully understanding this definition we come to recognise that God must exist.

Although Anselm addresses his proof to God almost as a prayer, it may be easier for us to grasp if we present it in a standard philosophical form: with a list of numbered premises leading to a conclusion.

1. God is the greatest conceivable being (or as Anselm puts it *'that than which nothing greater can be conceived'*).[24]
2. Even a fool (someone who doesn't believe in God) can understand that God is the greatest conceivable being.
3. (From Psalms 14 and 53) The fool says there is no God in reality.
4. (From 2 and 3) The fool is convinced that God, the greatest conceivable being, exists only in his understanding and not in reality.
5. It is greater to exist both in the understanding and in reality, than merely in the understanding.
6. (From 5) The greatest conceivable being, if it is genuinely the greatest, must exist both in the understanding and in reality.
7. (Conclusion from 1 and 6) Therefore God exists both in reality and in the understanding. Moreover (from 4 and 6), the fool really is a fool, as he is denying the existence of the greatest possible being, i.e. a being which must exist if it is genuinely the greatest!

Anselm's argument can be made clearer if we take out his passages about the fool. These passages are meant to show that the atheist is guilty of an absurdity, namely believing that something that must exist (God) doesn't exist! However, Anselm's argument works just as well if we focus only on those parts that prove God exists (and leave out the parts that reveal the fool to be a fool). There are two crucial aspects to Anselm's argument: first his definition of God as the greatest conceivable being, secondly his assumption that existing in reality is greater than existing in the understanding. From these two premises it becomes clear why St Anselm believes 'So truly, therefore, thou dost exist, O Lord, my God, for thou canst not be conceived not to exist' *(Proslogion 3)*. We can present the essence of Anselm's argument in standard philosophical form thus:

1 God is the greatest conceivable being.
2 It is greater to exist in the understanding and in reality rather than in the understanding alone.
3 Therefore the greatest conceivable being, God, must exist in the understanding and in reality.

Who is the greatest? Have a look at the two different scenarios in Figure 2.3.

There are two possibilities. Either God, the greatest conceivable being, exists only in our minds, or he exists in our minds and in reality as well.

1 Which scenario do you think is true? (Which universe do we live in?)
2 Which scenario do you think contains the greater being?
3 Are your answers to **1** and **2** the same? If they are different how can you account for the difference?

■ **Figure 2.3**

Scenario 1: The greatest possible being only exists in people's understanding

Scenario 2: The greatest possible being exists in people's understanding and in reality

In Scenario 1 people can imagine a powerful being, God, who has created and designed the world, who can perform miracles, who is the source of all morality, and who is omnipotent. Unfortunately, in this scenario, God exists only in people's imagination, and hasn't really created the world. Compare this with Scenario 2 where people can also imagine such a powerful being, except in this scenario the being actually exists, and has in fact created and designed the world, performed a few miracles, and so on. The question St Anselm might ask is which scenario has described the greater being: Scenario 1 or 2? Atheists (Anselm's fools) allege we live in Scenario 1, where the greatest conceivable being exists only in our imagination. But Anselm's point is that an imaginary greatest possible being cannot be the *greatest*, because it is possible to conceive of an even greater being, namely one which actually exists and so is actually able to perform miracles and create the world,[25] as in Scenario 2. By comparing these two possibilities, a God who is imaginary and a God who really exists, we begin to understand that God, in order to be genuinely the greatest, must exist in reality. Another way of making the point is to consider that a God who didn't exist wouldn't be the greatest possible being so to be genuinely the greatest he just has to exist.

The activity above brings out some of the reasons why Anselm thinks it's greater to exist in reality than merely in the understanding (the imagination). But here is another activity that might also bring out why Anselm's assumption is a plausible one.

Imagine your perfect partner.

1 Write down all the amazing qualities such a person would have. Now suppose that there is someone, somewhere in the world, who corresponds to your fantasy.

2 Would you rather go out with the real person, or with the purely imaginary one? Why? Why not?

If, in the activity above, you decided that you'd rather go out with someone who has all the qualities of your perfect partner and actually exists in flesh and blood as well (rather than make do with a perfect but imaginary partner) then you are agreeing with Anselm that it is better to exist in reality rather than simply in the mind.

We have seen that Anselm's ontological argument for God's existence springs from his understanding of God. By analysing what 'God' means (the greatest conceivable being) Anselm comes to realise that he must exist, because he is the greatest, and that those who deny his existence don't really understand the kind of being he is.

1 The philosopher Arthur Schopenhauer (1788–1860), referred to the ontological argument as a 'sleight of hand trick' and 'a charming joke', and the argument strikes many people as suspicious in some way. Have a look at each premise and each step in his argument: where, if anywhere, do you think the trickery lies in Anselm's argument?

2 What other things could you prove the existence of, using an argument like St Anselm's? Try the following format to prove the existence of whatever you like:

1 So-and-so is the greatest conceivable such-and-such.
2 It is greater to exist in reality and in the understanding.
3 Therefore so-and-so, if it is to be genuinely the greatest such-and-such, must exist.

Gaunilo's criticism

Before we look at Anselm's second version of an ontological argument, it is worth examining a criticism made by one of his contemporaries, the monk Gaunilo of Marmoutier. Gaunilo suspected that something was amiss with Anselm's argument and rejected it in his work entitled 'On Behalf Of The Fool'. Gaunilo truly believed in God, but objected to Anselm's move from understanding God to be the greatest possible being to the conclusion that God must exist in reality. Gaunilo argued that we can use this method to define anything we like into existence, so long as we claim it has the property of being the 'greatest' or 'most excellent'.[26] But the real existence of such things, even of God, would always be doubtful without further evidence.

Gaunilo

For example: it is said somewhere in the ocean is an island . . . And they say that this island has an inestimable wealth . . . it is more excellent than all other countries . . . Now if someone should tell me that there is such an island, I should easily understand his words . . . But suppose that he went on to say . . . 'since it is more excellent not to be in the understanding alone, but to exist both in the understanding and in reality, for this reason [the island] must exist'.

'On Behalf of the Fool', section 6

Gaunilo uses his counter-example of the perfect island to undermine Anselm's proof, and we can summarise it as follows:

1 We can imagine an island which is the greatest conceivable island.
2 It is greater to exist in reality than merely in the understanding.
3 Therefore the greatest conceivable island must exist in reality.

We can see Gaunilo structures his argument in the same way as Anselm's, but it leads to a questionable conclusion: there may be no such island despite what worshippers of Ibiza may say. For Gaunilo, using an ontological argument to prove that a perfect island exists doesn't actually work, as the existence of the island is always going to be in doubt until we find real evidence for it. The fact that we can imagine such an island (and as Anselm would say it then exists in my understanding) has no bearing on whether the island does in fact exist. Instead, according to Gaunilo, we must demonstrate as a 'real and indubitable fact' the excellence and greatness of the island. The same doubts can be raised over Anselm's argument for the existence of God. The fact that we can conceive of the greatest possible being does not imply that it actually exists, and the fool is right to say he can conceive God as not existing. Gaunilo goes on to say that the fool would be right to demand that we must prove that God is *in fact* (and not just by definition) the greatest conceivable being.

St Anselm's second version of an ontological argument

Anselm wrote a *Reply to Gaunilo* in which he defends his ontological argument, and draws upon his second version of it. This revolves around an extension to his definition of God, namely that he cannot be thought of as non-existent.

Anselm

God cannot be conceived not to exist . . . That which can be conceived not to exist is not God.

Proslogion, Ch. 3

To help us understand why Anselm makes this claim, let us once again compare two conceptions of God and ask which is the greater being: 1) a God who *can* be conceived of as not existing, or 2) a God who *cannot* be conceived of as not existing? To Anselm it is pretty clear that the second conception of God is greater: because God is the greatest conceivable being it must be impossible to conceive of his non-existence. In fact the idea of a non-existent greatest possible being is a contradiction in terms, claims Anselm, and so only a fool could think that God existed only in his or her mind.

This goes some way to defeating Gaunilo's counter-example. Gaunilo is right to say an island, or any other physical thing, can be imagined not to exist: for example, we can imagine the sea level rising, or volcanic activity making the island disappear. However, it is impossible to imagine the greatest conceivable being, God, as not existing: for if you could you wouldn't be imagining the *greatest* being. The implication here is that an island, or any other physical thing, is dependent upon other physical things for its existence: if those things were to change then the island might not exist. However, God's existence is not dependent upon anything, and so no variation in the universe could cause God not to exist.

Philosophers employ two rather technical terms to distinguish between these two types of existence, although Anselm himself didn't use these terms. Islands, and all physical things, have a CONTINGENT existence, in other words they depend upon other physical things for their existence. This means that for any physical thing certain changes in the state of other physical things could mean it would no longer exist. So, as we saw, the existence of any island depends on the existence and state of the sea surrounding it, and the tectonic plates supporting it. If these were to change then the island might cease to exist. In fact it is logically possible for any physical thing not to exist. Now, Gaunilo seems to be suggesting that God, like an island, has a contingent existence in this sense and so he too can be imagined not to exist. However, Anselm's definition of God states that his existence is *necessary*. Because he is the greatest conceivable being he depends upon nothing else for his existence. This means that he would have to exist no matter what the world happened to be like and so no changes in the state of other things will have any impact on his existence.

Gaunilo attempted to undermine Anselm's ontological argument by using it to show that all manner of perfect things, including God, could exist, but they could easily be imagined not to exist. However, Anselm claims Gaunilo's attempt fails because he doesn't understand that God is a necessary being, i.e. God (and only God) cannot be conceived of as not existing. Once again Anselm believes that he has shown that the very nature and meaning of God entails that God must exist.

ACTIVITY   Consider the proposition 'God exists'. (You may want to refer back to page 28.)

1 What is the subject of this proposition?
2 What is the predicate?
3 From Anselm's perspective, in what sense might you say the subject contains the predicate?

▶ criticism ◀ The theological genius of the Middle Ages, St Thomas Aquinas (1225–1274), rejected Anselm's proof in favour of his own five ways of proving of God's existence.

Because we do not know the essence of God, the proposition ['God exists'] is not self-evident to us.

Summa Theologica 1:2:1

Aquinas

Aquinas agreed that some things were self-evident, and could be known to be true *a priori*: for example, that 'man is an animal'. But in order to know these things we must be able to define both the subject (man) and the predicate (being an animal). However, humans have a limited intellect, and it is impossible for them to understand or define the nature of God. According to Aquinas, Anselm is overstepping the mark when he claims to know that God is the greatest conceivable being. Our minds cannot truly grasp what it means to call God this. Now, if the concept of God is not one that we can genuinely understand, then Anselm's argument cannot get off the ground. For if we can't really grasp the idea of God in the first place, then we are hardly in a position to know what must or must not follow from that idea, so Anselm's ontological argument fails.[27]

Descartes' ontological argument

Perhaps because of the success of Aquinas' own cosmological proof of God's existence, ontological arguments lay abandoned for several centuries. They were eventually revived by René Descartes (1596–1650). In the *Meditations on First Philosophy* Descartes sought certain and indubitable knowledge, and he began by subjecting all his beliefs about the world to extreme doubt. He famously discovered that he could not doubt his own existence, and so he knew he existed, but he wanted to go further than this in his search for knowledge. He believed that if he could prove the existence of God then this should provide the secure foundations for his beliefs about the world. However, because he didn't trust his own senses, he would have to prove God's existence to be true *a priori*, and this meant using an ontological argument.

ACTIVITY   Go back to Chapter 1 and remind yourself of the properties that the God of the philosophers was said to possess. Would you say that 'existence' should now be included as one of his properties?

We do not know whether Descartes was familiar with Anselm's proof, but the one he constructed took a very similar form. We can reconstruct Descartes' argument in the following way:

1 God is the supremely perfect being.
2 A supremely perfect being contains all supreme perfections.
3 Existence (as well as omnipotence, omniscience, benevolence, etc.) is a supreme perfection.
4 (Conclusion, from 2 and 3) Therefore God, a supremely perfect being, exists.[28]

As with Anselm's argument, Descartes' argument relies upon a particular definition of God, in this case that he is 'a supremely perfect being'. Descartes then analyses this concept of God and notes that a supremely perfect being would have to be perfect in every possible way, in other words, he would have to possess every possible perfection. So he would have to be all-powerful, all-good, all-knowing, etc. Now, it seems clear to Descartes that existence is a perfection just as being all-powerful, all-good, and so on are. In other words, as Anselm argued, it is better or more perfect to exist than not to exist. And so it follows that 'existing' must be an essential property of the perfect being. In his proof Descartes brings out what Anselm presupposes, namely that an ontological argument assumes that 'existence' is a predicate (or a property) that belongs to the concept of 'God'. By making this assumption both Descartes and Anselm are able to conclude that 'God exists' is true by definition, because the subject ('God', who contains all perfections) already contains the predicate ('exists', which is a perfection).

Descartes

From the fact that I cannot conceive of God without existence, it follows that existence is inseparable from him, and hence that he really exists.

Meditations V

Descartes also agrees with Anselm on the type of existence God must have: God is a necessary being. Descartes argued that it is impossible to imagine God as not existing, just as it is impossible to imagine an uphill slope existing without a downhill slope, or a triangle without its internal angles adding up to the sum of two right angles. God's existence is a part of his essence as the supremely perfect being. Because God is perfect his non-existence is impossible, in other words God necessarily exists.

In the eighteenth century, Immanuel Kant, himself a Christian philosopher, claimed to have conclusively refuted the type of argument put forward by Anselm and Descartes.[29] In his *Critique of Pure Reason* Kant coined the term 'ontological argument' to refer to this kind of proof. He offers two main objections to the argument: first, that even if existence is a necessary property of God that doesn't entail that God actually exists; secondly, that existence cannot be a property of God nor of anything else. Let's examine the criticisms in the order they appear in the *Critique*.

Kant's first criticism

Kant begins by provisionally granting Descartes' claim that 'existence' is a part of the meaning of 'God'; in other words the proposition 'God necessarily exists' (let's call this P_1) is true by definition, or ANALYTIC. But, says Kant, it does not follow from the fact that this proposition is true by definition that God actually exists in reality. Kant believes that it is possible to accept a proposition as true by definition (in other words to accept that the subject and predicate are inseparable) and yet to deny that there is anything in the world to which the subject refers.[30] Figure 2.4 gives one way of imagining the inseparability of various subjects and some of their essential predicates. For example, a shape, in order to be a triangle, must necessarily have three sides; if the shape lost the property of 'having three sides', then it would no longer be a triangle.

■ **Figure 2.4**
Inseparable predicates

All the black segments are inseparable predicates: if we try to take them away from the concept of the subject, the subject ceases to be what it is.

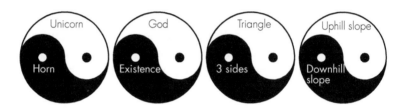

Figure 2.5 gives some examples of predicates that are separable from their subject. So the essence of the subject isn't affected if you take away or change any of these predicates. You could see a unicorn that's very happy, or deeply sad, but it would still be a unicorn. However, if you saw a unicorn without a horn you'd have every right to say 'that's not a unicorn, that's a horse'. Having a horn is an essential (an inseparable) feature of being a unicorn; suffering from manic depression isn't.

■ **Figure 2.5**
Separable predicates

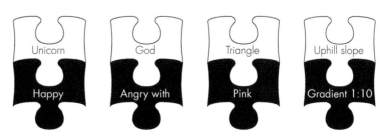

So, looking at the proposition (let's call it P_2) 'Unicorns are horned horses', we know this is true by definition because 'a horse with a horn' forms part of our definition of 'unicorn'. But of course it does not follow from this that there are any unicorns; that is to say, we can deny that there are any horned horses in the world. As Kant puts it, with propositions that are true by definition,[31] we cannot separate the subject from the predicate but we can still deny the existence of both the subject and the predicate together. The most we can infer about reality from P_2 is that '*if* unicorns do exist then they necessarily have horns'.

For Kant it is the same case with P_1 'God necessarily exists'. We might accept, along with Descartes, that 'necessary existence' forms an essential part of our definition of 'God', because it is one of his perfections. But it does not therefore follow that there is a God, as we can deny that there are any necessarily existing beings in the world. The most we can infer from P_1 is that '*if* there is a God then he must necessarily exist'.

So what Kant is arguing here is that we cannot move from the realm of definitions and concepts to reality in the manner that ontological arguments attempt. It is one thing to talk about our concepts and a very different one to talk about what exists in the real world. Descartes is free to define God however he likes, and it may well be that the proposition 'God exists' is true by definition. But that tells us only about the definition of the *word* 'God' and nothing about the *existence* of God in the world. Nothing in the definition can ever bridge the gap to tell us what must exist in reality.[32]

Kant's second criticism

Kant, however, was not satisfied with this criticism and sought to destroy the most important assumption made by ontological arguments: namely the claim that existence can be a part of our definition of God. To do this he tries to show that existence cannot be a property of God, because it is not a property at all. As he puts it:

'Existence' is obviously not a real predicate.

Critique of Pure Reason[33]

Kant

experimenting with ideas

To begin to see what Kant means by this, try the following exercise.

1 Imagine a piece of paper.

2 Picture it in detail in your head: what does it look like, where is it, what is it made of, how big is it? Write down a description of the paper, starting with the phrase 'The piece of paper I'm imagining is . . .'

3 Now add the following features to your picture-image of the paper:

- ■ is splattered with chip grease and batter
- ■ is made of eye-catching lime green paper
- ■ says the words 'Congratulations, you've won a trip of a lifetime' at the top
- ■ is scrunched up in a gutter
- ■ exists

4 Which of these further features changed your image of the paper?

In the exercise your initial description of the paper contained a number of predicates, to which we invited you to add some more. These additional predicates should have enriched your original idea of the paper: in other words, they have added to the concept by giving it new properties. However, what happens when you add the last feature and imagine the scrunched-up, greasy paper *existing*? Does this make any real difference to your idea?

Kant thinks not. He proposes that a genuine predicate is one that really does *describe* the thing we're talking about and so adds a descriptive property to it and enriches our concept of it. However, 'existence' does not do this: it adds nothing to our concept of a subject, and hence cannot be a genuine predicate. If I think of something as existing, the idea is the same as if I think of it as not existing. The properties it has are the same in both cases. So Kant is saying that a genuine predicate describes the subject. Since the predicate '. . . exists' does not describe its subject it is not a genuine predicate. This means that existence is not a property that a thing can either have or not have.

Kant makes his point by asking us to imagine 100 Thalers, coins used as the currency of his day: we might think of them as gold, heavy, round, musty, old. According to Kant's rule, these are all genuine predicates as they all change our concept of the '100 Thalers'. However, if we now add the concept of 'existence' to our description then nothing changes: there is no difference between our idea of '100 coins' and of '100 coins that exist'. In contrast, if we add the words 'covered in pink anti-theft paint' to the description then our concept definitely changes.

Kant concludes that 'existence' (unlike 'covered in pink anti-theft paint') is not a genuine predicate. If he is right, then ontological arguments fall apart because we cannot treat existence as one of the properties that God has. It is essential to the ontological arguments of both Anselm and Descartes that 'existence' is a part of what we mean by 'God'. But if existence is not a predicate, then 'existence' does not belong to our definition of 'God', and ontological arguments fail.

Russell's criticisms of ontological arguments

The second criticism proposed by Kant anticipates a problem raised by philosophers of language in the first part of the twentieth century. Philosophers such as Gottlob Frege (1848–1925) and Bertrand Russell (1872–1970) thought that there was a real difference between the surface structure of language and the true logical structure that underlies it, and that we must be careful not to confuse the two. For example, on the grammatical surface a statement like 'Nothing matters' seems to have a straightforward subject–predicate structure. However, on closer inspection we find that the term 'nothing' doesn't name or refer to anything, and is not a genuine subject. So sometimes what appears on the surface to be a subject (or a predicate), can be shown by further analysis not to be a genuine, logical subject (or predicate).

Existence quite definitely is not a predicate.[34]

Russell

The suggestion is that there is a similar deceit when it comes to the word 'exists'. 'Exists' seems to function as a normal predicate, appearing as a verb after a subject, so just as we can say that 'Bill laughs', 'Jesus saves', 'the lion sleeps', we can also say 'God exists'. However, Frege and Russell would agree with Kant that 'exists' is not a genuine predicate, as it does not describe a property of the subject. Frege argued that 'exists' is really just a shorthand way of saying 'there are *some* objects in the world that this concept refers to'; in other words to say that lions exist is to say that there are things in the world to which the concept of 'lion' corresponds. It is not to say that lions have a very special property known as existence.

Take another example. When we say 'A moon-jumping cow exists', we are not adding something new to our description of 'cow'. We are not saying 'A cow is a four-stomached ruminate which jumps over moons *and exists.*' All we are saying is that the description 'four-stomached ruminate which jumps over moons' corresponds to some object in the real world.

Figure 2.6 represents how Russell might analyse the claim that 'The cow that jumped over the moon actually exists.'

Another way to see the point is to contrast propositions like 'All cows eat grass' with 'All cows exist'. While the predicate 'eat grass' tells us something meaningful about the habits of cows, the apparent predicate 'exist' seems oddly tautological. For obviously all the cows that there are must exist, otherwise they wouldn't be all the cows. Similarly, compare 'Some cows

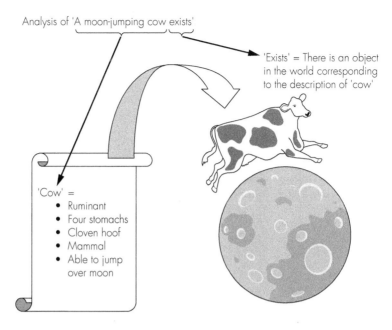

Analysis of 'A moon-jumping cow exists'

'Exists' = There is an object in the world corresponding to the description of 'cow'

'Cow' =
- Ruminant
- Four stomachs
- Cloven hoof
- Mammal
- Able to jump over moon

■ **Figure 2.6**

are mad' with 'Some cows exist'. Again, using 'exists' in this way is rather odd. The oddness seems to come from the fact that this sentence treats existence as a real predicate; suggesting that there are cows, some of which happen to have the property of existence, and others of which don't. But we can't properly describe some cows as existing, as though there were others that don't, because, of course, there aren't any others. There just aren't any non-existent cows. These observations suggest that to say that something exists isn't to describe it or to ascribe a special kind of property to it, but rather simply to say that there is such a thing in the world.

If Russell is correct then 'existence' is not a predicate, but is simply a term that informs us that there is something in the world corresponding to a particular description. When we say 'God exists' we are simply saying 'there is something in the world corresponding to our concept of "God": namely a being who is omnipotent, omniscient, benevolent, etc.' (see Figure 2.7 overleaf).

Russell's analysis of 'existence' profoundly damages the ontological arguments of Descartes and Anselm. These sought to show that 'God exists' was true by definition because 'existence' was a property and so part of the meaning of 'God'. We now find that 'existence' cannot be a property of God, or of anything. In order to show 'God exists' is true we need to find something in the world corresponding to our description of 'God', and this means producing empirical evidence for such a being.

■ **Figure 2.7**

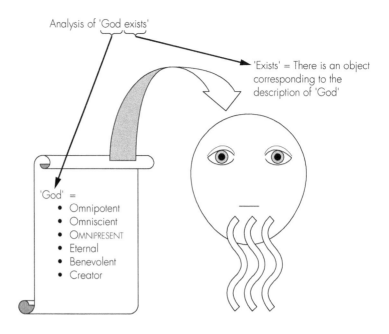

Analysis of 'God exists'

'Exists' = There is an object corresponding to the description of 'God'

'God' =
- Omnipotent
- Omniscient
- OMNIPRESENT
- Eternal
- Benevolent
- Creator

ACTIVITY
1 Go back and re-read Anselm's and Descartes' ontological arguments. Then re-read the criticisms of these arguments.
2 For each criticism identify which parts of Anselm's or Descartes' argument it undermines: for example, which premise does the criticism try to show as false, or which step does it show as invalid?

Modern revivals of ontological arguments

more difficult

Because of their beauty and potential power, ontological arguments have continued to intrigue and inspire philosophers of religion. In the twentieth century there have been versions or interpretations by Norman Malcolm (1911–1990), Alvin Plantinga (1932–) and Karl Barth (1886–1968) amongst others. Both Malcolm and Plantinga focus on claims about God's status as a necessary being, i.e. one who must exist. It is difficult to do any justice to the complexities of Malcolm's and Plantinga's arguments here. However, we have tried to give a brief summary of them below.

Malcolm believes that St Anselm got things right in his second version of the ontological argument. As with this version, Malcolm's argument rests on the claim that God's existence is necessary, although this claim is ambiguous. It may mean that the proposition 'God exists' is a necessary truth (in the same way '2 + 2 = 4' is a necessary truth). Or it may mean that God's existence is necessary in that he possesses a special quality called 'necessary existence'. This ambiguity is a possible source of criticism against Malcolm.

We can think about Malcolm's ontological argument in the following way. Consider four possibilities concerning God's existence:

1 God's existence is *necessarily false* – it is logically impossible for any being that has God's properties to exist.
2 God's existence is *contingently false* – it is possible that a being with the properties of God could exist, but it just so happens that there isn't such a being.
3 God's existence is *contingently true* – it is possible that a being with the properties of God could exist, and it just so happens that there is such a being.
4 God's existence is *necessarily true* – it is logically necessary that any being with the properties of God exists.

Malcolm would argue that **2** and **3** simply cannot apply to a being like God. This is because God is the greatest conceivable being, and as such he must be unlimited, independent and eternal. However, **2** and **3** suggest that his existence is contingent, i.e. limited by and dependent upon other factors. For example, for Malcolm there is a crucial difference between an eternal being, and a being who just happens (contingently) to exist forever: eternity is a quality of God whereas eternal duration is not. Malcolm argues that, because God is the greatest conceivable being, God's existence cannot be contingent, and thus the claim that 'God exists' cannot be contingently true (or false).

This leaves either **1** or **4** as the remaining possibilities. Statements that fall under category **1** are logically contradictory propositions, such as 'This square is round' or 'That bachelor is on his fifth marriage'. Malcolm argues that there is nothing logically contradictory about the claim that 'God exists'. This leaves **4** as the only remaining possibility: God's existence is necessarily true. For Malcolm this doesn't mean that 'existence' is a predicate of 'God', instead it means that 'necessary existence' is a predicate of 'God'. Malcolm believes he has shown that because God is the greatest conceivable being he must be a necessary being, and therefore he must exist.

▶ criticism ◀ Plantinga criticises Malcolm's argument, and offers his own ontological argument in its place.[35] Plantinga's objection to Malcolm is that it is possible for God to exist contingently (possibility **3** above) without God losing his independence or his unlimited or eternal qualities.

Plantinga's own ontological argument takes a slightly different approach to Malcolm's. What we mean when we say that 'God necessarily exists' is that God exists in every possible universe: i.e. there is no possible universe that doesn't contain God. Why is this so? Well, as with all ontological arguments, Plantinga accepts the definition of God as the greatest conceivable being (a being with 'maximal greatness' is Plantinga's phrase). A God that exists in all possible universes is greater than one that exists in only some universes. Therefore God, in order to be the greatest, must exist in every possible universe. This is the same as saying that God necessarily exists.

Conclusion

Ontological arguments can be seen in two ways: first as proofs of the existence of God, secondly as an expression and exploration of what 'God' means to the believer. It is unlikely that the arguments will sway an atheist. Critics of the arguments have strived to show that you cannot define something into existence, no matter how clever your definition.

However, ontological arguments may be more fruitfully read from within the framework of the believer. To the reflective believer the argument reveals what 'God' means, or who God is. Once you begin to understand God then you see that God's existence is of a different order to the existence of the rest of the universe. For the believer, God is a being unlike anything else because his existence stems from his own nature, and not from any external cause. His existence, as Descartes has it, is part of his essence and is therefore 'necessary' which suggests it is unlimited, independent, without a cause, without a beginning, and without an end.

Karl Barth argues that St Anselm's ontological argument should be read more as an exploration of faith than a proof of God's existence. Barth points out that Anselm's argument is framed at the beginning and the end as a prayer. As St Anselm says at the beginning of the *Proslogion*:

Anselm

> *I do not seek to understand so that I may believe, but I believe in order to understand.*

Proslogion 1

This seems to suggest that for Anselm philosophical analysis (in the form of his ontological argument) takes a back seat to faith. He does not use philosophy in order to prove to himself that God exists; instead he uses philosophy to help him explore and understand his own faith.

Cosmological arguments

Introduction

Hume

....
What was it then that determined something to exist rather than nothing?[36]
....

In this section we briefly sketch the source of cosmological arguments in Plato and Aristotle before focusing on Aquinas' three types of cosmological argument.

Cosmological arguments appeal to our intuition that the existence of the universe (along with everything else) needs an explanation. In its most basic form, a cosmological argument attempts to understand and answer the question 'Why is there a universe rather than nothing at all?' Humans thirst for answers to 'why' questions, and looking up at the stars at night it's easy to move from asking 'Why are we here?' to asking 'Why is any of this here?' Many people feel that the existence of the universe demands an explanation, that there must be some reason why it is here. The cosmological arguments propose that an explanation for the existence of the universe cannot be found within the universe, but must be located in some external source or cause. This external cause, the arguments claim, must be God. Moreover, the arguments conclude that God doesn't need an explanation, and doesn't have an external cause, because God is his own cause: his existence is necessary.

So, like ontological proofs, cosmological arguments claim that God has a necessary existence (in contrast to the universe, which is dependent upon God for its existence). However, unlike ontological proofs, cosmological ones base their conclusion that God exists on our experience of the universe.[37] So their premises are only knowable *a posteriori*.[38] The type of reasoning involved in such proofs, rather than being purely deductive as in an ontological argument, is inductive reasoning. The arguments proceed from what we know of the universe through experience and draw conclusions about what lies beyond our experience, namely the existence of God. These two labels, *a posteriori* and inductive, apply to all proofs for the existence of God except ontological arguments.

Why are you doing this?

1 On the right-hand side of a piece of paper write down the following event: 'This book lands on the floor.'

2 Now just to the left of it write down another event that caused the book to land on the floor. (Perhaps you were told to drop it by a teacher, or perhaps you were bored with it.)

3 Now to the left of this event write down another event that caused the event in **2** to happen.

4 Keep going as long as you can, writing down a cause for each event.

Your sheet of paper should look something like Figure 2.8

■ **Figure 2.8**
A chain of causes and effects

Event 4   Event 3   Event 2   Event 1

You probably found that the chain of cause and effect appears to have no end and could go on for ever. But you may also have wondered how, in that case, the whole chain got started in the first place. Proponents of cosmological arguments reckon that chains like this just have to get started by something and that this something must be God. To see how these arguments work in detail we must begin in the ancient world where they were first articulated.

The contributions of Plato and Aristotle

Plato

Shall we say then that it is the soul which controls heaven and earth.

Laws (Book X, 897c)

The origins of various forms of cosmological argument lie in the works of two ancient Greek philosophers, Plato (428–348 BC) and Aristotle (390–323 BC). In the *Laws* (reproduced in Hick, ed., *The Existence of God*) Plato categorised different kinds of motion or change. His most important distinction was between things that had the power to move or change both themselves and others (which he termed 'primary movers') and things that could only move or change others once they had been moved (called 'secondary movers'). For Plato, primary movers were the ultimate source of change, as they alone possessed the power spontaneously to cause motion.

Plato argued in the *Laws* that only souls could be primary movers, and that whatever causes the whole universe to change and move must also be a soul. So Plato's contribution to cosmological arguments is the suggestion that the universe is dependent on some ultimate, intelligent primary mover.

Read through the following passage and identify which are primary and which are secondary movers.

'The crowd gathered round the pool table like mosquitoes drawn to the lights above the bar. Fast Eddie was in trouble and he knew it. As he lent down to line up the cue beads of sweat slipped from his cheek onto the green baize. The cue clicked forward and balls ricocheted around the table, but found no pocket. Fat Sam moved up to take his turn, driven by his hunger for the thousand bucks that lay piled on the counter. The cue seemed a mere extension of his fingers, as he smoothly potted ball after ball after ball.'

The series must start with something, since nothing can come from nothing.

Metaphysics, Beta 4 (999b)

Aristotle

Aristotle also believed that all changes in the universe must come from some ultimate source. In the *Metaphysics* he put forward an argument to prove that there must be an 'unmoved mover' who is the ultimate cause of the universe. His argument asks us to consider two competing claims: that the universe has an ultimate cause, and that the universe has no ultimate cause. By showing that the second claim is not possible, he leaves us with only one option, namely that there is an ultimate cause. We can represent his attack on the second claim as follows (Figure 2.9):

■ **Figure 2.9 Aristotle's proof that there must be an unmoved mover**

1 The chain of causes and effects has no beginning, there is no ultimate cause.

2 (From 1) In which case, nothing caused the chain.

3 But if nothing caused the chain there would be no chain at all (one of Aristotle's metaphysical assumptions is that nothing comes from nothing).

4 However, there clearly is a chain of causes and effects, so the original assumption (that there is no ultimate cause) must be false. The only other possibility is that there *is* an ultimate cause, one that lies behind the chain of causes and effects, and which itself has no cause.

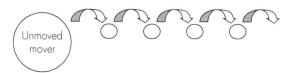

The argument we have presented here, on the basis of Aristotle's argument, is known as a REDUCTIO AD ABSURDUM. This means taking a point of view and reducing it to absurdity in order to show that it is false. The absurdity here is in step 3 as clearly there is a chain of cause and effect: after all the universe undoubtedly exists. But as step 3 follows on from step 2, and step 2 follows from step 1, Aristotle feels entitled to reject these claims as well. Having shown that step 1 – that the chain of causes has no beginning – is false, he has proved that there must be an ultimate cause, which itself has no cause.

Medieval theologians built on the work done by Plato and Aristotle in their construction of cosmological arguments demonstrating God's existence. These cosmological arguments fall roughly into two types: causal arguments and arguments from contingency. 'Contingency' in this context roughly means the dependency upon other things of the universe and all it contains, but we shall examine this concept in more detail below. Amongst Christian philosophers St Anselm put forward a very succinct cosmological argument,[39] but it was St Thomas Aquinas who explored the proofs in most detail. Aquinas made it his life's work to assimilate into Christian theology the rediscovered philosophy of Aristotle,[40] and he incorporated Aristotle's ideas in his own cosmological arguments for God's existence.

The five ways of St Thomas Aquinas

In his book the *Summa Theologica* Aquinas offers five ways in which God's existence can be demonstrated, and the first three ways are all forms of cosmological arguments:[41]

- first way – the argument from motion
- second way – the argument from causation } Cosmological arguments
- third way – the argument from contingency
- fourth way – a type of moral argument (see Chapter 3)
- fifth way – a type of teleological argument (see pages 63–64 below).

The first way and the second way are both forms of causal cosmological argument, and they seek to show that certain general features of the world (causation and motion) must be dependent upon a higher source, which is uncaused or unmoved, namely God. The third way is a cosmological argument based on the contingency of the universe, and it aims to show that the universe is dependent on a necessary being, God.

Aquinas' arguments from motion and causation: the first and second ways

Aquinas' first and second ways of proving the existence of God have a similar structure, and are 'causal' versions of cosmological argument.[42] Both begin by noting there are features of the world that we all experience: in the first way it is the existence of motion, in the second way it is the existence of causation. One possible explanation of such features of the universe is that they have existed forever. However, Aquinas argues that this explanation must be false by showing that there cannot be an INFINITE REGRESS of movers or causers. He does so by using a type of *reductio ad absurdum* similar to the one outlined above. Aquinas then goes on to show that these features need an explanation that lies beyond the ordinary chain of motion or causation. Because an infinite regress is not possible, the only other explanation is a cause or a mover that does not fall under the ordinary rules governing causation or motion. Such a being would need no further explanation, it would be the source of all causation without itself having a cause, it would be, as Aristotle said, the unmoved mover. Aquinas says that we call such a being 'God'.

We can summarise the first and second ways as follows:

The first way is the argument from motion (which for Aquinas included any type of change):

1 There are some things in motion or a state of change, for example, wood burning in a fire.
2 Nothing can move or change itself – in Plato's terms everything is a secondary mover.
3 Imagine everything was a secondary mover – then there would be an infinite regress of movers.
4 (*Reductio ad absurdum*) If 3 were true then there would be no prime mover and hence no subsequent movers, but this is false.
5 (Conclusion) There must be an unmoved prime mover (the source of all motion/change) whom we call God.

The second way is the argument from causation:

1 There is an order of efficient causes (every event has a cause).
2 Nothing can be the cause of itself.
3 Imagine this order of causes goes back infinitely – then there would be no FIRST CAUSE.
4 (*Reductio ad absurdum*) If 3 were true then there would be no subsequent causes, but this is false.
5 (Conclusion) There must be a First Cause (the source of all causes) and this we call God.

ACTIVITY
1 Go to www.epistemelinks.com, click on e-texts, select 'Aquinas', then select *Summa Theologica*.
2 Locate, and print off, Part 1, section 2, Third Article, entitled 'Whether God Exists'.
3 Read through the first and second way.
4 Identify in this original text where you think the premises outlined above are.

Criticisms of Aquinas' arguments from motion and causation

When we consider the chain of causation or of motion, it is easy to think of it temporally, with each event preceding and causing the next event. In this interpretation, a cause refers to the factor that brought about the effect. The chain of causation is thus one that goes backwards in time, with God, the First Cause, at the beginning starting the whole thing off, rather like a finger knocking over the first of a chain of dominos, or winding up a clockwork machine (see Figure 2.10).

■ **Figure 2.10**
God as the (temporal) First Cause

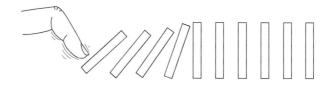

▶ criticism ◀ If we take the 'temporal' interpretation of causation then the cosmological argument seems to show that a First Cause, God, once existed and once created the universe. However, it is crucial to believers that God is still present to act upon the world and still cares about the world; this after all is the God of Abraham, the God described in the Bible. So the 'domino-flicking' First Cause may have satisfied a pagan philosopher such as Aristotle, but such a view is not one that a Christian philosopher such as Aquinas could subscribe to.

However, there is another interpretation of the chain of causation that lends itself better to the belief that God, as the First Cause, is acting on the world here and now. This interpretation sees 'causation' in terms of the factors that sustain an event, or keep it going once it has begun. For example, a farmer may plant a seed, and so cause the seed to grow in that patch of land, but it is the particular qualities of the seed, together with a fertile environment, that sustains its growth into a mature plant. The chain, or order, of causation can be thus seen as a hierarchical one with God as the ongoing and ultimate sustaining cause of the universe.[43]

■ **Figure 2.11**
God as the (sustaining) First Cause

In the diagram we can imagine tracing the cause of a tree back to its seed, then to the weather conditions that enabled the seed to grow, then to the movement of the earth round the sun that created the weather conditions. But the cosmological argument claims to show that ultimately it is God who causes all these things.

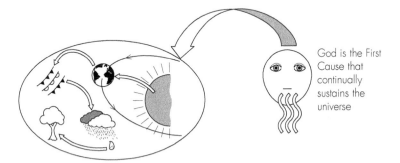

God is the First Cause that continually sustains the universe

▶ criticism ◀ At first sight the first and second ways appear to rest on a contradiction. On the one hand Aquinas says that everything must have a cause (nothing can cause itself), but he then concludes that something must exist that can be the cause of itself, namely God. So the original assumption is contradicted by the conclusion.

A defender of a cosmological argument might say that this is precisely what the *reductio ad absurdum* is supposed to prove: that there has to be at least one exception to the rule 'everything must have a cause'. If there weren't such an exception, then the universe would have no cause and would never come to exist. But if there is an exception, let's call it the First Cause, then it must be something without a cause, in Aristotle's terms an 'unmoved mover'. This defence has similarities to Anselm's defence against Gaunilo, namely that when we are talking about God we are dealing with a being unlike anything else, a being who has a special form of existence.

▶ criticism ◀ However, a critic might come back with the response that if we're going to allow for exceptions to the rule 'everything must have a cause' then why make God the exception? Couldn't we just as well make the universe itself the exception? In other words we would be saying that everything that occurs within the universe must indeed have a cause, but **51** the universe as such doesn't. The existence of the universe requires no further explanation: it simply is. This would rule out the need to posit God.

Alternatively, it can be asked of the cosmological argument, why must God be the ultimate cause and why is God the point at which our search for an explanation for the existence of things must end? Why, in other words, does the existence of God not require any further explanation? David Hume (1711–76) offers the following warning against searching for an explanation beyond the physical universe:

Hume

If the material world rests upon a similar ideal world, this ideal world must rest upon some other; and so on, without end. It were better, therefore, never to look beyond the present material world.[44]

■ **Figure 2.12**
Why stop our explanations at God?

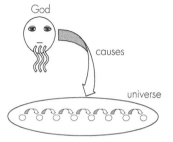

Hume suggests that seeking explanations beyond the physical universe will lead to an infinite regress of explanations. So perhaps we would do better to stop our search for explanation with the universe: either accept it has no explanation, or find an explanation for the universe that lies within the universe.

► criticism ◄

A further criticism arises from Aquinas' claim that an infinite regress of causes or movers is absurd. Aquinas seems to be confusing a (very long) finite chain of causes, for which there would indeed have to be a first cause to begin the chain, with an infinite chain of causes. In the first instance, it's true, if you take away the first cause, then everything else disappears. But in the second instance there is no first cause to take away; the series of causes is *infinite*. J.L. Mackie gives the example of a series of hooks, all hanging from each other.[45] With a finite series of hooks, each one hangs on the one above it, until we reach the last (or first) hook, which must be attached to something. Take away the wall attachment and the hooks fall – that seems to be how Aquinas is imagining the chain of causes and effects. But with an infinite series of hooks, each is attached to the one above, and so on forever: there is no first hook attached to a wall.

So philosophical critics of cosmological arguments seem prepared to admit that an infinite regress is after all possible, and that there is no need to postulate a 'First Cause'. However, by admitting this possibility such critics might be undermining a key weapon in the armoury of philosophy, what we might call the 'infinite regress FALLACY'. Philosophers often aim to show a position is flawed precisely because it results in an infinite regress. However, we've just seen that some critics of cosmological arguments are proposing an infinite regress of causes as a coherent and valid alternative to a First Cause. Such critics can't have it both ways: either they hold onto the infinite regress fallacy, which is a useful tool against many a suspect idea, or they discard the fallacy in order to undermine such cosmological arguments. Sadowsky says that philosophers stand to lose more by jettisoning the infinite regress fallacy, than by abandoning this line of attack on cosmological arguments.[46]

▶ criticism ◀

It is possible to criticise the argument from causation by questioning Aquinas' account of causation. One of Aquinas' main premises is the assertion that there is a series of causes such that every effect has a cause. The Scottish philosopher David Hume put forward a view of causation that, if correct, undermines Aquinas' assertion. Hume believed that we never actually experience causation; it is something our minds impose upon our perception of the world as a result of past experience. So, although we think we see one snooker ball cause another to move when it strikes it, all we in fact see is one ball move toward another until they touch, then the second ball move away (see Figure 2.13). We add the concept of 'cause' to this experience, once we have seen it happen frequently enough, but we can easily think of a particular event as not having this cause.[47] If Hume is right, then we have no knowledge of any 'chain of causes and effects', and this goes some way to undermining the first premise of the argument from causation.

■ Figure 2.13
According to Hume we do not observe 'causation'

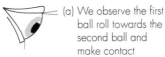 (a) We observe the first ball roll towards the second ball and make contact

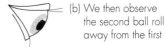 (b) We then observe the second ball roll away from the first

However, Hume's account of causation is a controversial one that many philosophers have taken objection to. A defender of cosmological arguments such as Elizabeth Anscombe would say that Hume's concept of causation is a strange one, stemming from an unreasonably sceptical view of the world. Anscombe agrees that it may well be possible for us to imagine an event without having one cause or other.[48] For example in Figure 2.13 we can imagine that the first snooker ball didn't cause the second ball to move; perhaps it is a trick snooker table where the balls are moved by hidden magnets or wires. But even if it is possible to imagine an event without the cause we think it has, it is impossible for us to imagine an event as genuinely having no cause at all. And, so long as every event has some cause or other, then Aquinas' argument can indeed get off the ground.

▶ criticism ◀

Bertrand Russell suggests that a further angle of attack on Aquinas' concept of causation might be drawn from quantum physics.[49] Since the 1920s, theoretical physics has raised the question of whether there are indeterminate events taking place at a subatomic, quantum, level that have no cause at all. This invites the possibility that other events have no cause, including the appearance of the universe itself. If this is a genuine possibility then it undermines Aquinas' first premise: the certainty that everything must have a cause.

▶ criticism ◀

As well as his scepticism about the concept of causation, Hume offered a further criticism of cosmological arguments that undermines Aquinas' position.[50] Hume argues that if we have explained the cause of each event in the series, then it is unreasonable to ask what caused the whole series. Take any series of events; let's say the separate appearance of five Inuit people in New York City.[51] Upon investigation we find that each of the Inuit is there for a different reason, and we are able to fully explain their presence in New York. According to Hume it would be unreasonable for an investigator to then say 'I agree you have explained why each Inuit is here, but I want to know why the whole group of five is here.' There is nothing more to say: an explanation of why each individual is there is enough; to demand an explanation of the whole group is unreasonable. This has become known as the FALLACY OF COMPOSITION: it is the fallacy of thinking that because there is some property common to each part of a group, this property must apply to the group as a whole. Russell gives a further example of this: it is true that every member of the human species has a mother, but it is a fallacy to conclude from this that our species as a whole must have a mother.[52] Similarly, every event within a series may indeed have a cause, but it is a fallacy to conclude that the whole series must have a cause. So 'cause and effect' is taken to be a concept which applies to events occurring in the universe, but it is a mistake to then try to apply the concept to the universe as a whole. If Hume is right, then Aquinas is mistaken in thinking that there must be a First Cause that started the chain of cause and effects, and this type of cosmological argument fails.

ACTIVITY   Which of the following claims are guilty of the fallacy of composition?

1 Every nice girl loves a sailor. Therefore there is one sailor that all nice girls love.
2 Every journey has a destination, therefore there is one destination for all journeys.
3 All activities are aimed towards some goal, therefore there is one goal that all activities ultimately aim at.
4 Everyone in Tonbridge Wells voted Tory in the last election, therefore Tonbridge Wells is a Tory constituency.
5 Every proof of God's existence is flawed, therefore trying to prove God's existence is a flawed activity.

Aquinas' argument from contingency: the third way

Aquinas' third way is from a different tradition of cosmological arguments – ones that are based on the contingency of the universe and of everything in it. We have noted already that contingency has a close connection with the idea of dependency. So, for example, the existence of a forest is contingent upon the existence of the availability of water to the trees' roots; or the existence of our democratic system of government is dependent upon us having the freedom to vote for different parties. Contingency is also bound up with the idea of mortality or 'shelf life': contingent events occur and then stop, and contingent objects come into being then cease to be. So, once all the rivers are dammed, the forest disappears; take away our freedom to vote for different parties and our democracy will disappear. Finally contingency implies that things are not fixed: they could have been different if the past had been different. If the climate had been hotter, then the forest would never have existed; if Plato's experimental system of 'philosopher kings' had been proven to work, then there may never have been any need for democracy.

experimenting with ideas

What, if anything, is the existence of the following contingent upon?

1 Life on planet Earth
2 Your own existence
3 The continuing good health of your neighbour's cat
4 A successful marriage
5 Public trust in politicians
6 An acrobat balancing on top of a human pyramid
7 The whole universe

Cosmological arguments based on contingency claim that everything in the universe is contingent, and thus dependent upon something else.[53] They go on to argue that it is impossible for *everything* to be contingent; there must be a non-contingent being, i.e. a necessary being, upon which the contingent universe is dependent. This necessary being is God. Aquinas' third way is a slightly different version of the argument from contingency. In this argument he emphasises the 'shelf-life' aspect of contingent beings, i.e. the fact that they have an expiry date, they come and go, live and die, are generated and destroyed. In other words they are impermanent. Aquinas argues that if everything has an 'expiry date' then at some point everything will expire and cease to exist. Since this hasn't happened he concludes there must be a permanent being which has no expiry date, and which all impermanent beings depend on for their existence. Let us look at how he reaches this conclusion.

We find in nature things that are possible to be and not to be, since they are found to be generated and then corrupted.

Summa Theologica 1:2:3

Aquinas

Aquinas' third way can be divided into two parts as follows:[54]

Part one

1 Things in the world are contingent (they come into existence and pass out of existence).
2 Imagine everything was contingent; then there was once a time when everything had passed out of existence – i.e. there was nothing.
3 (*Reductio ad absurdum*) If 2 were true then there would be nothing now (as nothing can come from nothing), but this is false.
4 (Conclusion of part one) Therefore not everything can be contingent – there must be at least one thing that is necessary.

Part two

5 For every thing that is necessary it either has the cause of its necessity in itself or outside of itself.
6 Imagine every necessary thing has the cause of its necessity outside of itself.
7 (*Reductio ad absurdum*) If 6 were true then (as with the causal argument outlined above) there would be no ultimate cause of necessity.
8 (Conclusion of part two) There must exist a necessary being which causes and sustains all other necessary and contingent beings – this being we all call God.

In the first part of his argument Aquinas is saying that contingent and impermanent things cannot continually furnish the universe throughout its infinite existence. There must come a point in time when impermanent things all cease to exist: their expiry dates all coincide. In which case, Aquinas says, we would expect there to be nothing now. But that is plainly false: the world is still stocked full of contingent beings. Therefore there must exist a permanent (NECESSARY) being that guarantees the continuing existence of impermanent beings, even if they all expire at once. Figure 2.14 shows how we might try to picture this: we can see there is a point at which contingent beings all expire, but a necessary being sustains the existence of the universe over this 'gap' and generates fresh contingent beings.

■ **Figure 2.14**
God as a necessary being sustaining the universe

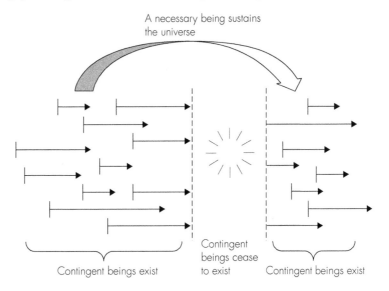

A necessary being sustains the universe

Contingent beings cease to exist

Contingent beings exist

Contingent beings exist

So Aquinas has established that there must exist a permanent, necessary being, which the universe (and the impermanent parts of the universe) depend on for their existence. In the second part of Aquinas' argument he considers whether such a necessary being is itself dependent on another necessary being, which in turn would be dependent upon another necessary being, etc. Aquinas denies the possibility of an infinite regress of necessary beings. There must, ultimately, be a necessary being who needs no other cause, but who is the cause of itself. So Aquinas concludes that there must exist a necessary being who needs no further explanation or cause, namely God.

Aquinas' conclusion: God is a necessary being

We saw above that if something is contingent then:

- its existence is dependent on other things
- it has a 'shelf life'; it came into existence and will one day cease to exist
- it might have been different (or might never have existed) if the past had been different.

What Aquinas', and other philosophers', cosmological arguments seek to prove is the existence of a non-contingent, necessary being. In contrast to contingent beings, a necessary being:

- has an existence that is independent of everything else
- is eternal; it has always existed and will never cease to exist
- has to exist; and it is impossible that it could be different, no matter how past, present or future circumstances might vary.

It is the existence of such a necessary being, one we call God, which Aquinas believes he has proved through his third way.

Criticisms of Aquinas' argument from contingency

▶ criticism ◀ Aquinas makes a clear connection (in premise 7 above) between the argument from contingency and the argument from causation. At least one criticism applying to the second way also applies to the third way. The third way relies on a *reductio ad absurdum* in order to prove that an infinite regress of contingent (and necessary) beings is impossible. However, we saw above that Aquinas may not have got his head round exactly what an infinite regress might be, and he may have been thinking of a very long finite series. We agreed that a finite series would need to come to an end at something with a sturdy support like an unmoved mover; but an infinite series does not need such support as it never comes to an end.

▶ criticism ◀ Aquinas seems to be saying that, over an infinite time period, all contingent things must come to an end, because they are impermanent, and that this would leave nothing left in existence. He concludes that there must be a necessary being that 'keeps things going' even when all contingent beings have ceased to exist. However, Mackie argues that Aquinas is committing a fallacy if he thinks that he can jump from 'every thing at some time does not exist' to 'at some time everything does not exist'.[55] Thus it might be the case that there is an infinite series of overlapping, yet contingent, things in the universe. If this were a possibility, claims Mackie, then there would be no need to hypothesise the existence of a necessary being.

▶ criticism ◀ A further criticism arises from Aquinas' conclusion that God is a necessary being. Some philosophers have argued that we can talk about necessary propositions, but we cannot talk about necessary beings. The concept of 'necessity' only applies to the truth of statements, not to things that exist. In the light of this account of necessity, perhaps the real meaning of the statement 'God is a necessary being' is that 'the proposition "God exists" is necessarily true'.[56] We saw above (note 30) that Hume and Kant challenged the assumption that the term 'necessary' could be applied to propositions about existence, as in the claim 'God exists'. They argued that a claim was only necessary when its denial entailed a contradiction. So, for example, we know that 'bachelors are unmarried men' is necessary because when we deny it (e.g. by saying 'bachelors are married men') a contradiction results ('unmarried men are married men').[57] However, both Kant and Hume argue that existential propositions, such as 'Ghosts exist' or 'Socrates once existed', can always be denied without self-contradiction. Even Aquinas accepted that 'God exists' was not self-evident and could be meaningfully denied.[58] Hence Kant and Hume agree that we cannot say about anything which exists that it is necessary. If this is the case (and not all philosophers agree with this analysis of necessity) then the conclusion of Aquinas' third way is seriously undermined.

We have now outlined some of the specific criticisms offered against the three ways, but two more general criticisms remain: do Aquinas' arguments prove the existence of a God who is worthy of worship? And does the universe really cry out for an explanation?

Do Aquinas' arguments prove the existence of God?

Aquinas is very careful not to overstate his conclusion in each of his proofs of God's existence. So, as he presents them, his cosmological arguments demonstrate the existence of an unmoved mover, an uncaused First Cause and a necessary being. Aquinas states that we refer to these three ultimate explanations for why the universe exists as 'God', but he goes no further than this in his conclusion.

▶ criticism ◀ Even if we accept Aquinas' cosmological arguments as sound, we might criticise them for failing to prove the existence of a being who is worthy of worship, either the God of the philosophers or the God of the Bible. After all, it is possible to imagine a First Cause which does not have some of the essential properties of God, and which may not be personal or benevolent or omniscient. For example, Plato and Aristotle believed in, and attempted to demonstrate, the existence of a supreme intellect that governed and caused the universe. But of course they did not believe in God as described by religious believers. We might argue that Aquinas has failed to add the essential religious ingredients to his cosmological arguments that would demonstrate God's existence.

However, when looking at the conclusions of Aquinas' arguments we should remember that he believed that there were limits to human understanding, and that his proofs had to remain within those limits. For Aquinas, we can never, through our own intellectual efforts, come to know God's essence: no proof can demonstrate who or what God is. The most reason can tell us is what God is *not*.[59] In order to understand the positive aspects of God we need the help of divine revelation, either directly through personal experience, or indirectly through a revealed text, like the Bible. This was one reason why Aquinas rejected ontological arguments, as they went beyond human reason by asserting that we could understand and define God's essence. So Aquinas' three ways were never intended to reveal the nature of God, only to demonstrate that there was some ultimate explanation for the existence of the universe. If the arguments are sound, then they will dramatically undermine the atheist's position, even if they don't exactly prove the existence of a Christian God.

Does the universe really need an explanation?

At the beginning of this section we mentioned that cosmological asrguments sprung from a very real need many of us have to answer the questions 'why are we here?' and 'why does the universe exist?'. Cosmological arguments can be seen as complex and arduous expressions of this need for an answer. To some it may seem obvious that the universe is crying out for an explanation: it must have come from somewhere, there must be a reason why it exists. However, to others it is not so obvious.

▶ criticism ◀ Our final criticism is put very well by Bertrand Russell in a radio debate with Father Copleston. Part of this debate was a discussion of cosmological arguments and of what ultimately caused the universe:

I should say the universe is just there, and that's all.[60]

Russell

In the context of the debate, Russell is arguing that it is meaningless even to ask the question 'what caused the universe?'. We have already seen above Russell's reasons for saying this, namely that it is a fallacy to argue that, because the parts of the universe have a cause, therefore the whole must have a cause. But in his dismissal of Copleston's religious position, Russell is expressing something much more primitive than this. He simply does not feel a need for any ultimate answers; he does not think the universe is crying out for an explanation. For Russell the universe just is, period.

Cosmological arguments are attractive to people who feel that the universe is lacking something, and needs explaining. This feeling makes the conclusion that God is the ultimate explanation for why the universe exists more palatable. However, for people who do not see the universe in this way, a cosmological argument remains puzzling: if someone is seeking an explanation, then stopping at God seems arbitrary. Why not stop looking for explanations before you get to God? Or why not search for an explanation of why God exists? It may simply be that, as with other arguments for God's existence, they only make sense if you already have some faith. And if you do believe in God, then cosmological arguments help to reveal another facet of God: that he must be the unmoved mover, the uncaused cause and a necessary being.

ACTIVITY

1 Have another look at the summaries of Aquinas' three ways above.

2 Now go through each criticism identifying which part of Aquinas' arguments the criticism is aimed at: for example, identify the specific premise it undermines, or the invalidity of a particular step.

Teleological arguments

Introduction

> *Thou dost cause the grass to grow for the cattle, and plants for man to cultivate . . . Thou hast made the moon to mark the seasons, the sun knows its time for setting.*
>
> Psalms 104: 14, 19

In this section we look at two types of teleological arguments: the traditional ones based on analogy (including Aquinas' and William Paley's versions and the criticisms made by David Hume) and more modern ones based on inference to the best explanation (including a discussion of the ANTHROPIC PRINCIPLE).

The word 'teleological' comes from the Greek *telos*, which means end or goal, and *logos*, which means 'an account of' or 'the study of'. So originally 'teleological' referred to the study of final ends, but later it came to refer to the view that everything has a purpose and is aimed at some goal. So a teleological argument for God's existence is one that finds evidence that the world has been designed and given purpose by God.

Teleological arguments are also known under other names: we have seen that Kant called them 'physico-theological' arguments, a phrase that does not trip easily off the tongue. They are often referred to as ARGUMENTS FROM DESIGN, because they draw attention to the appearance of design in the universe as evidence for the existence of a designer – God. However, as Antony Flew and others have pointed out, strictly speaking they are arguments *to* design because they seek to show that the world has been designed.[61] Referring to them as arguments *from* design suggests that they argue from the premise that the world has been designed, which is to assume what they are supposed to be proving! For consistency we shall refer to them all as teleological arguments.

We have seen that cosmological arguments are concerned with the general questions concerning the very existence of the universe: why is there something rather than nothing, what caused the universe to exist? Teleological arguments, on the other hand, are concerned with the specific details of the universe: why does the universe possess the particular qualities that it does and how can we best explain them?[62] There are many puzzling features of the world that scientists, philosophers and theologians have sought to account for, including:

- the regularity and order of the world
- the way that everything in the world seems to be designed for some purpose
- the way that living things are so suited to their environment
- the fact that that life developed in the world at all
- the fact that conscious beings exist.

What connects these features is the apparent unlikelihood of them occurring by chance. A teleological argument tries to show that these features are not the result of chance, but provide strong evidence for the existence of God.

This proof always deserves to be mentioned with respect. It is the oldest, the clearest, and the most accordant with the common reason of mankind.

Critique of Pure Reason[63]

Kant

Because teleological arguments are based on our experience of the universe they can be categorised as *a posteriori* proofs, alongside cosmological arguments, arguments from experience, and arguments from morality. Like the other *a posteriori* proofs, teleological arguments tend to be inductive arguments, beginning with specific claims that fall within our experience (here's evidence of design in the world) and concluding with a claim about what lies beyond our experience (God exists). As we mentioned some teleological arguments are ANALOGICAL, i.e. they are arguments based on analogy, whilst others are *abductive* arguments, that is to say inferences to the best explanation, in that they begin with some evidence that needs explaining and conclude with the best explanation for this evidence.

We should remind ourselves of one of the differences between inductive and deductive arguments. Deductive arguments, like the ontological proofs of God's existence attempted by St Anselm and Descartes, are capable of providing a conclusive proof, so long as the premises are true and the argument is a valid one. In contrast an inductive argument, such as a teleological argument, cannot conclusively prove the existence of God even if it is based on true premises. At best a teleological argument can only show that God's existence is probable.

Aquinas' argument from analogy

In his fifth way Aquinas offers a version of a teleological argument, which we can summarise as follows.

1 Things that lack intelligence, such as living organisms, have an end (a purpose).
2 Things that lack intelligence cannot move towards their end unless they are directed by someone with knowledge and intelligence.
3 For example, an arrow does not direct itself towards its target, but needs an archer to direct it.
4 (Conclusion) Therefore (by analogy) there must be some intelligent being which directs all unintelligent natural things towards their end. This being we call God.

This argument makes use of a belief that Aristotle held (you may remember that Aquinas was a big fan of Aristotle), namely the view that everything in the universe has an end or purpose. Aquinas himself does not give any illustrations from nature to support this 'teleological view' of the world, but we can use any number of Aristotle's observations. For example, Aristotle notices that ducks have webbed feet,[64] and he argues that the reason for this is so that they might swim better. Every living organism, and nearly every part of a living organism, has a function aimed at some purpose according to Aristotle. For Aristotle this is not an indication of any plan or design, it is simply a fact about the nature of things.

Aquinas accepts Aristotle's belief that organisms have a purpose or function, but he rejects the Aristotelian view that this teleology (i.e. this purposefulness) could come about naturally. Instead he argues that there must be an intelligence lying behind the function of organisms: someone must have arranged the world so that ducks ended up with an efficient paddling mechanism for a reason. So in the fifth way Aquinas claims that unintelligent objects (such as an arrow) can only be aimed towards a goal (such as a target) with the guiding hand of an intelligent being (such as an archer).

However, the example of the archer aiming the arrow has two functions in Aquinas' argument. Not only does it illustrate Aquinas' view that unintelligent objects can only reach their goal with the help of a guiding intelligence but it also represents a stepping-stone to the conclusion that a guiding intelligence must lie behind the universe. It is only in another work, *De Veritate*, that Aquinas makes this second function clear. In this work, Aquinas expands on his archer example, and says, 'Similarly, philosophers call every work of nature the work of intelligence.'[65] The key word here is 'similarly', as it suggests that Aquinas thinks we can use the archer example as an analogy for the whole universe. His conclusion is that the universe, which is unintelligent yet goal-directed like the arrow, must have a guiding intelligence behind it, just as the archer aims and fires the arrow. This intelligent being, Aquinas concludes, we call God.

► criticism ◄ The key premise in Aquinas' argument is the claim that 'things that lack intelligence cannot move towards their end unless they are directed by someone with knowledge and intelligence'. However, this is a controversial premise insofar as it very nearly assumes what the argument is setting out to prove, namely that there is an intelligent being who created the universe. If the argument were to succeed a supporter of Aquinas would need to bolster this premise with further evidence and justification. There may well be good reasons for believing that (a) all living organisms and parts of organisms have a function, and (b) these functions must be the result of the actions of an intelligent being. But Aquinas hasn't provided us with these reasons, and his argument needs fleshing out.

► criticism ◄ Moreover, as Flew points out,[66] the appealing suggestion that natural organisms have been designed seems to go against all available evidence. It is pretty clear that when an archer fires an arrow, or when an architect designs a house, there is direction in the process stemming from some intelligent being. Yet we observe that most ducklings, acorns, embryos, etc. grow and develop very successfully without any interference from an intelligent being. And so the claim that some intelligent hand must directly shape the natural world simply isn't supported by our observations of it.

In the five hundred years after Aquinas the success of science changed the way people saw the universe. The traditional Aristotelian view of the universe, which placed the earth at the centre surrounded by unchanging heavenly bodies, was undermined by the work of Copernicus (1473–1543) and Galileo (1564–1642). The new discoveries showed that the earth was just one planet amongst many revolving around the sun. Isaac Newton (1642–1727) claimed to have discovered the laws of motion that governed the movement of all objects, and the universe came to be viewed as a complex machine. Some thinkers saw these breakthroughs as a threat to Christianity – indeed the new discoveries did undermine much traditional Church teaching – but others used the new science as evidence that the universe was a glorious work of divine craftsmanship. If the universe is machine-like then it needs a designer, just as an ordinary machine such as a watch needs a designer. This analogy between the universe and a watch was the basis for a teleological argument put forward by William Paley.

In Figure 2.15 there are five boxes, each containing an object: Box 1 contains a wrist watch; Box 2 contains a pebble; Box 3 contains a honeycomb; Box 4 contains a coin; Box 5 remains unopened.

1 Which of the objects in Boxes 1–4 would you say have been designed?

2 What do the designed objects have in common?

3 List all the things you would be looking for in the fifth object, in order to determine whether it had been designed.

■ **Figure 2.15**
What's in the mystery box?

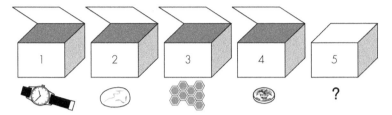

William Paley's argument from analogy

The Archdeacon of Carlisle, William Paley (1743–1805), put forward a very popular teleological argument in his book *Natural Theology* (1802). Paley imagines himself walking across a heath and first coming across a stone, which he strikes with his foot, then finding a watch on the ground. The same question occurs to him on both occasions: 'how did that object come to be here?'. In the case of the stone, for all Paley knows it may have lain there forever. However, in the case of the watch such an answer is unsatisfactory: there is something about the presence of the watch on the heath that demands further explanation.

So what is the difference between a watch and a stone in this case? What Paley actually notices about the watch is that:

■ it has several parts
■ the parts are framed and work together for a purpose
■ the parts have been made with specific material, appropriate to their action
■ together the parts produce regulated motion
■ if the parts had been different in any way, such motion would not be produced.

In the activity above you might have found further features that indicate some sort of design in a watch: e.g. its aesthetic appearance, or its complexity. We might think of this list as Paley's criteria for (or indicators of) design, and if an object meets these criteria then Paley will take it as evidence that the object has been designed. For Paley the watch on the heath has all the evidence of what he terms 'contrivance', i.e. design, and where there is design or contrivance there must be a designer or 'contriver'.[67] He concludes that the watch must have had a maker.

ACTIVITY   Draw a table like the one below.

1 Along the top, write in your criteria for design, referring to either
   a) the list you established in part 3 of the activity above, or
   b) the criteria Paley proposes.
2 For all the natural features listed, decide which criteria they meet.
3 Are there any natural features you can think of that don't meet any of the criteria?

	Criteria:				
Natural features	**1**	**2**	**3**	**4**	**5**
A snake's eye					
A peacock's tail					
The changing of the seasons					
The 'flu virus					
The solar system					

Paley

Every indication of contrivance, every manifestation of design, which existed in the watch, exists in the works of nature.

Natural Theology[68]

Having examined the watch and thereby established some criteria with which to determine whether something has been designed, Paley turns his attention to the natural world. He finds that all the indicators of design that we observed in the watch we can also observe in nature, except that the works of nature actually surpass any human design. This leads him to the conclusion that nature must have a designer wondrous enough to have designed such a universe.

We can summarise Paley's argument in the following way.

1 A watch has certain complex features (e.g. it consists of parts, each of which has a function, and they work together for a specific purpose).
2 Anything which exhibits these features must have been designed.
3 (From 1 and 2) Therefore the watch has been designed by a designer.
4 The universe is like the watch in that it possesses the same features, except on a far more wondrous scale.
5 (From 4 and 2) Therefore the universe, like the watch, has been designed, except by a wondrous universe maker – God.

Like Aquinas' fifth way, Paley's teleological argument is an ARGUMENT FROM ANALOGY. An argument from analogy typically works by comparing two things, and by arguing that because they are alike in one (observed) respect they are also alike in another (unobserved) respect. Paley's analogy between the watch and the natural world works like this.

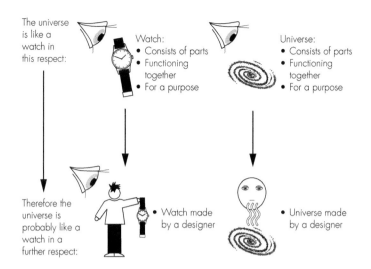

■ **Figure 2.16**
Paley's analogy between the watch and universe

1 Read through the following arguments from analogy.

a) In many ways a dog is like a cat, for example they both are warm-blooded mammals. Dogs give birth to live young, therefore cats do too.

b) A dog is like a duck-billed platypus, in that they are both warm-blooded mammals. Dogs give birth to live young, therefore duck-billed platypuses do too.

c) Just as a curry is a more stimulating dish if it contains a variety of flavours, so a nation will be more stimulating if contains a variety of cultures.

d) Just as a window box is more interesting if it contains a variety of flowers, so a garden will be more interesting if contains a variety of plants and trees.

e) We wouldn't let a wild animal control its owner, because the owner knows better than the animal what's in its interests. Therefore we shouldn't let the common people control the government because the rulers know better than the people what's in their interests.

f) We wouldn't let a child control its parents because the parents know better than the child what's in its interests. Therefore we shouldn't let students control an A Level class, because the teacher knows better than the students what's in their interests.

g) If you suddenly found yourself being used, against your will, as a life-support device for a famous violinist and knew it would last nine months, you would not have a moral obligation to keep the violinist alive. Similarly, if you suddenly found that you were pregnant, against your will, you would not have a moral obligation to see the pregnancy through to birth.

h) If you suddenly found yourself attached to a stranger who was acting as your life-support machine for nine months, and they're the only person who can keep you alive, then you have a right to be kept alive by that stranger. Similarly a foetus, whilst in the womb, has a right to be kept alive until birth by its mother.

2 What words or phrases indicate that an argument uses an analogy?
3 Which of the above did you think were strong analogies, and which were weak?
4 What do you think makes an analogy a strong or successful one?

William Paley takes great care in *Natural Theology* to outline, and then respond to, a number of criticisms people might make of his teleological argument. Here are some of the criticisms Paley anticipates:

A We may be in ignorance about how watches are made.
B The watch may sometimes go wrong.
C Some parts of the watch may appear to have no purpose.
D The watch might have come together by chance.

All of these criticisms would go some way to undermining Paley's claim that we know, just by examining a watch, that it has been designed. By implication of the analogy, they would also undermine Paley's claim that by examining the universe we can conclude it has been designed. Some of these criticisms are ones that David Hume put forward thirty years *prior* to Paley, and we shall leave a discussion of these problems until the next section.

▶ criticism ◀ In the meantime let us look briefly at criticism C. When Paley finds the stone on the heath he dismisses it out of hand: it doesn't seem to have any purpose, and certainly offers no evidence that the universe has been designed. It seems that if parts of the watch, or the universe, have no purpose then the conclusion that they have been designed is weakened. After all a designer wouldn't include pointless parts.

Paley's response to criticism C is as follows. He argues that there may be parts whose purpose we have not yet discovered, or that we don't understand and perhaps never will understand. It may well be that the stone is only a small piece in a wider puzzle, and we need to view the whole before we can see where the stone fits in.

David Hume's critique of teleological arguments

David Hume offered some of the most memorable criticisms of the design argument in his *Dialogues Concerning Natural Religion* published in 1779. In this book we listen in on three fictional philosophers discussing the nature of God:

■ Philo (characterised by his 'careless scepticism')
■ Cleanthes (characterised by his 'accurate philosophical turn')
■ Demea (characterised by his 'inflexible orthodoxy').

69

Near the beginning Cleanthes suggests a teleological argument that takes a similar form to Paley's version. Cleanthes argues that we can see the same effects in the world as we see in all manner of machines, namely that all the parts are finely adjusted to fit each other and work towards some definite purpose. Working through the analogy, Cleanthes' conclusion is that the cause of these effects must also be similar: just as the design of a machine is caused by human intelligence, so the design of the world is caused by divine intelligence. We can see that, as with Paley's version, this argument is based on an analogy (between a machine and the world), and as with Paley it moves backwards from observation of the effect (the machine/the world) to a conclusion about the cause (the designer/God).

Philo responds to Cleanthes' argument with a barrage of objections, many of which are also applicable to Paley's argument. Hume was an empiricist, and believed that all our justifiable beliefs come from observation and experience: 'a wise man proportions his belief to the evidence' was his guiding principle.[69] Such a starting point is very close to the critical scepticism of Philo, and many commentators assume that Philo's position is also Hume's.[70] We can classify the problems Philo/Hume raises with this teleological argument into three main types.

■ Problem 1: We have no experience of world-making

▶ criticism ◀ We can only recognise that certain sorts of objects, such as machines, have an intelligent designer because we have had direct or indirect experience of such objects being designed and manufactured. So it is by observation of the way in which watches, for example, come into being in our world that we learn that they require a designer. But if we had never had any experience of manufacture, engineering or design, then we would never suppose that an object such as a watch had been designed. Hume's point is that to know what has brought something about we have to have experience of its being brought about. So unless we have had some experience of other universes being made we cannot reasonably claim to know whether our own universe has been made.[71]

Paley may have been thinking of Hume's attack when he responded to criticism A above. Paley thinks that it does not matter if we have never seen a watch being made, and have no understanding of how it is manufactured. Paley asks 'Does one man in a million know how oval frames are turned?'.[72] Since the answer is doubtless 'no', then how is it we nonetheless are certain that they been designed? His answer is that there are certain intrinsic features possessed by certain objects which show that they are designed.

▶ criticism ◀ Hume's point cuts deeper than this though. It is indeed possible, as Paley says, for us successfully to infer that some unfamiliar object has been designed. But this is only because we can compare it to other manufactured objects that we've previously encountered. If we had absolutely no experience, direct or indirect, of the manufacturing process, then the object would remain a mystery to us. Yet we have no experience of the process that causes universes to come into being, as the universe is unique and there is nothing we can compare it to. The only experiences we have of the universe are of its separate parts, and these parts on their own cannot tell us about the origin of the whole. As Philo says, 'from observing the growth of a hair, can we learn anything concerning the generation of a man?'.[73] For Hume, if we have no experience of this universe being designed, and if we cannot compare it to other universes that have been designed, then we have no grounds for concluding that God or anyone else has designed it.

The arguments in the activity above (page 68) all relied on analogies. However, although two things might be similar in some respects, they might be very dissimilar in other respects.

1 Draw up a table like the one below. List the similarities and dissimilarities between each pair of things listed.
2 What is the impact of the dissimilarities on the arguments in the activity above? (page 68)

	Similarities	**Dissimilarities**
a) A dog *and* a duck-billed platypus		
b) A curry *and* a nation		
c) A window-box *and* a garden		
d) A wild animal *and* the common people		
e) The child–parent relationship *and* the student–teacher relationship		
f) Acting as a life-support machine for a violinist *and* carrying an unborn child		
g) A machine *and* the universe		

■ Problem 2: Arguments from analogy are weak

An argument from analogy claims that, because X is like Y in one (observed) respect, they are therefore probably alike in some other (hidden) respect. However, arguments like this are only reliable when the two things being compared have lots of relevant similarities. A reliable example of an argument from analogy might be this: I notice that you and I behave in similar ways when we miss the nails we are hammering and hit our thumb; from this I infer that you and I have similar sensations following thumb-hammering incidents. I conclude, by analogy with my own case, that when you smash your thumb with a hammer you feel pain. This conclusion seems justified even though it is impossible for me to feel your pain. It is justified because you and I are similar in at least one important way: we both share a similar human physiology. The question is: does a machine have enough relevant similarities with the universe to support the conclusion that they were both designed?

▶ criticism ◀ Hume (through the character of Philo) argues that the universe is not at all like a machine, not even a vast and complex one. Hume suggests that the universe resembles something more organic than mechanical; it is far more like an animal or vegetable than 'a watch or a knitting-loom'.[74] If so, the appearance of function and purpose amongst the parts of the universe is due more to 'generation or vegetation than to reason or design'. And since a vegetable does not have any designer; since its organisation appears to develop by some blind natural process, we have no reason to suppose that the universe is designed. Perhaps it simply grew! Now, it may seem rather absurd to compare the universe to a giant vegetable, but this is partly Hume's point: it is only as absurd as comparing the universe to a machine. For Hume there is nothing to choose between the world–machine analogy and the world–vegetable analogy: both are equally flawed comparisons. Flawed because, as we've said, for an argument from analogy to be reliable the two things being compared need to be alike in all the relevant ways. Unfortunately in both Cleanthes' and Paley's teleological arguments the two things being compared (a man-made object and the universe) are hardly like each other at all. Therefore Cleanthes (and Paley) cannot conclude, on the basis of the analogy with a machine, that the universe has a designer.

1 Read through the left-hand column in the table below and identify in the right-hand column who you think made (or caused) each particular thing (or effect). We have connected one as an example.

Effect	Cause
a) A stylish and ergonomic wooden shelving unit	A) A five-year-old girl
b) A modern slave labour system	B) An unshaven and smelly carpenter
c) A simple metal ruler	C) A murderer and common thief
d) A classic racing car	D) An engineer working from his London garage
e) A miniature cottage made from small plastic building blocks	E) A power-hungry megalomaniac
f) A shoddy, badly made, wooden table	F) A team of world-class designers
g) One small piece of a quilt	G) A vegetarian who hates the sight of blood
h) A stunning sixteenth-century painting of Jesus being entombed	H) A 90-year-old woman
i) An efficient legal system	I) A smart and trendy carpenter

2 What reasons can you give for each decision you've made?
3 What problems are there with reasoning backwards from effects to causes in this way? (Hint: G is a possible description of Adolf Hitler.)

Problem 3: The argument does not demonstrate the existence of God

One of the main assumptions on which Cleanthes' teleological argument rests is that 'like effects have like causes',[75] i.e. two things that are similar in their effects (probably) have similar causes. Both Cleanthes and Paley must make this assumption if they are to conclude that the universe has a designer:

1 Machines and the universe exhibit similar features of design ('like effects').
2 Therefore they have both been designed by some intelligent being ('like causes').

Yet neither Cleanthes nor Paley examines in detail how far the likeness of causes can extend, both being happy to move quickly to the conclusion that the designer of the universe is God.

Philo, however, takes the idea of 'like causes' and gleefully runs with it, bringing out some potential absurdities in comparing the universe with machines. He finds that by staying true to the analogy he arrives at possible causes of the universe that are nothing like a perfect, unique God. So, he makes the following points.

1 Complex machines are not usually the product of a single brilliant designer. Instead teams of people are involved in their design and construction. So, by the 'like causes' principle, the universe may also have been designed and created by many gods, not by a single deity.

2 We can take the analogy to its extreme by fully 'anthropomorphising' the designers of the universe, i.e. making them very similar to humans. For example, the designers and constructors of complex machines are often foolish and morally weak people. In the same way the gods who built the universe may well be foolish and morally weak. Humans involved in manufacture are both male and female, and reproduce in the usual fashion; so perhaps the deities are gendered and also engage in reproduction (like the gods of ancient Greece and Rome).

3 In most cases complex machines are the product of many years of trial and error, with each new generation of machine an improvement on its predecessors. By the 'like causes' principle then 'many worlds might have been botched and bungled' (as Philo says) before this one was created. In other words this universe may be the product of trial and error, one in a long line of 'draft' universes, and may well be superseded by a better one in the future.

4 Where there are design faults in a machine we usually infer that the designer lacked resources or skills, or simply didn't care. The universe appears to contain many design faults (particularly those that cause needless pain and suffering). For all we know this is because it was created by a God who lacked the power, skill or love to create something better (or perhaps, Philo muses, it was created by an infant or a senile God). As Philo says, the most reasonable conclusion of this argument is that the designer of the universe 'is entirely indifferent . . . and has no more regard to good above ill than to heat above cold or drought above moisture'.[76] This is a far cry from the all-loving God envisaged by Cleanthes and Paley.

This last objection, which draws on the problem of evil (see Chapter 3 below), may not be fatal for a teleological argument. Paley acknowledges the possibility of an attack from this quarter in criticism B above. But Paley argues that it is not necessary that a machine be perfect in order to be designed; all that is important is that the machine exhibits some sort of purpose. We shall see when we examine the problem of evil that the existence of God isn't necessarily incompatible with the presence of apparent design flaws (like unnecessary pain and suffering) in the universe.

It may also be possible to side-step Philo's criticisms by conceding that we can say very little about the designer of the universe purely on the basis of a teleological argument. This would take the sting out of Philo's attacks, as the conclusion of such an argument would simply be that a designer of the universe exists and would make no claims about what such a designer is like. In this case Cleanthes and Paley need only show a common thread of intent in the design of a machine and of the universe: just as the machine's design is the result of intentional action so is the universe's design. For Robert Hambourger, a modern supporter of teleological arguments, so long as we concede that the universe exhibits elements of design, even if only in parts and even if other parts are flawed, then this 'would be enough to show that something was seriously wrong with the atheist's standard picture of the universe'.[77] If we admit the possibility of design then we also admit the idea of an intentional act lying behind the design, and this would undermine the atheist's position.

However, we have now moved a long way from the optimistic claims, made by supporters of teleological arguments, that we can see God's handiworks in nature. Hume's Philo concludes that the very most that teleological arguments are able to establish is 'that the cause or causes of the universe probably bear some remote analogy to human intelligence'.[78] Such a tentative conclusion is unlikely to persuade anyone of the existence of God, unless they already believe in him.

ACTIVITY Re-read Paley's teleological argument. Where do you think Hume's criticisms really hit home? For each proposed criticism decide:

a) whether it undermines a premise, and, if so, identify which premise

or

b) whether it undermines the structure of the argument, i.e. the steps it takes towards the conclusion.

The challenge of Darwin

Traditional teleological arguments, based on the analogy made between the natural world and human artefacts, faced further criticism when Charles Darwin's (1809–1882) work on natural selection was published.

Much of the persuasive power of an argument like Paley's lay in examples of design taken from the natural world: it seemed obvious that the intricacy of a human eye and the beauty of a peacock's tail could not have come about by chance; they must have been designed. However, Darwin's *Origin of Species* (1859) provided an account of how such perfectly adapted features could and did come about, not by any intelligent designer, but by the struggle of every generation of species to compete, survive and reproduce. Darwin's theory of evolution became widely accepted as the best explanation of the features that William Paley puzzled over, namely that:

- living organisms consist of individual parts
- these parts are framed and work together for a purpose
- they have been made with specific material, appropriate to their action
- together they produce regulated motion
- that if the parts had been different in any way such motion would not be produced.

Darwin

The old argument from design in nature, as given by Paley [. . .] fails now that the law of natural selection has been discovered. We can no longer argue that, for instance, the beautiful hinge of a bivalve shell must have been made by an intelligent being, like the hinge of a door by man. There seems to be no more design in the variability of organic beings . . . than in the course which the wind blows.[79]

Nevertheless, we should give Paley's argument its due. The eye seems to be a precision organ precisely put together to perform a particular function. Before Darwin, the only explanation going for the existence of such features was the existence of a designer. What Darwin did was to give us an alternative account of how such design can appear. Random mutation plus the pressures of natural selection is the designer of all living organisms: it is not an intelligent or purposeful designer, but a blind unthinking mechanism.

But Darwin's theory did not extinguish teleological proofs altogether. Some theologians incorporated evolution into their arguments; Richard Swinburne, for example, assimilates evolution into the 'machine-making' nature of this mechanical universe.[80] So those features of design in the natural universe, although not directly caused by God as previously suggested by Paley and others, are still the result of the evolutionary mechanism built into the universe by God.

Other theologians changed their tack altogether, moving away from analogy as the basis for a teleological argument. We shall now turn to look at the second type of teleological argument, which views God as the best explanation for the special 'design' features the universe exhibits.

experimenting with ideas

For each of the following observations, decide whether **a)**, **b)** or **c)** is the best explanation for what was seen:

1 Ilham has been all around the world, studying thousands of birds, but he has never seen a white raven. This is because:
  a) All ravens are in fact black.
  b) All ravens are in fact black up until the year 2010, after which they might become any colour of the rainbow.
  c) All ravens that Ilham is about to see quickly change their colour, like chameleons, so that they appear black to him.
2 People in Cadiz harbour see the masts of ships disappear as they move away from port towards the horizon. This is because:
  a) The human eye is limited in its range: it can only see up to 29 miles in the distance.
  b) The earth is round.
  c) The masts don't actually disappear. It's the heavy mists in the air above the Atlantic Ocean around the coast of Spain that makes them seem to disappear.
3 Hayley found a rock on a heath, and brought it home as an ornament. But she found it interfered with the digital radio that it was placed next to. This is because:
  a) The rock is a magical stone, out to take vengeance on humanity for its destruction of Mother Earth.
  b) The rock is a lodestone, and has strong electro-magnetic fields that interfere with other magnetic fields such as those in digital radios.
  c) It was sheer coincidence that the radio broke soon after the rock was put next to it: there is no connection between the two events.
4 Blaine needs to throw six 6s in a dice game in order to win – he picks up the dice and rolls exactly six 6s. This is because:
  a) Blaine is a cheat and switched the ordinary dice for loaded dice when it came to his turn.
  b) It is entirely possible to roll six 6s purely by chance, and that's just what happened here.
  c) Blaine is naturally lucky: good fortune has shone on him throughout his life, and this is just another example of his good luck.

5 Hudson watches a cuckoo lay an egg in the nest of a robin. The cuckoo chick hatches and shifts itself around until all the robin eggs have fallen out of the nest. Eventually only the cuckoo is left, and the robin spends all day foraging for food to feed this parasitic bird. This is because:

a) The cuckoo egg was laid in the robin's nest by accident, and when it hatched it moved around too vigorously, which unfortunately knocked the robin eggs out of the nest.

b) God designed cuckoos as parasitic birds in order to destroy the eggs and chicks of unsuspecting robins.

c) Cuckoos have evolved behaviour over millions of years which exploits the maternal instincts in other bird species like robins.

　　i) Explain why you have made your choices.
　　ii) Make a list of all the things that make an explanation strong.

Tennant's argument to the best explanation

All teleological arguments begin by asking why the universe contains the specific features that it does: regularity, beauty, order and purpose. We have seen that some teleological arguments proceed by analogy to show that these features were designed by God, just as machines were designed by humans. Other teleological arguments advance in a different way, by asking how these features can be explained and concluding that God is the best explanation. Teleological arguments to the best explanation typically proceed along the following lines.

1 We see in the universe the presence of certain special features (orderliness, regularity, beauty, life, self-conscious beings, etc.).
2 These features, either collectively or individually, cannot be adequately explained by the natural sciences such as physics or biology.
3 The presence of these features (both collectively and individually) can be made sense of by the existence of God.
4 Where an explanation makes sense of certain features that cannot be explained otherwise, then we can conclude it is probably right.
5 Therefore God exists.

The fourth premise stems from an idea known as 'inference to the best explanation'. This was termed 'abduction' by the American philosopher C.S. Pierce (1839–1914) as an alternative to induction and deduction, although it is now viewed simply as another form of induction. The suggestion is that for any data that needs explaining we should believe in whichever hypothesis best explains the data. From engaging in the activity above you will have drawn up your own list of what makes an explanation a strong one, but it may have included the following.

- Simplicity: we should favour simple explanations over more complex ones, if they explain the same thing equally well (this is known as Ockham's Razor).
- Explanatory power: we should favour the explanation that is able to account for the greatest amount of the data.
- Predictive power: we should favour explanations that can be used to make predictions that can then be tested.
- Cohesiveness: we should favour explanations that best fit with those tried-and-tested beliefs that we currently hold.

The question is, when it comes to accounting for the orderliness, regularity, beauty, etc. of the universe, is God the strongest hypothesis?

Teleological arguments to the best explanation are able to build a cumulative case for the existence of God. F.R. Tennant (in *Philosophical Teleology*, 1930) draws on a range of features that we observe in the universe, all of which seem to demand an explanation; he concludes that God is the best hypothesis we have to explain their occurrence. Tennant recognises that each feature on its own may be explicable through the natural sciences, but together they form an overwhelming case for God's existence. He includes the following features as ones that are best explained by the existence of God.

- The intelligibility of the universe to humans: because it is ordered and regular rather than chaotic, our scientific investigations are able to unravel its laws.
- The possibility of organic adaptation: the process of evolution enables beings to adapt to their environment.
- The adaptation of the inorganic world to life: this planet is able to generate and support life, through its geology, climate, atmosphere, position in the solar system, etc.
- The beauty of nature: from the microscopic to the cosmological, the natural world astounds believers and non-believers alike with its beauty and sublimity.
- The existence of morality: humans are able to identify good from evil and to work to achieve the good.
- The emergence of human beings: evolution has progressed to produce humans who have the ability to contemplate the universe, appreciate its beauty and seek what is good within it.

For Tennant each of these features taken individually is very difficult to explain from a naturalistic perspective, i.e. one that remains only within the realms of the world of nature. When we consider the existence of all of them collectively, then the task of explaining them naturalistically becomes even harder. Only God provides an adequate explanation of why a barren, inanimate world gave rise, first to life, then to human beings capable of contemplating the universe and reflecting on their place within it. Tennant believes that the world is the way it is, and we are the way we are, because of God's guiding intelligence behind his creation.

ACTIVITY

1 How might an atheist scientist seek to explain each of the features mentioned by Tennant?

2 Without referring to God, how else is it possible that all of these features could occur together in a single universe?

▶ criticism ◀ David Hume suggests an alternative to teleological explanations in his *Dialogues Concerning Natural Religion*. Hume argues that it is at least possible that the universe is ordered and life-supporting as a result of chance and not intelligence.[81] This theory is often referred to as the Epicurean Hypothesis, after the ancient Greek philosopher Epicurus (341–270 BC) who proposed that the universe exists in the way it does as a result of the random movements of a finite number of atoms. Over an infinite period of time these atoms will take every possible position, some of them ordered, some of them chaotic. It just so happens that the physical universe is currently in a state of order, and that, by chance, beings have evolved that are capable of reflecting on the universe and why it is here. Hume argues that, although this may be a remote possibility, it cannot be disregarded as a plausible explanation for the so-called design in the universe.

The Epicurean Hypothesis, unsurprisingly, has not found favour with theologians, who continue to seek for scientific grounds for saying that God, not chance, is the best explanation for design in the universe.

A long time ago in a universe far away there lived the Yahoos, a species of self-conscious, carbon-based alien life forms. At a certain point in their intellectual evolution the Yahoos began to ponder the mysteries of the universe, where it came from and why they were here. Some of them argued that the universe was purposeful, with each part contriving to enable the evolution of the Yahoos themselves. The Yahoos believed that such a finely adjusted universe, which had resulted in the existence of Yahoos, clearly required an explanation.

1 Which explanation best accounts for the existence of the Yahoos:
   a) a teleological explanation, relying on the guiding intelligence of God; or **b)** an 'Epicurean' explanation, relying on blind chance?

2 Are there any other explanations that might account for the existence of the Yahoos?

3 Are the Yahoos justified in their belief that the universe has been perfectly adjusted so that they might come into existence? Why/Why not?

Anthropic teleological arguments and the Anthropic Principle

What strikes Tennant as most odd about the universe is the extraordinary list of physical conditions that have to be in place for human life to be possible. Human life is only possible because the universe exhibits very precise chemical, thermal and astronomical features, whose origin can be traced back to the Big Bang.[82] According to this way of thinking, the likelihood that this chain of events (extending over billions of years and culminating in the appearance of life on earth and conscious intelligent beings) could occur by pure chance is so unimaginably low that we are forced to conclude that there must be a guiding hand behind the process. It is this that leads him to the conclusion that it is no coincidence that everything on Earth is just right for human existence; God intended it to be that way.

■ **Figure 2.17** *The long chain of events leading to life on earth and eventually human beings*

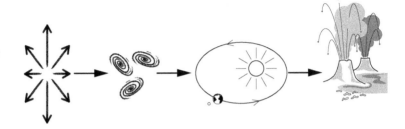

From the theists' perspective the work done by scientists on the Big Bang in the past fifty years has actually strengthened their case for God's existence. After all for even the most primitive of life to occur billions of years after the Big Bang certain very precise and unusual conditions need to be met. Is it really conceivable that it was pure chance that brought about these conditions? And it is not just the conditions for life on Earth that are incredibly unlikely. Here is a list of some of the conditions that have been cited as necessary for the emergence of human beings.

■ The Big Bang had to occur exactly as it happened, without variation. The scientist Paul Davies has maintained that if the strength of the initial event had varied by one part in 10^{60} (that's a 10 followed by 60 noughts!) then there would have been no Big Bang. This is equivalent to the accuracy an archer would have to have in order to hit a one-inch target from twenty billion light years away.[83]
■ There needs to be a precise balance in the values of constants that govern gravitational force and the weak nuclear force in every atom. Without this there would be no expansion of the universe, and so no formation of stars

or planets. Yet it's been speculated that the two forces need to be balanced to an accuracy of one part in ten thousand billion, billion, billion, billion.[84]

- Stars must have formed, and within them carbon atoms created from the fusion of hydrogen and helium atoms (carbon is an essential component of organic matter).
- A life-containing planet, such as Earth, needs to be at a precise distance from the sun in order to have just enough light and heat to maintain life once it has emerged.
- There must be the development of self-replicating DNA in the 'primeval soup' on the planet.
- There must take place the same random mutations that led to the natural selection of mammals, and eventually the emergence of our ancestors on the African plains.[85]

In fact when we consider all the physical conditions that the universe had to possess for humans to evolve then, as Russell Stannard puts it, 'there seems to be a conspiracy to fix the conditions'.[86] But, by positing the existence of God, this series of amazing coincidences is explained in one fell swoop: they are not coincidences, but the product of God's design. We can build up the argument as follows:

1 For human life to come into existence certain very specific, and unconnected, physical conditions need to be in place.
2 All these physical features are found to be in place in this universe.
3 Either these special features have occurred by chance (the 'Epicurean Hypothesis') or by Intelligent Design (the 'God Hypothesis').
4 The probability of all these features occurring by coincidence is minute.
5 Therefore the most likely explanation for these life-enabling features is Intelligent Design (the God Hypothesis).
6 Therefore God exists.

This type of argument can be described as an 'anthropic teleological argument', because its premises explore those special features of the universe needed to produce *human beings*, and 'anthropic' means 'relating to human beings' (from the Greek *anthropos* meaning man or human).

▶ criticism ◀ Discussions of the 'God Hypothesis', which explains why the universe seems so finely tuned for human existence, have led to the construction of the so-called Anthropic Principle (AP). There have been many formulations of the AP, and this has led to confusion about its exact meaning. Different versions of the AP have been developed both to support (e.g. by Tennant) and undermine (e.g. by Carter) the belief in God. But the original version of the AP, proposed by Brandon Carter in 1974, says that we have no reason to be surprised that the universe is the way it is, because if it were any different then we would not be around to be surprised.[87] It is only when explanation-seeking creatures like humans evolve that they start seeing the features that led to their own existence as special. It is true that the particular way that the universe did turn out was incredibly unlikely, but that doesn't mean that we can turn around and say that it couldn't have happened by chance. After all, it had to turn out one way or another and whichever way it did turn out would appear incredibly unlikely after the fact. If the initial conditions had been different the universe would have turned out very different. It could have resulted in the evolution of Yahoos or Houyhnhnms, instead of humans. It would then be the Yahoos or Houyhnhnms who marvelled at the amazing contrivances of the universe that led to their existence. It might have evolved without any intelligent life. In such a case the way it turned out would have been just as incredibly unlikely, the only difference would be that there would have been no one around to be surprised. This implies there is nothing inherently special about the features that led to life, and there is no need to posit God in order to explain them. The problem with the anthropic teleological argument is that it treats our own existence as of prime importance, as the most remarkable thing that requires explaining. But humans are only one of a great number of incredible things that the universe has thrown up, and only one of an even greater number of things that it might have thrown up had it been slightly different.

▶ criticism ◀ A less respectful criticism of anthropic-type teleological arguments comes from the American writer Mark Twain. Twain's short and scathing article 'Was the World Made for Man?' attacks the human-centred view of the universe that he felt some theologians held. He takes great delight in imagining how millions of years of evolution were needed to make oysters and fish (and coal for the fire) just so that we might have a light and tasty snack for tea. He concludes his article with the following sarcastic observation:

Man has been here 32,000 years. That it took a hundred million years to prepare the world for him is proof that is what it was done for . . . If the Eiffel tower were now representing the world's age, the skin of paint on the pinnacle-knob at its summit would represent man's share of that age; and anybody would perceive that that skin was what the tower was built for. I reckon they would.[88]

▶ criticism ◀ The question we've been addressing is whether God is the most probable explanation for the special features of the universe that have resulted in human existence. However, it only makes sense to talk about probabilities where we are able to compare the chances each outcome has of taking place. For example, when we flick a coin a few hundred times we can work out that there is a 50% chance that the coin lands heads side up. But Hume has already pointed out that this universe, or at very least our experience of this universe, is unique. We are therefore in no position to calculate the probability that this particular universe has of existing; we just don't have any other universes to compare it to. Thus we are also in no position to conclude whether God, or pure chance, is the most likely explanation for this universe.

Of all the proofs of God's existence, teleological arguments are the most reliant on empirical observation and scientific theories. For this reason we might think that they would be the most vulnerable to scientific criticism; and yet they have consistently proved to be resilient and adaptive. Teleological arguments have managed to incorporate developments like the mechanical universe of Galileo and Newton, Darwin's theory of evolution and recently the Big Bang theory. As they respond to science, so teleological arguments have shifted their focus from one special feature of the universe to another: from wondering at the place of the Earth at the centre of the universe, to puzzling over the perfect spiral of a snail's shell, to calculating the probability of carbon atoms forming.

An atheist might find this unacceptable. After all a theory that shifts and adjusts according to the prevailing intellectual wind seems to be unfalsifiable, that is to say, there would appear to be no way of demonstrating that it is false. Theories that cannot be disproved are regarded by some as meaningless and this is an idea we will be examining more closely in Chapter 5 (page 192). However, the popularity of teleological arguments with ordinary believers and religious philosophers is undiminished. We are still struck by the beauty and orderliness of the universe, whether in the equations of theoretical physics, or in watching a thunderstorm in the mountains. To an atheist, it is a wonder that chance has led to such things and to our being here to appreciate them. To a theist, beauty and order are evidence of God's guiding hand. But neither is likely to be persuaded by the arguments of the other. Perhaps what is needed to settle the question of God's existence is direct and personal experience.

Arguments from religious experience

The types of religious experience

One of the most compelling reasons for believing in God is seeing him for yourself. After all, if someone has had a personal encounter with God then they have an immediate justification for believing that he exists. This is in contrast to the cosmological and teleological arguments, which offer only indirect evidence for God (such as the existence of an orderly universe) and which have to fill the gap between the evidence and God through a number of other premises. It would seem as if an argument based on direct experience has no gap to fill because the evidence (experiencing God) leads immediately to the conclusion that God exists.

Before we look at how an argument based on religious experience might be constructed, we should look first at the types of experience that might count as religious. Richard Swinburne has categorised religious experiences into five types.[89] The first two types are public experiences, in that they can be witnessed by anyone present:

1 Everyday occurrences that some people experience as the work of God. For example, anyone can watch the sun rise but for some this is experienced in a profoundly religious way.
2 Extraordinary occurrences or miracles, such as the resurrection of someone who was pronounced clinically dead weeks earlier.

The next three types are private experiences as they are only accessible to the individual having them:

3 Unusual experiences which are imbued with religious significance (e.g. dreams or visions). The individual who has had the experience is able to talk about it and put it into words.
4 As with 3, these experiences are particular to an individual. But in the case of this type of experience the individual cannot describe them, they are beyond words (e.g. mystical experiences).
5 The final type of experience is also private to the individual, but non-specific. So someone comes to feel the 'presence' or a 'guiding hand' of God in his or her life, but this isn't attached to any particular feeling or vision or personal experience.

Read through the religious experiences, past and present, described below.

1 Which of Swinburne's categories do you think each one falls into?

2 Imagine you were the person having each of these experiences. Which would convince you that God existed?

a) 'The angel of the Lord appeared to Moses in a flame of fire out of the midst of the bush . . . God called out to him . . . And Moses hid his face, for he was afraid to look at God.' (Exodus 3:2–11)

b) Blaise Pascal, a French mathematician, described an encounter with God thus: 'From about half past ten in the evening until half past midnight. Fire. God of Abraham, God of Isaac, God of Jacob, not the God of the philosophers and scholars. Absolute Certainty: Beyond reason. Joy. Peace.'

c) In nineteenth-century France, a young girl called Bernadette saw the Virgin Mary in a cave. She was struck by the peace, calmness and love emanating from Mary.

d) You wake up in the middle of the night certain that you are being watched from the door. In the morning you think you can see a handprint on the frame (later you find out that a saint was martyred nearby a thousand years ago).

e) 'And thus, with the flash of one hurried glance, it attained to the vision of THAT WHICH IS. And then at last I saw Thy invisible things . . . but I could not sustain my gaze; my weakness was dashed back, and I was relegated to my ordinary experience.' St Augustine, *Confessions*, Chapter 17

f) In 1996 in Senegal a farmer cut open a watermelon and found the name of God written inside it.

g) 'I saw a light from heaven, brighter than the sun, blazing around me and my companions. We all fell to the ground, and I heard a voice saying to me in Aramaic, "Saul, Saul, why do you persecute me?" ' (Acts 26:13–14)

h) C.S. Lewis, author of the Narnia Chronicles, experienced over the period of a year the increasingly clear presence of God in his life. One night he fell prostrate on the ground and put all his faith in God.

i) In front of a crowd of thousands at Wembley Stadium an American Evangelical Miracle Worker invited the Holy Spirit into the body of a woman with a limp; immediately she could walk normally again.

j) In 1995 in New Delhi a statue of Ganesh, the elephant-headed God of Wisdom, drank milk from a spoon that was held in front of it.

Swinburne's categorisation is useful, but he hasn't captured what religious experiences *feel* like to the people who have them. When we read the many accounts there have been of religious experiences (whether public or private) we find that they are strikingly similar in their effect: full of awe, terror, fascination and love. The German theologian Rudolf Otto coined the term numinous (from the Latin *numen* meaning 'divine power') to describe the experience that humans have when they encounter the holiness of God. For Otto our encounter with God is a distinct and recognisable experience which has certain features that set it apart from all other experiences. One of the key features is the feeling of being 'a creature, abased and overwhelmed by its own nothingness' in the face of God.[90] This 'creature-feeling', as Otto calls it, captures the idea that the cause of the religious experience is external, not internal: people feel the presence of God as a power that exists outside of them, it does not come from within.

Otto uses the Latin phrase *mysterium tremendum et fascinans* ('a terrifying and compelling mystery') to try to convey the simultaneous feelings of terror and attraction that characterise our experience of the numinous. The term 'mysterium' conveys the 'otherness' of God, a being whom we cannot comprehend and who is completely alien to us. 'Tremendum' captures the overwhelming terror of encountering God, and Otto describes the experience as full of dread and awe. Finally the word 'fascinans' sums up the feeling of wonder and rapture that believers feel during religious experiences: they are drawn to God at the same time as they are in awe of him.

There are many forms of religious experience (such as enlightenment in Buddhist traditions, or mystical experiences of nature[91]) but it is the numinous experience that perhaps forms the strongest reason for concluding that God exists. In the sections that follow we look at a proof of God based on numinous experiences and the objections that can be made to this proof. In Chapter 3 we shall examine another type of significant religious experience: miracles.

Constructing an argument from experience

On the basis of people's numinous experiences it is possible to build a simple proof of the existence of God. We can categorise arguments from experience into two types: type A, which are based on my own experience, and type B, which are based on the experiences of other people.

Type A:

1 I have had an experience that I am certain is of God.
2 I have no reason to doubt this experience.
3 Therefore God exists.

Arguments like this are based on what Richard Swinburne calls 'the principle of credulity'. 'Credulity' means 'willingness to believe' and Swinburne is claiming that the way things seem to us (in our experience) is a good guide to the way things actually are (in the world).

Type B:

1 I have heard sincere reports from others of their experiences of God.
2 I have no reason to doubt the veracity of these reports.
3 Therefore God exists.

This type of argument relies on another principle identified by Swinburne, namely the 'principle of testimony'. 'Testimony' refers to the reports made by other people, such as giving a statement in a court of law or, in a more everyday sense, telling someone of the latest gossip in the office. Swinburne's claim is that generally, unless we have special reasons for not doing so, we should believe what other people say.

Both A and B types of argument are built on *a posteriori* premises. They begin with the claim that some people (in the first instance me, in the second other people) have directly experienced God. They then make the assumption that, based on our usual experiences, we have no reason to doubt our senses or the word of others. And if this is the case, so the arguments go, then we have good reason to say that there is a God.

One of the great advantages of these arguments is their reliance on direct experience; after all, our experiences form the most important source of our knowledge of the world. And, generally speaking, experience of a thing is strong evidence for the existence of that thing. The argument from experience treats experiencing God no differently from experiencing anything else. You believe this book exists because you have had a direct and immediate experience of it. You believe the beast of Bodmin Moor exists, because it bit your arm off. Similarly, people come to believe God exists because he appears to them as a numinous experience. But should our experiences of God be treated in the same way as any other experience, and should we trust others or ourselves when it comes to mysterious and unique encounters? These are the questions that we shall now turn to.

Should we trust our own religious experiences?

ACTIVITY   Refer back to the examples of the religious experiences in the activity on page 86.
   How might a strict materialist, someone who did not believe in anything supernatural or religious, go about explaining them?

The principle of credulity tells us that we should trust our own senses, believe what we see and what we hear (unless we have special reason not to). Our fundamental beliefs about the meaning of life, the universe and everything will be affected by our decision to trust our senses following a religious experience, so we must be very careful that this trust is well-placed.

▶ criticism ◀   It has been pointed out[92] that people who experience God may have put themselves into an unusual mental state. In the Christian tradition, mystical experiences often follow from long periods of fasting. Medieval mystics would starve themselves in order to promote the heightened state of awareness necessary to have an experience of the divine. South American shamans often spend several days taking drugs to help them enter the spirit world. And Jesus meets Satan face-to-face, but only after forty days and forty nights of surviving in the desert without food.[93] Is it surprising, we might ask, that mystical experiences occur once the brain is in such an altered state? We have good reason to doubt the testimony of people who have experienced God by these means. As Bertrand Russell says, from a scientific point of view there's no distinction between a man who eats too little and sees God and a man who drinks too much and sees snakes.[94] In other words the fact that someone has an experience of what they take to be God is no guarantee that they have actually seen God.

Recently psychologists working with V.S. Ramachandran at the University of California have found that some people with temporal lobe epilepsy experience intense spiritual feelings during epileptic seizures. Ramachandran's hypothesis is that there is a biological basis to religious experience: heightened activity in the left temporal lobe of the brain in turn floods all the senses (sights, sounds, etc.) with an overwhelming emotional experience[95] which is very similar to the accounts that believers give of their numinous experiences. The 'temporal lobe' hypothesis is very attractive to atheists as it offers a tidy naturalistic explanation for the mysterious nature and intensity of religious experiences. However, it is currently still only a hypothesis and cannot yet account for all numinous experiences.

In defence of the argument from experience Brian Davies suggests that it may well be the case that we could not experience God unless we were in a special mental state.[96] Perhaps it's necessary to go through a special preparation (such as meditation or fasting) in order to reach a state of mind where we can finally come into contact with the divine. So the fact that such preparation is a precondition of our having mystical experiences doesn't establish that these experiences are fake. After all, there are all kinds of perfectly genuine experiences which require special preparation. To use Davies' example, in order to see the whole of Paris we have to assume an unusual physical location, such as climbing up the Eiffel Tower. But this doesn't mean that the experience of seeing the whole of Paris isn't genuine.

Moreover not all religious experiences happen to people who are in an abnormal mental state. Sometimes ordinary people, in stable mental states, are going about their daily lives when they unexpectedly have a religious experience, for example Saul on his way to Damascus.

▶ criticism ◀

Even if we accept that such experiences appear to occur without the person being in any heightened state of awareness we may still be suspicious of their veracity. After all, as sceptics are keen on pointing out, our ordinary experiences of the world are often incorrect. Our senses often deceive us. We are subject to all kinds of optical illusions, for example straight sticks can appear bent when they're half-immersed under water. Couldn't experiences of God be like this: an illusion or some other confusion of our senses?

Again we may offer a counter-argument to this. The fact that we sometimes discover that our senses have misled us doesn't warrant us in generalising this fault to further experiences. After all, we recognise that our senses are sometimes deceptive by using those very same senses to detect the deception. I recognise that the stick is really straight, by pulling it out of the water and taking a closer look. This suggests that the observation that we can sometimes be deceived by our senses presupposes that they are not always deceptive and that they can be used to correct our errors. We recognise errors because they occur against a background of perception which we take to be non-deceptive. This means that in general we can indeed rely on our senses, and if there is no good reason for supposing that a particular perception is deceptive it is reasonable to suppose that it is not. So, if I have a religious experience and there is no reason to suppose that it is some sort of illusion, then I am warranted in trusting it.

We've noted that arguments from experience appear to treat experiences of God in the same way as experiences of any other person. But is experiencing God really just like experiencing anyone else? Our ordinary experiences of people come in the form of sense data, of shapes, sizes, tones, etc. We can easily say of people what they look like, where they are, how long they have been there, how many of them there are. But there are problems with the claim that God can be an object of experience in the same way that other people are. This is because of the special nature of God:

■ he is incorporeal – so does not 'look like' anything
■ he is everywhere – so it doesn't make sense to say 'there he is'
■ he is outside of time – so he was always there, or never there.

So an experience of God is not like any other kind of experience, and the question remains: how do we know whether this experience, the one we're having now, is an experience of God?

If we are to have an experience of something, then we must first possess the mental framework necessary for us to recognise it. How do we know that the square white box is a computer? It's because we *recognise* it as such; it conforms with the concept and mental image of computers that we already possess. Aquinas has argued that we can never really know who God is because he is beyond our understanding. If this is the case then how is it possible to recognise God? And if we can't recognise God then how can we know that it's God whom we are experiencing in our spiritual vision? Here's how we might present this argument:

1 To experience X as X we must first recognise X.
2 In order to recognise X we must possess an understanding of what X is.
3 We can never understand God.
4 Therefore we can never know that our experience of God is in fact God.

A theologian might respond by saying that experiences of God *are* different from ordinary experiences in that they do not need prior understanding and recognition. For Rudolf Otto a numinous experience is one that carries with it both the feeling of belittlement and the knowledge that it is a divine power that is causing our belittlement. 'The numinous is thus felt as objective and outside the self.'[97] This is because religious experiences are self-authenticating: their truth and reality are guaranteed as a part of the experience. In other words, if you have such an experience you just know it is authentic. However, the claim that they are self-authenticating in this sense may strike us as horribly circular:

'I had a vision of God the other day.'
'How do you know?'
'Because visions of God are always truthful and real.'
'Yes, but how do you know that your experience was a "vision of God"?'
'Because visions of God are always truthful and real.'
'But how do you know it was truthful and real?'
'Because it was a vision of God.'
etc.

A person having such an experience may be completely convinced of its authenticity, but cannot guarantee that it really is authentic without begging the question; that is to say, without presupposing what they are trying to prove. It is always possible that what appeared to be a genuine experience of God was in fact the devil in disguise or a hallucination. It seems as if there are often reasons why we should sometimes doubt our own experiences, especially when they are one-off experiences. First, our mind is easily affected by the physical state of our brain, by what we eat and drink, by the various systems (e.g. lymphatic and limbic) that affect our brain, by our emotional states, etc. Secondly, we are sometimes deceived by what we see or hear (as in the example of the stick in water, or mirages or optical illusions). Thirdly, if we have had no prior experience of God then how can we recognise an experience as being one of God?

But to someone who has had a numinous experience these objections are academic. As a result of the experience they now believe in God, and whether they have good grounds to believe in his existence becomes irrelevant.

Should we trust the religious experiences of others?

The problem with the private, inner experiences of other people is that it is hard for us to check whether what they are saying is true. They might be lying when they say they've got a headache, or they're tired, or they're anxious about work. But if a person says they've seen some incredible sight that goes beyond their own personal inner world then it is reasonable for us to expect to be able to confirm this for ourselves. Suppose a girl claims to have seen Elvis Presley busking outside the local library. If this were true we would expect to be able to visit the library and see Elvis busking for ourselves. If this amazing event was unrepeatable, if it left no evidence or if it could not be experienced by anyone else, then we would say that the claim that 'Elvis busked outside the library' had not been established.

Numinous experiences are private, accessible only to the individual having them, so we might expect not to be able to check the veracity of these reports. But numinous experiences are not like experiences of inner aches, pains or queasiness. This is because they point beyond themselves – to a cause that is external and independent of the experience, namely God. Because religious experiences are used to make claims about things that exist (God) we would expect to be able to confirm their truth, in the same way that we expected to be able to confirm whether Elvis was outside the library. Unfortunately religious experiences are also private, so there is no means of checking whether a numinous experience was in fact an encounter with God, in other words there is no means of corroboration.[98] So the private nature of religious experiences makes it impossible for us to check their truth, and we lose grounds for believing in the veracity of the religious experiences of other people.

The British empiricist A.J. Ayer makes a similar point when he says that it is impossible to verify the existence of God.[99] God is not an ordinary object of experience; he is IMMATERIAL and transcendent, unlike Elvis Presley or the beast of Bodmin Moor. In the case of the beast, we have agreed methods for establishing whether or not it exists. We can set up traps, use infra-red cameras, send out troops of boy scouts to hunt for panther droppings, etc. Because we have such agreed methods it is meaningful to talk about whether or not the beast exists. And if enough people claim to have seen it, and agree on what they saw, we will have good reason to believe it exists. But compare this with the case of God. God may occasionally reveal himself to a select few, but we have no means of subsequently confirming that it really was God. He doesn't leave any footprints behind that we can check, there are no agreed signs we could look for that would establish that he was there. Moreover others cannot repeat the experience. Many people have been back to the road to Damascus, but none have been able to verify what St Paul saw. All this means that religious experiences are unverifiable and therefore it would be unreasonable to believe in them.

Davies counters this objection by pointing out that whether or not the existence of something is independently verifiable does not affect whether or not it exists. The fact that we can't verify something doesn't mean it doesn't exist, it just means that we can't *know* that it exists. If someone has an experience of being kidnapped by aliens, for example, we may have no means of verifying whether the experience is genuine since our technology might not be advanced enough to detect alien abduction techniques and equipment. But this failing in our technology has no bearing on whether or not the abduction actually happened.

John Hick also defends the argument from experience against the verifiability objection, claiming that there is indeed a method of verifying the existence of the Christian God's existence.[100] We may not be able to make independent checks in this life, but we will be able to at the end of our lives when we come face to face with God and are judged. This kind of proof he terms 'eschatological verification', normally meaning the kind of verification that comes at the end of time. This is not the kind of verification we'd expect in science, but, he argues, it does suggest that it is at least meaningful to talk about the experiences we have of God.

▶ criticism ◀ A further argument against the principle of testimony is that there is no uniformity in the way people describe their experiences of God. In particular, people from different religions claim to have had visions of very different deities. Christians may see Mary, Hindus may see Vishnu, and so on. But they can't all be right, the objection goes, and we have no reason to privilege one religion's experience over any of the others. And so it seems that none has any real claim to be the truth. To see the point, let's return to the beast of Bodmin Moor. Let's suppose that three separate people claim to have seen the beast. One claims it looked like a great bull with six legs, another like a large red, fire-breathing lizard, another like a huge shaggy dog with eyes like saucers. Surely, in a case like this where there is little corroboration between the different witness statements, we'd be inclined to suppose that none of these experiences could be trusted. By contrast if all three said it was a large black cat we'd be more inclined to believe them. Now, religious experiences are far more like the former case than the latter. Surely, if these experiences were genuine we'd expect different people's experiences to agree on various points. If they have genuinely seen God then they would describe the same kinds of experiences.

To counter this we might point out that it simply isn't true that different religions and different individuals describe very different religious encounters. They may differ in detail, but there could be a core to the experience which is common to all. This core might be defined as the experience of something 'holy'. We've seen that Rudolf Otto described numinous experiences as *mysterium tremendum et fascinans* – a terrifying and compelling mystery. Believers from all religions report the same kinds of feelings: of being overwhelmed, of humbling awe and fear, accompanied by love and peace. These experiences have no ambiguity about them, witnesses are all certain of what has happened. The fact that the experiences vary slightly, from religion to religion, may be explained by saying that they are seeing different aspects of the same thing (like looking at Mount Everest from different angles).

A number of further objections to believing the truth of other people's religious experience come from David Hume, in his critique of miracles. We shall examine Hume's criticisms in some detail in Chapter 3.

ACTIVITY   Look again at the two types of argument from experience (see page 87).

For each of the criticisms, identify whether it is aimed at undermining a particular premise (and state which one) or whether it is aimed at the validity of the argument (and state which step).

Key points: Chapter 2

What you need to know about **arguments for the existence of God**:

1 Arguments consist of reasons put forward to support a conclusion. In a deductive argument the reasons, if true, guarantee the truth of the conclusion. In a strong inductive argument the reasons give good grounds for accepting the probable truth of the conclusion. The reasons, or propositions, that support an argument may be known to be true *a priori* (without further need for empirical evidence or observation) or *a posteriori* (on the basis of observation and experience).

2 Ontological arguments for God's existence are deductive arguments, and their premises are alleged to be *a priori*. A typical ontological argument works as follows. We can define God as 'the greatest being imaginable'; it is, of course, greater to exist in reality than simply in the imagination; therefore, in order for God to be the *greatest* possible being he must exist in reality. In other words it is part of the essence of God that he exists. Unfortunately it seems as if ontological arguments can be used to prove the existence of the 'greatest possible anything', even absurd things like islands. The problem seems to be that they treat 'existence' as if it were just another property of an object, like being red or round. Philosophers of language have argued that 'existence' is a number-word, like 'one' or 'some' or 'all', and not a property. Recent revivals of ontological arguments have focused on the idea of God's necessary existence.

3 Cosmological arguments are inductive arguments, resting on general observations about the universe. They aim to show that the universe requires an explanation of some sort, a cause, and that this cause is God. Aquinas' cosmological arguments rest on the claim that an infinite regress of a particular process or relation (motion, causation, dependency) is absurd, and that the only alternative is that there is an ultimate starting point, namely God. Some critics have doubted whether the universe, or its processes, needs any explanation at all, whilst others have wondered why God doesn't need an explanation.

4 Teleological arguments are inductive arguments based on observations about specific features of the universe, namely the ordered, regular and purposive appearance of the world and its inhabitants. The most influential teleological arguments have rested on an analogy with designed objects. Many features of designed objects (having parts which work together, functioning to fulfil a purpose) seem to be shared with living creatures and their environment. It is therefore supposed that living creatures were also designed, along with their environments. However, arguments based on analogy are most reliable when the two things being compared are very similar; but the universe (for example) does not resemble a watch (for example) closely enough for us to be able to draw any conclusion about whether it was designed.

5 Arguments from religious experience are of two sorts: either based on one's own experience of the numinous, or on the testimony of others who claim to have had such experiences. Numinous experiences have an immediate effect on those who have them. Such is their power that they are said to lead directly to the conviction that God exists. Critics have sought to offer non-supernatural explanations of religious experiences, often drawing attention to the unusual mental state of those who have them.

3

The challenges to believing in God

Introduction

In Anthony Burgess' novel *Earthly Powers* a writer is sent to Buchenwald, a Nazi concentration camp, at the end of the Second World War. 'What was the smell? All too human . . . A compound of longstanding urine, diseased faeces, rancid fat, old rags, gums ravaged by trench mouth, cheese. Gorgonzola cheese . . . It was the smell of myself, of all humanity . . . I wanted to have [Bishop] Carlo with me here to smell the ripe gorgonzola of innate human evil and to dare to say that mankind was God's creation and hence good . . . Man was not God's creation, that was certain. God alone knew from what suppurating primordial dungheap man had arisen.'[101]

We have seen how natural theology, in the form of arguments for God's existence, can reveal in more depth what it means to believe in God, even if the arguments fail to convince non-believers. But belief in God is not just belief in God's existence. There is a whole framework of beliefs that accompany the belief that God exists, for example beliefs about what attributes God possesses, about how God acts on the world, and about how people should act in the world. These beliefs, which are corollaries of belief in God's existence, present challenges that the atheist thinks may prove fatal to belief in God. One of the most immediate and pressing challenges is the question of how the belief in God can be reconciled with the immense suffering that humans endure.

George Orwell captures even more powerfully the pain that human beings are capable of inflicting on one another: 'If you want a picture of the future, imagine a boot stamping on a human face – for ever.'[102] The evil actions of human beings, described so sickeningly by Orwell and Burgess, present one of the greatest challenges to believers. In this chapter we look at this and other challenges and at how believers might respond to them.

The challenge to God

We can identify challenges to a belief in God as coming from two sources: first, those problems that believers encounter as part of their spiritual journey; secondly those problems raised by non-believers in order to question or undermine theism. To the atheist it may seem as if the believer is committed to holding beliefs that are irrational, inconsistent or meaningless. Over the next three chapters we look at how the believer might respond to these three challenges.

- In this chapter we look at claims that belief in God is based on inconsistent or contradictory ideas (e.g. that God is good but allows evil to exist in his creation).
- In Chapter 4 we look at the claim that belief in God is irrational or non-rational.
- In Chapter 5 we look at the claim that belief in God is meaningless.

In the left-hand column of the table below are some of the properties attributed to God by believers; in the right-hand column are properties attributed to the universe by believers.

a) Try to come up with as many problems with the concept of God as you can by combining two or more properties from either column (e.g. 2 and D). You may find that a single property is problematic in itself.

b) How might a believer go about resolving these problems?

Properties of God	Properties of the universe
1 God is omnipotent	**A** Evil exists in the world
2 God is omniscient	**B** Humans have freewill
3 God is omnipresent	**C** There is evidence of God in the world
4 God is benevolent	
5 God is beyond understanding	**D** Humans can have private thoughts
6 God has freewill	**E** God intervenes in the world
7 God defines morality	**F** The universe is governed by physical laws
8 God is outside of time	
9 God acts morally	**G** The universe exists in space and time
10 God is immaterial	

c) You can play a version of this game online if you visit www.philosophersnet.com/games/whatisgod.htm.

In doing this activity you may already have discovered some of the problems associated with evil, miracles and morality which have concerned philosophers over the ages. We shall be returning to these below, but let us first examine some of the other accusations that an atheist might make against the believer.

One problem concerns the claim that God is all-powerful or *omnipotent*. J.L. Mackie, amongst others, argues that if we examine the idea of being literally all-powerful we quickly find that it is incoherent.[103] To see why, we need to recognise that being all-powerful means being able to do anything. So, consider the task of creating a stone so large that God himself could not lift it. Can God perform this task or not? Well, if he *cannot* then there is at least one thing he cannot do, and so he would not be omnipotent. But, on the other hand, if he *can* successfully perform this task then there is something else he cannot do, namely lift the stone he has created. So either way there is something an omnipotent being cannot do. It seems to follow that it is impossible to be literally all-powerful. There just have to be limits to the power a being has to perform certain tasks, and if so then omnipotence isn't a possible attribute of any being.

Perhaps the swiftest solution to this problem comes from St Thomas Aquinas who argues that God's power is bound by what is logically possible, but he is still omnipotent. He cannot perform actions which contradict reason. This means he cannot create round squares, or married bachelors; and in the same way he cannot create stones that he cannot lift. But within the limits of the logically coherent his power is indeed boundless.

The atheist may generate similar, non-trivial questions, such as 'Can an omnipotent God create something that later he will have no control over?' for example humans who have FREEWILL. This is a more serious problem for the believer since it touches on our own nature and our relationship to God. If God is truly all-powerful, then we do not have sole power over our own actions. On the other hand, if he were truly all-powerful he should be able to give us sole power over our own actions. So, once again, either way there is a limitation on his power.

There is also a problem arising from God's omniscience (the claim he is all-knowing) when combined with the claim that human beings have the freedom to choose their own course of action, at least some of the time; in other words, the claim that humans have freewill. If God really knows *everything*, then it seems as if he must know the future, and, in particular, he must know what choices we are going to make. But if God knows what action I will perform before I decide to do it, then I cannot have chosen to do otherwise than I did. But if we cannot choose otherwise, then the actions we appear to choose are not really freely chosen at all. I may feel as though I freely choose to take tea rather than coffee with my breakfast, but God knew all along that I would choose tea. I couldn't have done otherwise than 'choose' tea, and so it seems this choice was predetermined. It follows that the feeling of free choice is just an illusion.

Now, faced with this dilemma, the believer could give up their commitment to human freedom. Perhaps we are all just robots living out our predetermined lives. But this view of humankind does not sit at all well with the notion that we are responsible for our actions, and with the associated claim, so crucial to most religious systems, that we are accountable to God for our choices. In Christian theology, for example, it is often said that at judgement day we will have to answer for our actions before Christ, and that if we are found wanting we will be subject to eternal damnation. Now, if I have no genuine choice about the sins I have committed, then I appear to have good reason to feel aggrieved by this arrangement. If God knew I would sin, and made me so that I would sin, then what do my sins have to do with me? If I couldn't help it, why punish me? Surely God is the only person responsible for all the crimes of humanity!

Clearly then, denying humans freewill has not been a popular option for believers, since it appears to put the blame for all sin onto God. But neither do believers normally wish to surrender claims to God's omniscience. So how can the problem be resolved? One approach is to say that God's omniscience arises because he is outside of time, or ATEMPORAL, so he is able to survey the whole of time in one go. This means that for him there is no future or past; or rather, future and past co-exist on a continuum laid out before his gaze. Human actions are not predetermined and we freely choose to act as we do. But, at the same time, God is able to see what actions we so happen to choose. Just because God knows what I will do, this doesn't mean that I was somehow forced to do it. To understand this thought, consider our own knowledge of the past. Think back to a choice that you made recently, say to have tea rather than coffee with your breakfast this morning. You now know that you chose tea; but the fact that you know that you chose tea doesn't mean that you didn't freely choose tea. You might have chosen coffee. In the same way, the thought goes, the fact that God can know what our choices will be doesn't mean that they couldn't be otherwise. He may know that I will choose tea with my breakfast tomorrow. But when the choice comes, I am still freely choosing tea over coffee, and it is still true to say that I could, if I wanted, choose coffee.

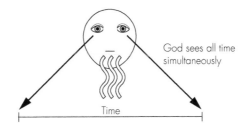

■ Figure 3.1 *God is atemporal*

God sees all time simultaneously

Time

God's atemporality makes sense if we think of him as the creator of space and time. If he has created time itself then he must stand outside it and so is able to survey the whole of it 'at once', as it were. However, this now leads us into a third difficulty with the concept of God. If he does indeed 'transcend' his creation, how is he able to intervene in the world, for example when producing miracles? If God is not in time, and he is not composed of ordinary physical matter, then how can he enter into the spatio-temporal universe and make things happen in space and time? To be atemporal and immaterial, yet act on matter and in time seems impossible.

experimenting with ideas

Consider each of the problems below. How might a philosophically minded believer respond to them?

1 God cannot make a stone so large that he can't move it. Therefore God is not omnipotent.

2 God cannot make a being whom he can control yet who has genuine freewill. Therefore God is not omnipotent.

3 God cannot know what a being with freewill is about to do. Therefore God is not omniscient.

4 God has created beings whom he knew would do evil to one another. So ultimately God is to blame for our wicked acts. Therefore God is not good.

5 God is outside of space and time. Therefore God cannot intervene in the world, and he cannot perform miracles.

6 God is perfect and all-powerful so his creation must be perfect too. Therefore he doesn't need to intervene in the world to improve things. So he would not perform miracles.

7 Ultimately, the God as described by the philosophers (omnipotent, benevolent, omniscient etc.) cannot possess all the properties they ascribe to him. The very concept of God is an incoherent one, and belief in such a God is irrational.

There are three further challenges to the coherence of belief in God that the believer must face. We examine each of these challenges in detail over the rest of this chapter.

First, the issue of whether God is able to intervene in his creation to perform miracles is a challenge believers have to meet. After all, the twin miracles of the virgin birth and the resurrection of Christ are the bedrock of Christianity. However, to some philosophers the concept of 'miracle' is simply incoherent: it depends on both the existence of physical laws that can never be broken, and on the fact that miraculous events break these physical laws. If it can be shown that the concept of a miracle is incoherent then the very foundations of belief in a Christian God are threatened.

Secondly, one of the oldest and most pressing concerns faced by the theist is the so-called 'problem of evil'. How is it possible that a loving and benevolent God allows such horrific pain and suffering to exist in the world? It seems as if God, who created a universe with all this horror, must be responsible for it, and if so this would seriously undermine both the God of the philosophers and the God of the Bible.

Finally we shall look at the claim that God is the source of our moral laws. If God creates right and wrong, then we would seem to have to accept whatever he commands as right. But this suggests that if he had commanded what we now think of as evil, say genocide or infanticide, then these actions would also have been morally good. But this seems crazy. Surely such actions could never be good even if God had commanded them. This way of thinking leads us to suppose that morality must be independent of God. But there are problems with this solution too. For if morality exists independently of God then God is himself bound by morality, which further limits his omnipotence.

The challenge of miracles

Introduction

Moses threw [the staff] on the ground and it became a snake, and he ran from it. Then the LORD said to him, 'Reach out your hand and take it by the tail.' So Moses reached out and took hold of the snake and it turned back into a staff in his hand. 'This,' said the LORD, 'is so that they may believe that the LORD, the God of their fathers – the God of Abraham, the God of Isaac and the God of Jacob – has appeared to you.'

Exodus 4:4–6

He cried with a loud voice, Lazarus, come forth. And he that was dead came forth, bound hand and foot with grave clothes . . . Jesus said unto them, Loose him and let him go.

John 11:44

Miraculous events like these pose two challenges to the believer: (i) Is the idea of a miracle a coherent one? (ii) Is it ever rational to believe in miracles? Miracles lie at the heart of Christian belief, first in the virgin birth of Jesus, and secondly in his resurrection after his crucifixion. Both of these events confirm that Jesus was not a mere prophet or spiritual leader but he was the Son of God. So any challenge raised regarding the coherence or impossibility of miracles is an important one and must be met by the believer.

But before we can deal with either of these challenges we must first ask what a miracle is, or what it is that makes an event a miraculous one. We often see the word 'miracle' used in newspapers to describe rare or unusual occurrences (such as winning the lottery with your first ticket), or events that go against the ordinary run of things (such as being the only survivor of a plane crash). But in the context of religious philosophy the concept of 'miracle' has a technical meaning and it is this that we need to investigate.

experimenting with ideas

Consider the following events and ask yourself whether each is a genuine miracle.

Once you've considered each one, ask yourself what it is that makes an unusual event a miracle. What do miracles have in common?

1 In 1997 an unemployed Welsh miner dreamt of winning the lottery. The next week he correctly chose five numbers and the bonus ball, earning himself £100,000.

2 In 1936 a school prayed for the safe recovery of a fellow pupil who had recently developed cancer. The girl survived against all odds and lived well into her seventies.

3 In 1945 a British pilot was shot down over Germany and fell 10,000 feet without a parachute. He landed with only a few minor injuries.

4 In 1917 in the Portuguese village of Fatima two children saw the Virgin Mary. A crowd of thousands gathered in the afternoon and watched the sun spin violently and fall from the sky.

5 In 1995 an effigy in India was seen to 'drink' milk, thus fulfilling a 2,000-year-old prophecy.

6 In Nebraska in 1950 the members of a church choir all arrived 10 minutes late for their weekly practice, something that had never happened before. They found that just before they'd arrived the church had been destroyed by a huge explosion, which would have killed them had they been on time.

We might consider miracles as a special category of religious experience, as outlined in the previous chapter, but there are two very important differences to the numinous experiences that Rudolf Otto described:

■ Miracles tend to be public, i.e. events that occur 'out there' in the real world, so that many people can witness them. Ordinary religious experiences are often 'private', e.g. internal visions or feelings.
■ Miracles are *supernatural* in some way, and cannot be explained away by the sciences. It is at least possible to provide some sort of naturalist explanation for ordinary religious experiences.

There are two philosophers, one a believer and one a sceptic, who have offered influential definitions of miracles. The first is Aquinas in his *Summa Contra Gentiles*, the second is Hume in his *Enquiry Concerning Human Understanding*. Aquinas identifies three types of miracle, all of them caused by God:[104]

1 events which are incredible, but which remain within the ordinary course of nature (e.g. someone suddenly being cured of an illness);
2 events which are incredible and which go against the ordinary course of nature (e.g. a blind man suddenly being able to see);
3 events which are incredible and which go against the laws of nature (e.g. the sun spinning and falling from the sky).

Hume gives a more succinct definition of a miracle:

a transgression of a law of nature by a particular volition of the Deity or by the interposition of some invisible agent.[105]

Hume

He goes on to offer a series of criticisms against this idea of a miracle, and we shall examine his account of miracles later on.

Write down examples of events which would fall into each of Aquinas' three categories of miracle. Which of these examples would also meet Hume's definition?

The important point to notice about these and other definitions of miracles by philosophers is that they refer to a divine cause: it is God who has intervened in the world. But, for the contemporary Christian philosopher Richard Swinburne, an event is not a miracle simply because a law of nature has been broken by God.[106] There must also be some sort of religious significance or purpose to the event, for example God strengthening our faith, or revealing his plan or his love. So, for example, if God were to intervene in the ordinary course of nature to perform some trivial act, such as to turn someone's hair blue, or make it snow on your wedding day in July, it would not be a miracle. A miracle, according to this view, cannot just be some silly prank. Swinburne's definition also rules out many of the events typically referred to in ordinary language as 'miraculous', such as a loved one surviving a plane crash, or David Beckham scoring a free kick in injury time. For while such events might go against the ordinary course of nature, or at least be highly unusual, and so might be thought to involve the intervention of God, they have no genuine religious significance.

Is the concept of 'miracles' a coherent one?

▶ criticism ◀ As with ordinary religious experiences, the stubborn non-believer will try to find a naturalistic explanation for the supposed miraculous event, however unlikely. For example, the parting of the Red Sea before the Israelites may be accounted for in terms of the unusual meteorological events of the region. Alternatively, the reliability of the witnesses to the supposed miraculous events may be questioned. For example, the events reported at Fatima in 1917 may have been a consequence of mass hysteria. The point is that, for each example of a miracle that the believer gives, the inventive non-believer will always be able to respond with some alternative explanation which need not make any reference to divine intervention. So to the committed atheist none of Aquinas' three categories of miracle is safe.

experimenting with ideas How might the imaginative atheist try to show that the suggested miracles in the activity on page 103 are not in fact miracles? What naturalistic explanation might they give for each of these incidents?

▶ criticism ◀ Another problem raised by atheists is why God elects to intervene in the world on some occasions, but not on others. For example, why does he intervene to correct this person's faulty eyesight, but allow someone else to go blind? Why does he rescue this person from the wreckage of a terrible plane crash, but allow the rest to die? What possible logic is there to these decisions? What criteria is God using to decide when, where and on whom to perform a miracle? God's miraculous interventions appear to the atheist to be arbitrary.

In response the believer is likely to say that miracles are signs of God's grace. The question of 'why this miracle and not that one' cannot be answered by providing the non-believer with a series of boxes she can tick in order to work out when a miracle is due or deserved. (Is it a life-threatening situation? ☑, Are the people involved religious? ☒. Will performing this miracle strengthen their faith? ☑ etc.) To the believer, God really does move in mysterious ways, and is not answerable to an earthly ethics committee that is out to judge his actions.

The question of when God decides to intervene is also linked to the problem of evil. Both atheists and believers often ask themselves 'Why does God not intervene when it really counts, to relieve us from pain and suffering?' The eighteenth-century French philosopher Voltaire was particularly troubled by this; he wondered why God did not intervene miraculously to prevent the deaths of thousands of devout Christians in the Lisbon earthquake.[107] Someone concerned by the problem of evil might also ask why God moved the sun in 1917 at Fatima, but in the very same year failed to prevent the slaughter in the trenches on the Western Front? Why would God busy himself with making a statue weep blood in Sicily while letting tens of thousands of people drown in a tsunami? We shall return to questions such as these when we look at the problem of evil.

One response given by believers themselves is that the definition of miracles, at least as given by Hume, is flawed. From the perspective of some atheists, God is seen as a kind of magician, a performer out to impress us with his box-of-tricks, or a superhero, out to put all wrongs to right. When Herod wanted Jesus to perform some miracle (or as Tim Rice would have it 'Prove to me that you're no fool, walk across my swimming pool.'[108]) he demonstrated that he had no understanding of the real meaning of Jesus' miracles. As the theologian Ninian Smart says, miracles 'occur in the context of a personal situation, and one which has special religious significance'.[109] So miracles have a specific purpose and they convey something about God to those who witness them or are responsive to them.

▶ criticism ◀ A further problem with miracles is a technical one which we encountered above: if God is timeless or atemporal then how can he act within time to cause miracles?

However, this can be solved in various ways. First a believer might say that God is in time and is everlasting (this is known as God's *immanence*). This means that God has always existed, and will always continue to exist, but it also means that he exists in time and hence is able to act upon the universe.[110] Secondly a believer might argue that because God is omnipotent there are no limitations on what he is capable of doing. Through his omnipotence, God is able to act on the world, and perform miracles, despite being outside of time. Finally a timeless God could have created the universe, along with all the laws governing the universe, and 'built into' his creation certain miraculous events that seem to go against these laws. In the same way, a computer programmer can design a word-processing package that contains a few surprises for the user (such as the head of the Queen popping-up the millionth time that the '£' key is pressed).

▶ criticism ◀ Another closely related problem concerns how we are to explain why God would need to perform miracles. A perfect being would surely have created the world properly in the first place with no need to meddle in it afterwards like a bad engineer tinkering with his machine to ensure it runs properly. If the Israelites' escape from Egypt was part of his original plan for his world, for example, then why not arrange things so that they could escape in advance, rather than have to intervene on the day and part the Red Sea?

One response open to the believer is once again to argue that God doesn't actually intervene, but builds miracles into the original plan. So God will have arranged things in advance such that the Red Sea would part at the most opportune moment. Note, however, that this view involves an adjustment to the definition of miracles. No longer do they involve direct divine intervention; rather they are events that go against the ordinary course of things as far as we understand them, but which are caused in the same way as all other occurrences in the world as part of God's mechanical universe.

▶ criticism ◀ We come now to a conceptual problem with miracles, namely the claim that the very definition of miracle reveals them to be impossible. Consider the following argument.

1 A miracle is an intervention by God in the world which breaks a law of nature.
2 A true law of nature is a law that describes and explains all past events and all future events.
3 (From 2) An event that breaks a law of nature demonstrates that this 'law' was not a genuine law – it simply means we were making a mistake in calling it a law.
4 (From 3) Therefore no event can really violate a law of nature (if it is a genuine law).
5 (From 1 and 3) Therefore a miracle (an event that violates a law of nature) can never occur.

So a miracle is impossible because no *genuine* law of nature can be violated, yet miracles must violate the laws of nature, otherwise they are not miracles. This argument tries to show that the concept of a miracle is incoherent: it is a contradiction in terms. No event can break a law of nature, since a law of nature is by definition inviolable. Figure 3.2 presents this argument in another way:

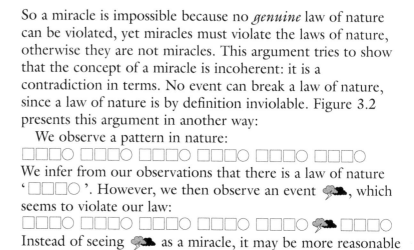

■ **Figure 3.2 *Can a genuine law of nature be violated?***

We observe a pattern in nature:

We infer from our observations that there is a law of nature ' '. However, we then observe an event , which seems to violate our law:

Instead of seeing as a miracle, it may be more reasonable to infer that we were wrong about our original law of nature ( ). The new evidence leads us to posit a new law of nature:

' '

Richard Swinburne responds to this criticism by claiming that if an event appears to have violated a law of nature then we have two options: first to reject the law, which is the route the atheist would take; or secondly to accept it as a universal law with the proviso that 'an exceptional non-repeatable counter-instance' to the law has occurred.[111] Swinburne suggests that the advantage of the second response is that it preserves the universal law as a universal law in those cases where it would be impossible to find an alternative theory that accounts for the 'exceptional counter-instance', i.e. the miracle, as well as all the other phenomena originally supporting the law. This defence appears to safeguard the *possibility* of miraculous events. However, we shall now examine an argument which claims that, whilst miraculous events might be possible, it can never be reasonable to believe that a miracle has occurred.

Is it ever rational to believe in miracles?

David Hume argues in Section X of his *Enquiry Concerning Human Understanding* that it can never be rational to believe in miracles. He offers several arguments to support this view, the first of which is based on his own sceptical empiricist beliefs. As Hume says 'a wise man proportions his belief to the evidence' and in the case of miracles the only evidence that most of us have are the stories and reports of other people. For Hume the question of reasonable belief in miracles comes down to the question of reasonable belief in the word (testimony) of people who say they have witnessed a miracle.

Hume points out an initial problem with the concept of 'miracle' that makes it irrational to believe they can occur. In order to believe in the possibility of miracles we have to accept at least two claims:

1 that there are laws of nature, based on the uniformity of past experiences; and
2 that a miracle is an event which contradicts this uniformity of experience.

By 'uniformity' Hume means 'no exceptions in human experience'; so, for example, there is a uniformity of experience 'that a dead man does not come back to life'. It is rational to believe this because it concurs with all that we have experienced about the deaths of people and the grief we feel because of this finality. In order for an event to count as a miracle it must be an exception to all our experience, for example a human dying then coming back to life days or weeks later. But because a miracle is an exception to all that we know and understand about the world it is therefore never rational to believe in it.

The case for miracles is undermined still further when Hume points out that belief in miracles is primarily based on the testimony or witness statements of others. A modern analogy might be so-called 'urban myths': it is never you yourself who witnessed the sinister or strange event, it is always a friend-of-a-friend who, say, 'worked in an office where a man died sitting at his desk and nobody noticed until days later'. Now, for Hume we need to balance the evidence when deciding whether to believe such tales. In order to believe in miracles we not only have to believe that miracles are possible, we also have to believe that the witnesses are telling the truth, and are not themselves lying, deceived or misinterpreting what they saw. But, Hume argues, it is always more reasonable to conclude that witnesses are lying or have been deceived, than to believe they have really witnessed a miraculous event. Why?

Hume's argument is that we are faced with a choice about what to believe: we must either believe that the person is lying or mistaken and the miracle didn't happen; or that the miracle happened and the person is telling the truth. Faced with such a choice, Hume argues, we can do nothing other than look to our past experience. We must work out which option fits better with what we know about how the world works. Now as it happens the evidence shows that, whilst people generally tell the truth, they do lie from time to time; they do exaggerate, they will kid themselves, and they can be deceived. In other words, people are not totally reliable in the way they recount events: their word does not always conform to reality. This is an important lesson of experience. It means that, whilst we should generally believe what people say, there will be occasions when we should not.

At the same time, miracles, by definition, do *not* conform with our past experience; in fact they go against all our experience, this is what makes them miraculous. As far as past experience goes, miracles just don't happen. So, when someone asks you to take their word that a miracle has occurred, they're asking you to believe them on the grounds that people are generally trustworthy, or in other words, that their word regularly conforms to reality. In doing so, they're appealing to the principle that one should believe things because they conform to past experience. However, and this is the problem, if you apply this principle consistently, you cannot believe them, because experience suggests that people tell the truth less regularly than miracles occur. Hume sums this up in a famous phrase, by saying that when people ask us to believe they have seen a miracle there is 'a mutual destruction of belief and authority'[112] meaning that we should not accept someone's word, if accepting their word means believing in something which is more out of kilter with past experience than people lying is. So when someone says they've witnessed a miracle, and they expect us to believe it, they are asking us to make an irrational commitment, namely to believe them despite the fact that what they've said is more unbelievable than that they are lying. But, if the miracle is more unlikely than a lie then we must assume we are dealing with a lie not a miracle.

experimenting with ideas

Read through the following and decide which would be rational to believe, and why/why not, according to Hume.

1 A thousand years ago a Viking ship sails round Europe until it reaches the north coast of Egypt. The Vikings are disappointed by the lukewarm refreshments that are given to them by the Egyptians, even though it is a boiling hot day. The Vikings describe how they bury frozen water underground in the winter so they can use it to cool drinks in the summer. The Egyptians have never seen ice before, as water never freezes in Egypt. Is it reasonable for the Egyptians to believe what the Viking sailors have said: that water can turn into a solid form?

2 Herodotus, the ancient Greek historian, hears about some Phoenician sailors who claimed to have sailed round the whole of Africa, and who witnessed that during their voyage the sun moved from arcing across the sky in the south to doing so in the north. Should Herodotus believe the sailors' story?

3 Two men, one who is partially sighted, the other with a damaged heel, ask the Roman Emperor Vespasian to cure them, as they believe he is capable of performing miracles. Following consultation with his expert doctors, Vespasian does partially cure them. Hundreds of years later David Hume reads about these 'miracles': should he believe that Vespasian did cure the two men?

4 A woman, claiming to be from the future, appears in Washington DC warning us about the dangers of exercise. She says that, in the future, research has shown that a healthy diet and regular exercise is the cause of ageing, and that we should eat a fat and sugar-rich diet, and do no exercise at all if we wish to live longer. Should we believe her?

5 You see a man claiming to be Christ at his Second Coming walk across a swimming pool in south London in the cold, sober light of day. You tell your friends about this. Should they believe you?

As a rule of thumb Hume says we should always believe the least miraculous thing. This means that the 'wise man' weighs up the probability of a miracle against the probability that those who witnessed it were lying, or were deceived. He concludes that we shouldn't believe people who've witnessed a miracle unless the idea that they might be lying is more miraculous still! Hence, it is always going to be more reasonable to suppose the witness is wrong than to suppose they are recounting something that actually happened. But does the number of witnesses make a difference? Consider the question in Figure 3.3.

■ **Figure 3.3 Which is more of a miracle?**
a) That all these people are lying or have been deceived, or
b) That a miracle has actually happened?

We have seen a miracle

Consider the following two reports of a miracle.

1 Mary comes home and tells her fiancé, Joseph, that she is with child having been miraculously affected by the Holy Spirit.

2 Mary and about 200 others claim to have seen the recently crucified and entombed Jesus walking around the garden of Gethsemane apparently fit and well.

Which would you be inclined to believe? Why? What would Hume say?

Hume is telling us that it is only reasonable to believe things which are based on past experience. But if this were the case then we might never come to believe in anything new or different. If it is only ever reasonable to believe in the occurrence of events which fit in with past patterns of experience then it seems it must always be unreasonable to believe others' reports of unusual or unexpected events, such as that men have landed on the moon or that a new species of tree frog had been discovered in the Amazon, or for an ancient Egyptian to believe that water is capable of turning into a solid form.

In defence of Hume, we might emphasise his point that what is reasonable to believe is what is most likely on the balance of evidence, where relative probabilities are based on regularities in past experience. Now, if NASA, the television news, the papers, etc. tell me that men have landed on the moon; if the Russians don't dissent from this story; if no reputable scientists claim it can't be true and so on, then we must ask ourselves what is more likely: either men have landed on the moon or there is a worldwide conspiracy inexplicably concocted to make it seem as if they have. In this case it is surely not unreasonable to suppose that the conspiracy would be the greater 'miracle'. Similarly, the appearance of a new species of tree frog in the Amazon may be new in some sense, but it fits in with our past experience reasonably well. Frogs, after all, do come in many guises, so a new sort is not so out of kilter with what the past suggests is possible. And scientists are generally pretty reliable in the way they report their findings, especially where there's no money at stake, so the greater unlikelihood here (the greater 'miracle') is that the scientist was lying. Contrast this with scientists claiming to have found a fire-breathing lizard the size of a rhino in the Amazon jungle. The existence of such a creature would be truly miraculous: it doesn't fit in at all with what we know about natural history. No creature has ever been discovered which can breathe fire. No living lizard has been seen that is as big as a rhino. In such a case, when balancing the probabilities, we probably would suppose that the scientists were lying. Although it's highly improbable that a scientist would lie to us about the existence of an Amazonian dragon – in balance it's far more likely that the scientist is lying than that there is actually a dragon living in the Amazon.

There is a further criticism we can make of Hume, however. Hume doesn't rule out the logical possibility of miracles, he simply says that it is unreasonable to believe in them when others tell us about them. But what would he say if we ourselves experience a miracle? Would he expect us to doubt our own eyes and ears, and seek some other explanation?

Read through the following situations and decide which explanation is more likely and why.

1 A man comes back to life.
   a) He was never dead, but was just in a coma.
   b) He was dead and it was a miracle.
2 Thousands of people claim to see the sun moving quickly around the sky in broad daylight.
   a) The sun was moving around the sky.
   b) The crowds of people were all mistaken in what they saw.
3 A close friend of yours says that she was born with her left arm longer than the right. She says that a group prayed intensely for her, and her arms grew to be the same length.
   a) She is not telling you the truth about her arm lengths.
   b) Her right arm did miraculously grow in length.
4 Hundreds of people report feeling better after visiting a holy shrine in Thailand.
   a) Their improvement in health is a coincidence.
   b) Their improvement in health is a direct result of the miraculous healing power of the shrine.
5 You are in a car crash whilst travelling at 70mph on a motorway. As you fly through the windscreen you feel yourself floating to the verge as if carried by an invisible power. The others in the crash have life-threatening injuries; you have a few cuts and bruises.
   a) You have been protected by angels.
   b) You had a lucky escape.

Hume goes on in the *Enquiry* to give a number of further arguments against believing in miracles.

1 He offers an explanation of why we are so inclined to trust the testimony of others when they tell us that they've seen a miracle. We tend to believe them because we desperately want to. We want to feel that the world is a mysterious place where good things can happen. Hume says such beliefs are comforting and agreeable. However, the fact that it would be nice if miracles occurred is not a good reason for believing that they do.
2 He then makes the point that it is normally in places where there is a lack of scientific knowledge that miracles seem to

occur. So, for example, there were many miracles during Biblical times before we had developed much scientific understanding of the world. In countries where science is widely understood there are few reported miracles. Hume's point here is that with a better grasp of the laws of nature which govern the universe, and with a more rational approach concerning what to believe, humans will be less inclined to believe in the occurrence of miracles.

While there may be some truth in Hume's observation, it is worth noting that more people witness miracles in the United States of America than anywhere else in the world. This might be taken as evidence that there is no connection between scientific understanding and scepticism about miracles.

3   Finally, Hume points out that many religions claim that particular miracles demonstrate that theirs is the true faith. However, each religion is also committed to saying that the so-called 'miracles' of all other faiths do not occur, and so do not help establish these faiths as the true faith. However, in rejecting the evidence for the other religion's miracles, one effectively undermines the evidence for one's own miracles. For if I have no stronger evidence than you do for the occurrence of a miracle, and yet am sceptical of yours, then, if I am to be consistent, I should be sceptical of my own. In other words, when I argue that other religions are wrong, and I apply the same standard of proof to my own religion, then I will have to reject my own religion's miracles too.

The challenge of evil

I didn't want to harm the man. I thought he was a very nice gentleman. Soft-spoken. I thought so right up to the moment I cut his throat.

The multiple killer, Perry Smith[113]

I form light and create darkness, I make peace and create evil, I the Lord, do all these things.

Isaiah 45:7

Write down a list of ten things that have happened in the world in the last fifteen years that you regard as evil – try to be as specific as you can.

What do these things have in common, i.e. what makes them evil? Are there different categories of evil?

What is meant by evil?

The problem of evil remains one of the most contentious and unsettling areas in the philosophy of religion. The problem is important to believers and non-believers alike: believers because they have to reconcile their belief in God with their day-to-day encounter with pain and suffering in the world; non-believers because the existence of evil is often cited as evidence against the existence of God. Unlike some of the other theological issues that we have encountered (Who is God? Can his existence be proved? Is he a necessary being?) the problem of evil is generated through our experience of life, and not simply through intellectual investigation. Before we outline the problem of evil in more detail we should first examine what is meant by 'evil' in this context.

Philosophers of religion have traditionally identified two sources of evil: natural and moral.[114] 'Natural evil' includes natural disasters, disease, and all the pain and suffering of sentient beings not caused by humans. 'Moral evil' refers to those acts of cruelty, viciousness and injustice carried out by humans upon fellow humans and other creatures.

Generally evil is taken to refer to those concrete and negative experiences that sentient beings have of the world. These negative experiences can be grouped into the physical (including hunger, cold, pain) and the mental (including misery, anguish, terror), and we can summarise these two types of experience as pain and suffering.[115] Pain and suffering are commonplace amongst sentient beings on this planet, and so evil confronts us on a daily basis.

St Augustine defines evil as that 'which we fear, or the act of fearing itself'.[116] The idea of fear as an evil in itself is echoed in Truman Capote's account of a horrific multiple murder (by two drifters, Perry Smith and Dick Hickock) and its aftermath in a sleepy mid-west American town in 1959. In the townspeople's panic following the murders there was a rush to buy locks and bolts to protect their homes:

Folks ain't particular what brand they buy; they just want them to hold. Imagination of course can open any door – turn the key and let terror walk right in.[117]

If we apply Augustine's account of evil to the situation that these townsfolk found themselves in, then we can identify both the cold-blooded murderers and the terror they leave behind as evil. But Augustine and Aquinas are careful to argue that evil is not a 'thing' (a mysterious substance or presence, for example) but is the absence of goodness. Their account of goodness was strongly influenced by Plato and Aristotle's understanding of 'good', which contained the idea of goal or purpose. For

Aristotle 'good' refers to the complete fulfilment of a thing's natural potential. So a good can-opener is one that is excellent at opening cans, it possesses all the relevant features (the Greeks would call them 'virtues') necessary for opening cans safely and efficiently. Similarly a good oak tree is one that has all the virtues of an oak tree (it has strong roots, is disease free, efficiently photosynthesises and produces numerous acorns).

[Evil is] nothing but the corruption of natural measure, form or order. What is called an evil nature is a corrupt nature . . . It is bad only so far as it has been corrupted.

The Nature of Good 4

Augustine

For Augustine, and Aquinas, evil is not a concrete thing, it is simply the 'privation of good', i.e. a lack of goodness, a failure to flourish or fulfil a natural purpose. We shall see later that this account of evil is fundamental to Augustine's explanation of why it exists. Augustine sees the world, as created by God, in terms of goodness; evil is introduced only later as some disorder within the goodness of God's creation.

experimenting with ideas

Refer to the examples of evil you gave in the activity on page 114.

1 Which of these evils would you prevent if:
  a) you were a billionaire
  b) you were Superman
  c) you were even more powerful than Superman?
2 In the case of **c)** are there any evils you would allow to persist – why/why not?

The problem of evil

The problem of evil affects all the theistic religions, which have as their object of worship a God who is the all-powerful creator of the world, and who cares deeply for his creation. We find the problem clearly stated in the works of both St Augustine and Aquinas,[118] but we can also find earlier versions dating back to Epicurus (341–270 BC). This is how Epicurus puts it:

Epicurus

God either wishes to take away evils, and is unable; or he is able, and is unwilling; or he is neither willing nor able; or he is both willing and able. If he is willing and is unable, he is feeble, which is not in accordance with the character of God; if he is able and unwilling, he is envious, which is equally at variance with God; if he is neither willing nor able, he is both envious and feeble, and therefore not God; if he is both willing and able . . . from what source then are evils? Or why does he not remove them?[119]

As John Hick (1922–present) puts it: 'Can the presence of evil in the world be reconciled with the existence of a God who is unlimited both in goodness and in power?'[120] More recently philosophers have identified at least two different formulations of the problem of evil: the *logical problem* and the *evidential problem*.

The logical problem of evil

The logical problem of evil is the assertion that believers are committed to holding two apparently inconsistent beliefs:

1 God is the all-powerful, wholly good and all-knowing creator of the universe.
2 Evil exists in the universe.

We can find one of the clearest statements of the logical problem of evil in J.L. Mackie's paper 'Evil and Omnipotence'.[121] Mackie tightens up the problem by adding a third proposition that really brings out the contradiction:

3 A wholly good being eliminates evil as far as it can.

ACTIVITY
1 Using these three propositions do you think it's possible for an atheist to construct an argument to prove that God cannot exist?
2 Write down any additional premises that would be needed to make the argument watertight.
3 How might believers criticise such an argument (which premises or steps would they deny)?

For Mackie, propositions 1, 2 and 3 cannot be held to be true simultaneously, so believers must give up at least one of them. It seems undeniable that there is pain and suffering (and a privation of good) in the universe, and thus 2 is true.[122] What about 1? The contradiction would disappear if believers jettisoned some, or all, of the qualities of God, as either he wouldn't be able to do anything about evil, or he wouldn't care. But as Epicurus points out, if God does not have the will to eradicate evil (he is not all-loving) or if he does not have the power to do so (he is not omnipotent) then he would no longer be God at all. We shall see that many proposed solutions to the problem of evil argue that evil is in some way good, or contributes to something good, in which case 3 can be surrendered without abandoning theism. It remains to be seen whether these solutions are successful.

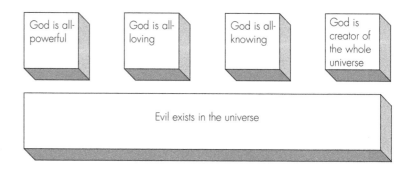

Figure 3.4 *The problem of evil*

It appears that not all of these beliefs can be true at once. Yet, evil certainly seems to be real, so does God not know about it? Does he not care about it? Is he unable to stop it? If we opt for any of these it seems that the God of the philosophers does not exist.

The evidential problem of evil

Darwin

God who could create the universe, is to our finite minds omnipotent and omniscient, and it revolts our understanding to suppose that his benevolence is not unbounded, for what advantage can there be in the sufferings of millions of the lower animals throughout almost endless time?[123]

Darwin's experiences as a biologist brought him face to face with the daily pain and suffering of animals. For many thinkers, including Darwin, David Hume and the contemporary philosopher William Rowe, the sheer amount of evil in the world weighs against there being a God who is omnipotent and wholly good. After all would an almighty, all-knowing, all-loving God allow such extraordinary pain and suffering to exist? Why doesn't he intervene to prevent earthquakes that kill tens of thousands, or viruses that kill millions? Why does he allow psychopaths and serial killers to unleash their cruelty onto innocent people? Why has he permitted genocide after genocide in the past hundred years?

This is not a logical argument, as it does not aim to show that the theist holds a set of inconsistent beliefs. Instead it is posing a question: Given the existence of evil, which of the following is the most reasonable hypothesis:

H1   that there is an infinitely powerful, wholly good God who created the world; or

H2   there is no such God?

For Hume and Rowe the existence of evil is clear evidence in favour of the second hypothesis. As Hume says:

Hume

We must forever find it impossible to reconcile any mixture of evil in the universe with infinite attributes . . . But supposing the Author of nature to be finitely perfect, though far exceeding mankind, a satisfactory account may then be given of natural and moral evil.[124]

William Rowe cites gratuitous and pointless evil as evidence that a theistic God doesn't exist at all.[125] As an example of gratuitous evil, Rowe describes the suffering of a fawn trapped and horribly burned by a forest fire, which lies in agony for several days before dying. The agony endured by the fawn seems to be pointless, and preventable, but Rowe accepts that such an example does not *prove* that God doesn't exist. However, he does maintain that such gratuitous evil makes it reasonable to believe in H2 and reject H1.

ACTIVITY   Refer to the examples of evil you gave in the activity on page 114.
    Think of as many reasons as you can why God might permit such evils to exist (write down every reason, no matter how absurd, or whether or not you believe it to be true).

Resolving the problem of evil

Since the problem of evil was first posed, theists have sought to resolve it without abandoning their belief in an all-powerful, all-knowing and all-loving God. There have been many proposed solutions to the problem of evil, but we can group the main ones into four types:

■ abandoning traditional theism
■ evil is necessary for good
■ evil is a means to a greater good
■ evil is the responsibility of humans – the freewill defence.

Of these, the last three preserve theism as a religious system, and solutions of this type have come to be termed THEODICIES.[126] We might further categorise such solutions as either 'strong' or 'weak' theodicies. A strong theodicy provides an explanation or justification of why God permits the existence of evil within his creation. A weak theodicy (or a 'defence') may not venture to explain why evil exists, but it does offer a defence of theism and shows that the existence of God is not incompatible with the existence of evil as the atheist claims.

■ Solution 1: Abandoning traditional theism

In the twentieth century some theologians proposed a radically different interpretation of what it means to believe in God. Two such revisionist theories stand out as offering potential solutions to the problem of evil: *theological* ANTI-REALISM and *process theology*. We shall examine theological anti-realism in more detail in Chapter 5 when we look at the philosophy of language, but in brief it is the claim that religious beliefs do not refer to anything in the real world. So, for example, belief in God does not imply belief in a being who exists 'out there' in the real world. Anti-realists differ as to what belief in God does imply, but it might include a commitment to a moral way of life, a cultural tradition, or a certain attitude and approach to the world.[127] From an anti-realist point of view the problem of evil is no longer a problem, as God is not a real being existing independently of our minds, and so could not have made the world differently or have intervened to prevent evil from happening.

Process theology, as inspired by A.N. Whitehead (1861–1947) and Charles Hartshorne (1897–2000), suggests that God is not omnipotent, as has been traditionally claimed within theism. As Whitehead puts it, God is 'the great companion – the fellow-sufferer who understands', so he is not separate from his creation, but a part of it and developing with it, influencing events but not determining them. Process theology, far removed from standard Christian theology, is able to solve the problem of evil by surrendering God's omnipotence. God remains able to affect his creation through his infinite persuasive powers, but he cannot eradicate evil or prevent evil from happening.[128]

A third solution to the problem of evil might be found amongst the religious sects who proposed that God is not the only powerful deity. In the Persian traditions of the Zoroastrians (founded in the sixth century BC) and the Manicheans (founded in the fourth century AD) a benevolent God vies with a malicious devil for control of the world. St Augustine himself was a Manichean for about nine years before converting to Christianity. Within these religions evil exists because of an evil deity, and it is not the responsibility of the benevolent God. However, as Augustine realised, such a dualist perspective undermines the absolute power of God, and is at variance with much that is written in the Bible. However, there is an ambiguity in the Old Testament as to whether God or the devil is the source of evil, and in some passages, for example the book of Job, the devil seems to carry out evil acts on behalf of God.[129]

▶ criticism ◀ It is clear that these types of solutions lead in a direction often far away from Christian teachings, and so they are unacceptable to many believers. However, for those who are attempting to make sense of the universe and of evil from a position outside traditional theism such solutions may be reasonable and plausible.

Solution 2: Evil is necessary for good

Augustine's 'aesthetic' theodicy
St Augustine provides one of the best-known theodicies, and argues that God is good and powerful, and created a perfect world. Evil was then introduced into the world because some of his creatures turned away from God. Augustine places particular blame on the fall of the angel Satan from heaven and on the failure of Adam and Eve to resist temptation in the garden of Eden. This, for Augustine, constitutes the original sin of humans. Through these sins God's creation was corrupted, and the natural goodness of the world disappeared: there was a 'privation' of the good. Augustine's theodicy thus places the blame for moral and natural evil on the freely chosen acts of God's creatures (humans and angels). We shall return to this when we review the freewill defence below.

In addition to his 'freewill' theodicy, Augustine also offers an explanation which suggests that evil is part of the natural balance of the universe. This is an aesthetic argument, an argument for the beauty of the universe, and Augustine draws an analogy with the use an artist makes of light and dark shades that create harmony and balance in a painting.

For as the beauty of a picture is increased by well-managed shadows so, to the eye that has skill to discern it, the universe is beautified even by sinners, though, considered by themselves, their deformity is a sad blemish.

Augustine

City of God, 11:23

How does this description of the world as being perfectly balanced fit in with the idea of original sin, and the imperfection that we have brought into the world? Well, Augustine says that this is a matter of perspective. It may seem to us, at a local level, that there is imbalance in God's creation: there is too much pain and suffering, and too much evil that goes unpunished. But Augustine claims that our sinful acts are ultimately balanced by the justice of God: after we die we are all judged, and sinners atone for their sins by being punished. So the beauty that Augustine is talking about is a kind of 'moral beauty' where ultimately justice is done, and the moral balance of the universe is restored.

But in parts of creation, some things, because they do not harmonise with others, are considered evil. Yet those same things harmonise with others and are good.

Confessions, 7:13[130]

Augustine

ACTIVITY   Do you agree with Augustine's comparison between the universe and a work of art? What problems are there with this analogy?

▶ criticism ◀   There are at least two pressing problems with Augustine's aesthetic theodicy. First, as Darwin pointed out, there is a vast amount of suffering undergone by animals which doesn't seem to be balanced by anything, even after the animals die. Augustine isn't really concerned with this type of suffering, and doesn't have much to say on it, except to suggest that nature needs to change and progress, and somehow the deaths of animals helps this to happen. Secondly, and more seriously, Augustine is left with having to justify the eternal pain of humans who are punished and go to hell. By explaining how the suffering caused on this Earth is balanced by the suffering of the wrong-doers in hell, Augustine has simply moved the problem of evil to the next life. Why does a benevolent, omnipotent, omniscient creator allow eternal pain and suffering to exist for those in hell?

1 In a world where everything is red, would it be possible to appreciate, or even recognise, the redness of the universe? If it is possible, how is it possible?

2 How might you go about teaching someone the meaning of the following terms without referring to the words in brackets:
   a) down (up)
   b) hard (soft)
   c) sad (happy)
   d) tall (short)
   e) good (evil)?

There is another way in which evil might be seen as necessary for good. This is the so-called 'contrast' theory. At some points in his theodicy Augustine seems to be hinting at something along these lines, but, as Hick points out, such a theory is in no way central to Augustine's theodicy.[131] The contrast theory is the idea that good only makes sense in contrast to evil; the two concepts trade off each other and so evil actually is necessary for good. If this is right we couldn't have a concept of good without a concept of evil, and we would be unable to recognise the good things and actions in the world without also perceiving the evil things and actions with which they are contrasted. Part of the implication is that in a world without any pain or suffering we would not recognise good acts and so would not applaud, or strive towards them. To use an analogy, a world without evil would be similar to a world with no colours other than red: we wouldn't be able to see the redness because we would have no (non-red) point of reference, nothing to compare it to.[132]

▶ criticism ◀ However, as Mackie points out[133] the contrast theory seems to set limits on what God can and can't do: he can't create good, or make us aware of good, without simultaneously creating evil. So if we wish to maintain that God is omnipotent then the contrast theory of evil must be abandoned. Because of this, a theist committed to God's omnipotence will probably not be tempted by this solution to the problem of evil.

▶ criticism ◀ However, there is a far stronger argument against the contrast theory: namely, that the two concepts don't in fact trade off against each other in the way they'd have to for the contrast theory to work. Good and evil are not opposites in the same way that 'up and down' are. With these latter you clearly cannot have one without the other. But the concept of good has certain intrinsic features which are not defined simply by opposition to evil. It is true that on the Augustine–Aquinas interpretation of evil they are logical opposites: evil means 'lack of goodness', and so is the exact counterpart to 'goodness'. However, by the more common understanding of 'evil' as being 'pain and suffering', good and evil are not opposites. As Hick points out, pain has a very different physiological structure and cause to pleasure, and it doesn't make sense to think of pleasure and pain as opposites.[134] Moreover, we can imagine a world in which everyone is good (perhaps a communist utopia, or a Christian Kingdom of God) and where no one does anyone else wrong. There is nothing inconsistent in the idea of such a world. It may be true that the people in it would have no need of the *concepts* good and evil, and might not recognise acts they performed as 'good'. But this is not the same as saying that they are not actually good, and, most importantly, is not the same as saying that their world would not be *better* than this world.

◾ Solution 3: Evil is a means to a greater good

One of the most appealing solutions to the problem of evil is to see evil as having some purpose and contributing to a greater or higher good. This could mean that evil is an enabler for other goods, and those other goods wouldn't exist without evil. Or it could mean that the universe is in some way a better place because of the existence of evil.

experimenting with ideas

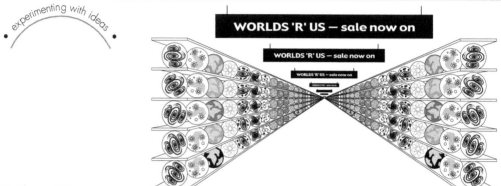

◾ **Figure 3.5**

You have a summer job as a shop assistant in **Worlds 'R' Us – the Ultimate in Universe Shopping**. One day God walks in and says he wants to buy a universe. More specifically he wants to buy the best possible universe (which he can easily do, given he is God). He browses through the billions of shelves, which contain every possible universe, and then asks you for more details of their specifications: the quantity of pain and suffering, the extent of freewill, the level of DETERMINISM, the degree of order and regularity, the balance and beauty in each universe. Eventually, after examining all the billions of universes in the shop, God comes up to the counter and says 'I'll take this one'; and that is the universe we now live in.

1 What 'health warnings' or 'unique selling points' would you have told God about when selling him this universe?

2 Do you think God made a good choice? Why/Why not?

3 Was there a better universe on offer? In what way would it have been better?

4 What do you think God was looking for in a universe (what 'specifications')?

Leibniz's theodicy

Leibniz

This supreme wisdom, united to a goodness that is no less infinite, cannot but have chosen the best . . . So it may be said that if this were not the best of all possible worlds, God would not have chosen any . . . There is an infinitude of possible worlds amongst which God must needs have chosen the best.

Theodicy Book 1, s 8

Gottfreid Leibniz (1646–1716) asks us to consider the situation of God as one of an all-powerful and good being whose task it is to select, from amongst all the possible universes that he could create, the one he will actually create. Now, given that God knows the whole histories of all the possible universes, and is wholly good, then the one he selected to create must be the very best one possible. As this universe is the one that God chose to create, it follows that, despite appearances to the contrary, it must be the best universe going, and every feature in it is an essential part of the divine plan. Therefore the pain and suffering of this world are just some of the many essential ingredients which go in to the construction of the best possible world. This means that all the evil which exists in this universe, must, in some way, contribute to making it a better place than every other possible universe. And if any particular occasion of pain or suffering were to be different from the way it actually is, then the world would overall be worse off. In other words, every single piece of evil, from the suffering of innocent children, to all the millions of people dying horrible and painful deaths from disease, famine and war, is all for the best. Of course, we are not able to see why each local instance of evil is necessary to the divine plan, and it is inexplicable to us why God should allow this or that person to suffer. But, as Augustine argued before him, for Leibniz this is because we do not have God's perspective on the whole of creation, and neither are we able to understand what the other options were.

▶ criticism ◀ Leibniz's position has had many critics, and the French philosopher and writer Voltaire (1694–1778) was one of the first to attack Leibniz's theodicy. In Voltaire's novel *Candide,* the character Dr Pangloss regularly announces that this is the best of all possible worlds. As the eponymous hero is tortured by religious fanatics, and as he watches his mentor Dr Pangloss be hanged, Candide wonders to himself: 'if this is the best of all possible worlds, what can the others be like?'[135] What Voltaire does is to confront the cool intellectual approach that Leibniz takes to the problem of evil with horrific pain and suffering in the world. He does not really refute Leibniz's theodicy, but it is certainly not easy to support it when faced with the concrete reality of pain and suffering.

Swinburne's theodicy

Richard Swinburne (1934–) argues that some forms of evil are the means to certain goods.[136] Swinburne accepts that God is omnipotent and could stop evil, but only at the price of sacrificing the virtuous acts which are the noble human response to its presence. So the existence of suffering makes higher-order goods possible. For example, courage and charity would not exist if there were no one in danger or in need. Swinburne has gone so far as to say that even the existence of Nazi concentration camps can be justified if they led to greater goods, such as acts of sympathy, co-operation and benevolence. He argues that it is better that we live in a world where we can work to reach these goods than in a 'toy world' where nothing threatens us and human actions have no significant consequences. After all, if there were no obstacles to our desires, no possibility of suffering, never the threat that our actions might produce evil outcomes, then our actions would be devoid of meaning, there would be no moral dimension to anything we did. So if there is to be any point to human agency and any space within the universe for making moral decisions, we need to live in a world where there are real challenges and our actions matter. Swinburne's conclusion is that God created a 'half-finished' universe (neither free from evil nor full of evil) which gives humans the opportunity to improve it from within. This does rely on the assumption that humans are free, and we shall examine this assumption when we look at the freewill defence below.

For each of the evils outlined below, think about what good could come of them.

1 Children starve in drought-ridden central Africa.
2 Homeless people, who are sleeping rough, freeze on the winter streets of New York.
3 Forest fires sweep round the outskirts of an Australian town, burning livestock and choking people.
4 A tidal wave destroys all the coastal villages of Indonesia.
5 The bubonic plague wipes out half the population of Europe in the fifteenth century.
6 A ruthless dictator sends his enemies to die in labour camps.

Swinburne's theory also goes someway to solving the problem of natural evil. If human actions are to have consequences that we can learn from and build on, then the world needs to be law-abiding. If God intervened with a minor miracle every time someone fell from a building, or cut themselves with a knife, then humans would not be able to anticipate consequences of their actions, nor formulate general laws of nature. It is only within a law-abiding universe that humans can learn from experience; and a law-abiding universe will contain natural disasters and all the pain and suffering of the fight for survival.

St Irenaeus (AD 130–202) and more recently John Hick have argued, along with Swinburne, that God allowed evil in his creation for a reason: so that we might make a journey towards the good.

Irenaeus' theodicy

Irenaeus

It was possible for God himself to have made man perfect from the first, but man could not receive this [perfection], being as yet an infant.

Against Heresies 4, 39, 1

Unlike Augustine, St Irenaeus does not take the view that human freewill (initially through the choices of Satan, Adam and Eve) caused evil to 'seep into' a perfect world. Irenaeus argues that humans must use their freewill to work towards moral and spiritual understanding, eventually achieving perfection in the next life. So for Augustine perfection existed in the past, at the moment of creation, and we have fallen from this state of grace; whereas for Irenaeus perfection will come in the future at the end of time.

■ **Figure 3.6a**
The Augustinian theodicy

■ **Figure 3.6b**
The Irenaean theodicy

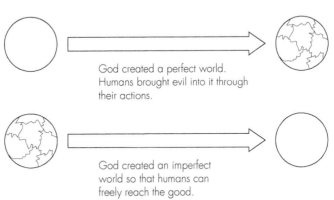

God created a perfect world. Humans brought evil into it through their actions.

God created an imperfect world so that humans can freely reach the good.

John Hick also takes a teleological approach, that is to say, he also argues that the imperfections and suffering of this world will eventually lead to a better state. For Hick the world is a 'vale of soul-making'[137] in which our souls are strengthened and matured by the struggle and suffering of this life. God maintains an 'epistemic distance' from us (that is to say, he doesn't provide us with the knowledge of what our destiny or purpose in this life is) so that we do not know what our purpose is and must exercise our genuine freewill in order to approach the good (a state of holiness).[138]

▶ criticism ◀ The claim that evil exists as a means to some other good (such as spiritual maturity or noble virtues) has been bitterly contested. Hick himself acknowledges that the distribution of misery in the world seems to be random and meaningless, so that it may be heaped upon those who seem least deserving.[139] In such cases it is hard to see what good can come of such evil. Dostoyevsky put forward a series of particularly painful examples of evil in his novel *The Brothers Karamazov*. The character Ivan Karamazov cites three cases of appalling and pointless cruelty to Russian children (to which could be added the holocaust in Belorussia in 1942,[140] or the Beslan school massacre of 2004), which in his view clearly give reason to reject God and the world he has created. Ivan does not deny the existence of God, but instead, disgusted at the universe God has created, he rejects God as a being who is worthy of worship.[141]

Read through the following two examples given by Ivan Karamazov.

1 A young girl, abused by her parents, wets her bed and is forced by her mother to eat her own excrement, before she is made to sleep in a freezing cold shed.

2 A boy throws a stone and injures a General's dog. The boy is stripped and sent out as quarry for a hunt. He is eventually caught and torn to pieces by dogs in front of his mother.

   a) How might these examples of evil be explained within Swinburne's theodicy and St Irenaeus' theodicy?

   b) Do you think these explanations are satisfactory?

▶ criticism ◀ The problem Dostoyevsky poses is almost a utilitarian one. For any theodicy that views the existence of evil as a means to an end we can ask 'is the end worth it?' In other words is God justified in creating a world that contains so much pointless and gratuitous evil in order to attain certain goals? For Ivan Karamazov the answer is no – there can be no goal so worth having that young children are allowed to be tortured in order that this goal might one day be reached.

Solution 4: Evil is the responsibility of humans – the freewill defence

In many of the most influential explanations of the existence of evil, particularly in St Augustine's and St Irenaeus' theodicies, human freewill is an essential element. We have seen that St Augustine argues that it was freewill that led to the original sin of Adam and Eve. This resulted in their subsequent expulsion from paradise by God, and the introduction of pain and suffering into their lives and the lives of all their progeny.[142] Augustine maintains that, although God created a perfect world, evil was introduced by the choices humans made, and thus it is the responsibility of humans not of God.

For St Irenaeus (and modern supporters such as Swinburne and Hick) freewill is necessary if we are to improve ourselves and the world, and to work towards spiritual maturity and noble actions. With this type of theodicy, evil is thus an unfortunate side-effect of God granting us freewill. But it is a price worth paying if there is also the possibility that human freewill can lead to salvation and redemption. In this sense then, solution 4 (the freewill defence) is connected to solution 3 (evil ultimately makes the world a better place).

Both the Augustinian and Irenaean freewill defences view moral evil as stemming from the free choices of humans. They also both view freewill as a positive quality that is a gift from God to humans. Peter Vardy offers a summary of the freewill defence as follows:[143]

1 The highest good for humans is a loving relationship with God.
2 Love must be freely chosen.
3 So God, who is all-powerful and loving, gave humans freewill (in order to achieve 1).
4 Genuine freewill means that sometimes humans will choose good, and sometimes they will choose evil (cruelty, viciousness, greed, etc.).
5 Therefore evil exists in order that humans may choose a loving relationship with God.

As both Hick and Swinburne point out, God does not wish to create a cosy 'toy world' for his human 'pets' to live in. So it is a mistake to look at the world and wonder why it isn't more pleasant for humans. A much greater good than pleasure is the relationship humans can have with God, and this can only be a genuine relationship if we have freewill. And, as we have seen, freely chosen evil is a terrible side-effect of freewill, but one that is worth it.

Let us now look at some of the most important criticisms that have been made of the freewill defence.

▶ criticism ◀ St Augustine's account of original sin is problematic in that it depends upon a literal interpretation of the first book of the Bible. For Augustine, the succumbing to temptation by Eve and then Adam in the garden of Eden is the real origin of sin and evil. Many believers do not now read the account of what happened in the garden of Eden as literally true, preferring to read it symbolically. Nor do many modern believers subscribe to the view that the angel Satan turned away from God, and that this too introduced evil into the world.

▶ criticism ◀ Antony Flew criticises the freewill defence on the basis of the very meaning of 'freewill'.[144] For Flew, freely chosen actions are ones that have their causes within the persons themselves, rather than externally. So when you have the chance to marry the person you love, your decision to do so will ultimately stem from the type of person you are: whether you find them funny, whether you fancy them, whether you 'click' with them, whether you trust them, etc. As long as your choice to marry is internal to you, that is to say, powered by your own character and desires, then it is freely chosen. Flew then goes on to say that God could have created a possible world in which all humans had a nature that was good, and yet in which they were free in Flew's sense. In such a world, humans would always freely choose to do the right thing. And such a world would surely be a better one than this.

However, Flew's attack on the freewill defence may be objected to on the following grounds. What would be the difference between Flew's 'naturally good' people, and automata or mere puppets who had been created always to act in a good way? It is important to theistic belief that God gave humans the freedom to choose to worship and love him, or the freedom to turn away from him. But in Flew's world, God seems to have manipulated the key parts of his creation (humans) in order to bring about his desired results. Imagine a hypnotist persuading someone they were in love: what would be the worth of this love? Just as we would question the value of the feelings manipulated in someone by a hypnotist, so we might question the value of the love felt for God by the 'naturally good' humans in Flew's world. Moreover, is a God who manipulates the end-results in the way Flew describes, a God who is worthy of worship?

▶ criticism ◀ J.L. Mackie offers another version of Flew's criticism, presenting it as a logical possibility, perfectly within God's omnipotent powers.[145] He argues that:

1 It is logically possible for me to choose to do good on any one occasion.
2 It is logically possible for me to choose to do good on every occasion.
3 It is logically possible for any individual to choose to do good throughout their life.
4 God is omnipotent and can create any logically possible world.
5 Therefore God could have created a world in which we were all genuinely free, yet we all chose to do good.
6 God did not create such a world.
7 Therefore either God is not omnipotent, or he is not wholly good.

So Mackie's attack on the freewill defence leads to a restatement of the logical problem of evil.

However, in recent years the logical problem of evil, as presented by Mackie and others, has been rigorously attacked by theistic philosophers, and the freewill defence remounted. Alvin Plantinga (1932–) rejects the idea that God can create an infinite number of possible worlds. For example, God cannot create a world in which humans aren't created by God. And even within the possible worlds that God could create there are limitations. For example, it is possible that there is some person (Plantinga names him Curly Smith) who has a corrupt nature such that, in every possible world that God could create, he will always choose to do at least one evil action. In this case, it is not possible for God (even an infinitely powerful and loving one) to create a world in which Curly is free yet always does good actions. Plantinga is offering a defence (what we called above a 'weak' theodicy) of evil, showing that the existence of evil is compatible with a wholly good and all-powerful God.

Once again our position on the problem of evil may come down to our prior beliefs about the universe. If we are committed atheists, then we may use the existence of evil to justify our atheism. However, it does not seem as if evil proves the non-existence of God. The most evil does is to show that belief in the non-existence of God is rational. From the believer's point of view the existence of evil is a lived and agonising problem. The Book of Job in the Bible underpins this, as God proves to the devil that Job will love him whatever his circumstances. The devil destroys Job's life, family, livestock, leaving him with nothing. Job's friends argue that he must have done something wrong. But throughout his trials, Job maintains his faith in God's righteousness, despite being in ignorance about why he is suffering so much. This story of faith in God, in the face of pain and suffering, is an inspiration to many believers. But the story of Job does not solve the problem of evil, it merely tells us how it is possible to live with evil and yet still believe in God. The story reassures believers, but frustrates atheists who will continue to ask how such a juggling act is possible.

The challenges of morality

Introduction

'Why do you call me good?' Jesus answered 'No one is good except God alone'.

Mark 10:18

It is a common assumption that belief in God goes hand-in-hand with moral goodness. Most people see religion as inseparable from morality, from the system of rules governing how we should live. When a comment is needed on a particular crime, or the latest moral outrage, the media often turn to religious leaders for their views and judgement. The media present members of religious communities as morally upright, and are quick to call them hypocrites when they behave in ways that display human weakness. In many countries politicians align themselves with religion because such allegiance carries the aura of moral respectability needed to win votes. So belief in God has strong moral connotations, but what precisely is the connection between morality and God? The question presents a further challenge to the philosophically minded believer, alongside the issues raised by miracles and evil. There are at least three philosophical approaches to this question:

1 to regard God as the source of morality
2 to take morality as evidence for God's existence
3 to consider God and morality as conceptually distinct.

The first two approaches emphasise the dependence of morality on God, the last approach sees morality as existing independently of God.

Read through the following statements and select the option that best reflects your own beliefs.

1 I think the 10 Commandments
   a) have no moral authority whatsoever
   b) were an effective method of convincing a whole society to be moral
   c) are an accurate record of the commands given by God to Moses.

2 If God did not exist then morality
  a) would remain unaffected because it is meaningless anyway
  b) would remain unaffected because it exists independently of
    God
  c) would cease to have any meaning.
3 If humans ceased to exist then morality
  a) would no longer have any meaning, because it's a human
    invention
  b) wouldn't have any application, although there would still be
    moral laws
  c) would remain, although it would exist only in God.
4 I should be moral because
  a) pretending to be moral is the best way of getting ahead in life
  b) I hate to see other people suffer or get hurt
  c) otherwise I shall be punished in hell.
5 If a believer heard God command them to sacrifice their own son
  on a mountain top
  a) he should see a psychiatrist
  b) he should ignore the command because it would be morally
    wrong to obey it
  c) he should obey the command, because all God's commands
    are good.

*If you answered mostly a): for you the status of morality is dubious; it
is perhaps a system of rules invented by humans in order to get by in
life.*
*If you answered mostly b): for you morality is not grounded in religion
or God, but in some way exists independently.*
If you answered mostly c): for you God is the source of morality.

There is a strong tradition within Western philosophy of
treating morality as conceptually distinct from religion.
Socrates asks, in Plato's *Republic*, why should we be moral?
And he is not satisfied with just any old answer. Acting
morally purely for prudential reasons (to avoid punishment or
find reward) undermines the value of morality and places
another value (self-interest) above it. Yet for many thinkers
saying that we should be moral because God commands us to
be, or because we shall reach eternal salvation, seems to be
just another prudential and self-interested reason.[146] By
placing the source of morality in God we are in danger of
making morality a means to an end: we act morally to suit
God's will or our own self-interest. For philosophers who see
moral values as the highest good this is problematic, in that it
undermines the value of morality and our own role as
autonomous moral agents.

Many philosophers have sought non-religious responses to
Socrates' question. Plato and Aristotle argued that we should

be moral in order to fully flourish as human beings. The utilitarians (Bentham, Mill) and their precursors (e.g. Hume) argued that we should be moral out of our natural sympathy for the welfare of others. Another type of answer, proposed by Kant, is that we should be moral because it is our duty to be moral (although we shall see below that God does have a part to play in Kant's theory).

However, even amongst atheists, there does seem to be a strong sense that morality is more fragile, or harder to justify, without the existence of God. The German philosopher Friedrich Nietzsche argued that the loss of faith in God which was taking hold of Europe in the nineteenth century required the forging of a new kind of morality. What he termed 'the death of God' would have a profound impact on our attitude to good and evil. Ivan Karamazov, in Dostoyevsky's *The Brothers Karamazov*, puts forward a pretty common point of view when he says that without a God 'everything would be permitted, even cannibalism'.[147] Jean-Paul Sartre (1905–1980) runs with this idea in his lecture *Existentialism and Humanism* and in fact he mocks those philosophers who, whilst rejecting God, have held onto some kind of objective moral system.[148] For Sartre, if there is no God then there is no possibility of any kind of objective morality: it becomes something invented by the individual through their actions.

In the rest of this chapter we shall look at the attempts made by Christian thinkers to delineate the relationship between God and morality. We focus on two ways of approaching the dependency of morality on God (see Figure 3.7). First we examine God as the source of morality, and the implications of this approach, namely the construction of a Christian Ethics. Secondly we examine morality as being an indicator of the existence of God, and the implications of this approach, namely the construction of an argument for God's existence.

■ **Figure 3.7 Two ways of exploring the dependence of morality on God**

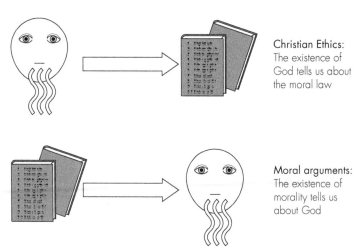

Christian Ethics:
The existence of God tells us about the moral law

Moral arguments:
The existence of morality tells us about God

God as the source of morality: Christian Ethics

For believers, God is the origin of moral laws and moral goodness. The task of Christian moral philosophers is to describe an ethical theory based on the teachings of Christianity, in other words to construct a Christian Ethics. This may seem like a fairly simple task; after all, unlike atheist or humanist philosophers, Christian philosophers have direct access to the moral law via the revelations of the Bible. However, constructing a Christian Ethics is still a heavily contested area of philosophy.

Christian Ethics has been described as dealing with 'what is morally right and wrong for a Christian'.[149] But there isn't just one single ethical code or theory that we can refer to as 'Christian Ethics'. We might mistakenly assume that the Bible is enough to provide believers with a consistent ethical theory by which they can live their lives. But Christian Ethics isn't simply the Decalogue (the Ten Commandments) as amended by Jesus; instead it is a combination of:

1 traditional Jewish ethics (from the Old Testament)
2 the teachings of Jesus (as recorded by the Gospel writers and Paul in the New Testament)
3 the interpretations of the Bible by the Church (e.g. in the form of the Creed, etc.)
4 personal revelation (direct guidance by God in specific instances).

It is also important to remember that there are many different kinds of Christian Churches, each with their own perspective on ethics: Catholic, Orthodox, Lutheran, Calvinist, Anglican, Evangelical, and numerous variations within these Churches.

The concept of a single Christian Ethics may be undermined by ambiguities within the Bible as to the code that Christians should live their lives by. Evangelical Christian writers such as Norman Geisler[150] and John Stott[151] are particularly sensitive to these ambiguities as these writers refer directly to the Bible as a means of finding guidance and solving contemporary issues. For example, Geisler recognises that the Old and New Testaments are contradictory in many ways, and that believers cannot simply select the bits that they like and reject the bits that they don't like. This type of *ad hoc* ethics is very dangerous as it can be used to justify and condone almost any practice. Instead Geisler argues that there are certain rules of thumb that we can use to determine whether a particular part of the Bible is still morally relevant. Geisler's rules are:

1 Ignore the ceremonial law of the Old Testament (e.g. in Leviticus) as it is no longer important.[152]

2 Ignore any laws that Jesus rejected, as Jesus offered a new covenant.

3 Ignore rules that are culturally specific (e.g. Paul's condemnation of men with long hair) as our culture is very different from that of Paul's or Moses'.

4 Ignore the actions of important people (e.g. David) from the Old Testament where they contradict the teachings of the rest of the Bible.[153]

▶ criticism ◀ The problem is that all of these rules of thumb are ambiguous and open to interpretation. Geisler himself can be accused of using a 'pick-and-mix' method when he applies the teachings of the Bible to contemporary moral dilemmas. Sometimes he takes from the Old Testament, sometimes from the Gospels, sometimes from Paul; sometimes he uses the example of figures from the Bible, sometimes he uses direct quotations about the law. The point is that the Bible can be used to support contradictory viewpoints (e.g. men and women are unequal, and men and women are equal), and Geisler's four rules don't prevent this from happening. Theologians have long tried to resolve these problems and inconsistencies, and below we are going to look at three specific theories that Christian philosophers have proposed: Divine Command Ethics, Natural Law Ethics and Situation Ethics.

God's will as the source of morality: Divine Command Ethics

The law of the Lord is perfect . . . the commandment of the Lord is pure.

Psalms 19:7–8

The Good consists in always doing what God wills at any particular moment.

Emil Brunner[154]

The claim that morality is determined by God's will, his commands or prohibitions, is known as the Divine Command theory. The origins of Divine Command Ethics (DCE) can be found in Plato's *Euthyphro* but has been since held by St Augustine and many other theologians. On the surface DCE is a simple idea, maintaining that an action is right if it is commanded by God, and wrong if God forbids it. For example, murder is wrong because God forbids it, and it is the very fact that God forbids it that makes it wrong. So it is not as if God has to consult the moral law, a law which was independent of his will, to see whether it is wrong or not. Now this seems to be fairly straightforward as an ethical theory, but there are many difficulties with it, some of which were raised by Plato in his dialogue the *Euthyphro*.

▶ criticism ◀

An initial difficulty with DCE concerns how we are to determine what God's will is, and how we are to apply it. Revelation is the most obvious answer, but the revelations of the Old and New Testament do conflict. Even assuming the Bible to be the word of the true God, it remains open to different interpretations. Moreover, there are many situations that we face which God's commandments do not address, for example those involving advances in biomedical technology. There are no commandments that deal with cloning or xenotransplantation or genetic engineering and so there are large gaps in the moral law, which believers have to improvise around. Moreover, personal revelations as to God's commands should be subject to the same doubts as religious experiences. Serial killers such as Peter Sutcliffe claim to have been told by God to kill and murder, but, as Jean-Paul Sartre says:

If I hear voices, who can prove that they proceed from heaven and not from hell, or from my own subconsciousness or some pathological condition?[155]

Sartre

This may not be a fatal objection to DCE, however, but only a practical difficulty that we inevitably face in our efforts to determine the moral law.

The Euthyphro Dilemma as a criticism of Divine Command Ethics

Is what is pious loved by the gods because it is pious, or is it pious because it is loved?

Euthyphro, 10a

Plato

In the *Euthyphro* Plato shows that DCE (or an ancient Greek version approximating to it) was inadequate as a system of morality. In it the character Euthyphro attempts to define morality as that which is the will of the gods, or in his phrase that which is 'loved by the gods'. Socrates raises the question of whether everything that the gods command must therefore be moral, or whether everything the gods command is 'moral' because they are following some external moral authority.

This choice has become known as the EUTHYPHRO DILEMMA, and it can be transferred very neatly to DCE. As a dilemma it offers two unpalatable options to a theist:

1 every action that God commands us to do (even cruel and despicable ones) is good
2 every action that God commands us to do is good because it accords with some other moral authority.

Let's examine the consequences of each option.

The first option is DCE taken to its logical extreme. So, God could command us to do completely trivial things (such as not stepping on the cracks in the pavement) and these would be morally right. God could even have commanded us to perform cruel, dishonest or unjust acts, which run counter to our moral intuitions. But according to this interpretation of DCE, a believer would be obliged to do these things and they would be morally right because God had commanded them. It is possible to find many examples in the Old Testament of God's commands that seem to us to be morally questionable: for example, the command to Moses to commit acts of genocide whilst on the journey to Canaan (Deuteronomy 3:2; Numbers 31), or the command given to Abraham to sacrifice his own son Isaac:

God tested Abraham and said to him 'Abraham . . . Take your son, your only son Isaac whom you love, and go to the land of Moriah and offer him there as a burnt offering.'

Genesis 22:2

In the original dilemma given to Euthyphro Socrates asks why we should worship a God who could command us to do horrific acts. But this interpretation of DCE forces us into a position where any act, however terrible, is good when it is commanded by God. This is a conclusion we might wish to avoid. As Job says:

It is unthinkable that God would do wrong, that the Almighty would pervert justice.

Job 34:12

However, Søren Kierkegaard (1813–1855) is quite prepared to accept that God may tell us to commit acts that require us to suspend our ethical beliefs, and that we would be obliged to carry out those acts. In *Fear and Trembling* Kierkegaard defends Abraham's decision to kill his son on the grounds that God has commanded it as proof of his faith.[156] In doing so Kierkegaard challenges the assumption that ethical values should be placed above all other values. For Kierkegaard there is a higher value, known only by God, and yet we must have faith in God's will if he commands us to perform an apparently unethical act. Such faith cannot be rationally explained, nor supported by evidence, yet faith may, in some situations, require the suspension of our ethical beliefs. It was just so with Abraham: he was, as Kierkegaard says, a 'knight of faith' and was prepared to murder his own son in the faith that he was doing it for some higher purpose or 'telos'. Kierkegaard refers to this as the 'teleological suspension of the ethical', where the will of God comes above mere ethics.

But Kierkegaard's position is also one that many believers would be uncomfortable with. Both Aquinas and Augustine believed that God cannot will evil because he is perfectly good, in an ethical sense. So it seems tempting to a theist to reject the view of DCE, that God could tell us to do anything and it would by definition be good. In which case, what makes God's commands good?

The only other option, and the preferred choice of Plato, is that good is independent of God's will, so that what makes his commandments good is that they conform with an external moral authority. In this case God doesn't issue commands which then automatically become 'good'; instead God issues commands which comply with a moral code that lies outside of God. This approach conforms with Plato's metaphysical theory of forms in which the good has objective reality discoverable by reason. However, for the traditional theist this is a problematic way of accounting for the goodness of God's commands. For if the moral law lies beyond God then we can by-pass God if we wish to be moral, and we can also wonder, as Plato does, why we should worship a God who is bound by the same moral rules as ourselves? So to many believers the second horn of the dilemma seems as unacceptable as the first.

Figure 3.8 *The Euthyphro Dilemma*

God's commands are good simply because they come from God

God's commands are good because they conform to an external moral source

The Euthyphro Dilemma, when applied to Christian Ethics, challenges the view that God's commands form the basis of ethics. Both options given by the dilemma are problematic for the believer: the first, as it makes acts of genocide and infanticide morally good; the second because it places morality beyond God. However, there are other theories of Christian Ethics that avoid the Euthyphro Dilemma altogether, and which find the source of morality elsewhere than in God's commands.

God's creation as the source of morality: Natural Law Ethics

If God's direct commands are not the source of morality, then perhaps the source lies in his creation, and the goals and purposes he has built into it. This teleological approach to Christian morality is known as Natural Law Ethics and it stems from the moral philosophy of Aristotle.[157] Aristotle believed that everything in the world had a function or a purpose, for example the function of the sun is to provide light and warmth, and the function of a plant is to grow and reproduce. Aristotle's idea that everything is aimed at some ultimate goal (an idea known as teleology, which you may remember from the discussion of teleological arguments in Chapter 2) suggests that there is a Natural Law that governs all living, and non-living, things.

If Aristotle is right and the universe and everything in it is teleological (aimed at some purpose) then his next point makes perfect sense: everything will benefit if it strives to fulfil its purpose. In technical terms we must strive to reach our highest good (referred to by later scholars as our *summum bonum*). For example, if a plant is successful in fulfilling its function, in other words if it grows big and bushy and has lots of offspring, then it is a *good* plant. And so an element of value, the idea of 'good', is an essential part of Aristotle's teleology. This is Aristotle's basic idea:

■ **Figure 3.9**

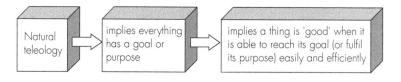

Natural teleology → implies everything has a goal or purpose → implies a thing is 'good' when it is able to reach its goal (or fulfil its purpose) easily and efficiently

experimenting with ideas

According to the ideas of Aristotle, what would make each of the following 'good'?

1 Can-opener
2 Politician
3 Venus fly-trap
4 Dung beetle
5 Snowboarder
6 Human being
7 Painting
8 Beach
9 Celebrity magazine
10 Website

However, Aristotle was not a theist, and did not believe in a personal God who had created and cared for the world. Therefore he did not give a religious account of why the world was governed by Natural Law in the first place. When Aristotle's writings were rediscovered in Western Europe in the thirteenth century it seemed clear to the scholastic philosophers that God was the key element missing from Aristotle's account. St Thomas Aquinas made it his life's work to reconcile Aristotle's philosophy with Christian theology. For Aquinas it was obvious that the Natural Law, which determines the teleological nature of the universe, was created by God, and this was the element missing from Aristotle's theory. So the laws of morality are ultimately governed by the Natural Law, and what is good is determined by what our purpose is.

For Aquinas we are able to discover the Natural Law for ourselves, and so we can use our intellectual abilities to work out God's purpose for us in this life (although our *ultimate* purpose lies in the next life). His conclusions about our purposes are as follows:[158]

- We should act virtuously. For Aquinas, 1 Corinthians 13:13 lays out the three most important 'virtues', namely faith hope and AGAPE (this means selfless love or charity) to which can be added the four virtues proposed by the ancient Greeks: courage, wisdom, temperance and justice.
- We should avoid sin (which for Aquinas meant failing to fulfil our purpose, i.e. engaging in activities that go against the Natural Law).
- We should live harmoniously in society, and have fruitful marriages.
- We should seek to learn about the world using our reason.
- We should worship God.

However, there are problems with Natural Law Ethics, many of them revolving around the arbitrary definition of what is 'natural'.

▶ criticism ◀ Some philosophers have argued that it is a fallacy to begin an argument with premises that simply *describe* the world (e.g. 'it is a law of nature that women can give birth and nurse children') and conclude with a statement that *prescribes* how we should live (e.g. 'therefore women should stay at home and look after children').[159] The fact that women can bear children does not imply that they morally ought to bear children, although this argument has been used to justify the home-bound position of women in many societies. Moving within an argument from a description (an 'is') to a prescription (an 'ought') is known as the is/ought fallacy and both Aquinas and Aristotle seem to be guilty of this logical error. (Note however, that not all philosophers agree that this is always fallacious.[160])

► criticism ◄ Natural Law theory relies on a teleological view of the universe that is no longer commonly believed. For example, Aristotle believed that the reason why sunflowers turn to face the sun was because they were trying to get as much sun as possible to help them grow. Of course, such teleological descriptions are still used in biology, but the modern biologist would regard them as only a manner of speaking. The theory of evolution from Darwin onwards has been highly successful in accounting for the apparent design of organisms, without any reference to God. The plant doesn't *really* have a purpose or goal, it has just evolved mechanisms which make it more successful than its competitors in reproducing. Natural Law theory describes a world which is unchanging, which has been pre-designed, and where everything has a purpose which it is striving towards. But evolutionary theory describes a world where organisms adapt and change, and in this case Natural Law, as conceived by Aquinas, does not apply.

► criticism ◄ The natural laws that Aquinas worked out seem to be determined by the age in which he lived. What may seem 'natural' to us in the twenty-first century (e.g. the lifestyle choice not to get married or have children) would seem completely unnatural to Aquinas. Accounts of what is 'natural' vary from society to society, and our awareness of this should make us suspicious when people make pronouncements about natural 'laws' that govern our behaviour and hold true for all times and places.

► criticism ◄ For Natural Law theory to work as a moral theory, Aquinas must be correct in saying that all of us have the same innate human nature. But we could argue that individuals are a distinct product of their environment, their heredity and their own free choices, and that there isn't a single human nature that we all have. Controversially, the French existentialist philosopher Jean-Paul Sartre argued that human beings have no nature or function at all.[161]

So Natural Law Ethics relies on a problematic view of 'natural' that is now hard to accept. To base a moral theory on human actions that are designated as 'natural' seems at best antiquated and at worst totally prejudiced. With the collapse of Natural Law Ethics in the twentieth century it made sense for Bishop John Robinson to announce that: 'There is no one ethical system that can claim to be Christian.'[162]

God's love as the source of morality: Situation Ethics

'You shall love the Lord your God with all your heart . . .
You shall love your neighbour as yourself.' There is no other
commandment greater than these.

Mark 12:30–31

Situation Ethics is a contemporary Christian moral theory
that rejects the absolute and rigid rules that both Divine
Command Ethics and Natural Law Ethics propose. Situation
Ethics arose out of the attention that modern Christians paid
to the Bible, as opposed to the creed of the Protestant or
Catholic Churches. The most famous supporter of Situation
Ethics is Joseph Fletcher who published his book *Situation
Ethics* in 1966[163] (although he did have many precursors,
most notably Anders Nygren who published *Agape and Eros*
in 1930).

The point of departure for Situation Ethics is the New
Testament, and in particular Jesus' statement that there were
just two commandments: to love God with all your heart,
soul and mind; and to love your neighbour as yourself. The
Greek word for love that is most commonly used in the New
Testament is *agape*. This is in contrast with the Greek term
eros, which has connotations of sexual love, or even of
uncontrollable desire or passion. *Agape*, on the other hand, is
love that is selfless: love for a partner, friends and family, but
also the compassion we may feel for strangers. *Agape* is
sometimes translated as 'charity'. Supporters of Situation
Ethics take Jesus' commandment 'to love' as the only
important moral principle that there is. As St Paul wrote in 1
Corinthians 13:13, 'So faith, hope and love abide, these
three; but the greatest of these is love.'

Fletcher argues that there are three main approaches to
Christian Ethics, but only one of them recognises love as the
central concept. The three approaches are:

1 The legalistic approach – which means making moral
  decisions on the basis of certain rules or principles. Both
  Divine Command and Natural Law Ethics take this kind of
  approach. The problem with a legalistic approach to
  Christian Ethics is that we can never have enough rules to
  deal with the ever-changing circumstances of human
  beings. So, for example, the new medical dilemmas
  revolving around genetic engineering cannot be resolved
  by appealing to old rules.
2 The antinomian approach – which means rejecting all rules
  and principles and making decisions on the basis of your
  'intuitions' as each moral dilemma arises. (The word is

formed from the Greek words 'anti' meaning 'against' and 'nomo' meaning 'law'.) The problem that Fletcher has with this approach is that different individuals have very different feelings about the same situation (e.g. whether or not to have an abortion) and this can only lead to moral chaos.

3 In between these two extremes lies the situational approach – which means accepting one rule: 'to do that which is the most selfless, loving thing'.

In Situation Ethics there are no generalisations or absolute rules because every situation is different, and must be judged according to the specific circumstances. What is important is that in each situation we are as loving (in the selfless sense) as we can be.

Although this type of ethical theory seems the most appropriate to many Christians today, it too has its own problems.

▶ criticism ◀ Situation Ethics makes two questionable assumptions. The first is that we all have the potential to be equally loving; and the second that people are capable of judging what is loving in a particular situation. But, with respect to the first issue, are we actually all as compassionate or sympathetic as one another? If sympathy or compassion turns out to be a genetic disposition that varies between individuals, then the degree to which we are capable of love will differ. The problem then will be that what is right in a particular situation would not be the same for everyone. As regards the second assumption, in order to make moral judgements based on love we need to have criteria to determine whether an action is genuinely loving or not. But no criteria seem to be forthcoming. Are we to judge a loving action by the amount of love that went into it, or the purity of the love, or the consequences of the love, or the type of love?

▶ criticism ◀ It seems clear that different people will interpret situations differently, and the only rule they have to fall back on (i.e. 'do that which is most loving') is frustratingly vague. So, within Situation Ethics, what is morally right will ultimately depend on who you talk to, what their understanding of love is, and what their understanding of the situation is. If Situation Ethics becomes a purely subjective morality, then it is not clear how it differs from an antinomian approach that rejects moral rules altogether.

The moral arguments for the existence of God

We saw (in Figure 3.7 on page 134) that there are two approaches a believer can take when exploring the relationship between God and morality: either moving from God to morality or from morality to God. In the first case we begin with the existence of God and use this to determine our ethical theories. In the second case we begin with the existence of morality and see what this tells us about the existence of God. In this section we look at this second approach in the form of moral arguments for God's existence: arguments that claim that because morality exists there must be a God.

It is possible to identify two types of moral arguments: theoretical arguments and practical arguments.[164] Theoretical arguments are 'truth-directed'. In other words they aim to show that certain things are the case, that certain statements are true, on the basis of premises carefully constructed to support a conclusion. The traditional proofs for God's existence (teleological, cosmological and ontological arguments) are all theoretical arguments in this sense. A moral argument of the theoretical type aims to show that God is the best explanation we have for the way in which we experience morality. Practical arguments on the other hand aim to show that having a certain belief is worthwhile or beneficial to the believer. A moral argument of the practical kind aims to show that my position as a moral agent will be improved if I come to believe in God.

Our moral ideal can only claim objective validity in so far as it can rationally be regarded as the revelation of a moral ideal eternally existing in the mind of God.

The Theory of Good and Evil[165]

Rashdall

Two of the most famous supporters of a theoretical moral argument for God's existence are Hastings Rashdall (1858–1924) and J.H. Newman (1801–1890). The moral arguments they propose are *a posteriori* arguments, beginning with our experiences of morality and concluding with the existence of God. The moral experiences they refer to might include: feelings of sympathy for other people; our inner conscience; feelings of guilt; or our experience of morality as obeying a moral law or commandment.

How would you be feeling in the following situations?
a) Identify those aspects of your feelings that might count as 'moral'.
b) Where do you think moral feelings come from? What is their origin? Why do we have them?

1 You are on your way to meet a friend and have lots of time to spare. You see a woman on her own, at the bottom of a flight of stairs, with a baby in a pram and some shopping.

2 You stumble across an illegal sporting activity whilst out for a walk in Kent: dozens of rabbits have been tied to pegs in the ground, and a man is jumping around in a sack, stamping on them. It seems as if the bystanders are betting on how many rabbits he can stamp on in one minute.

3 You discover that at your former school there are no longer any detentions, but students are instead sent to the biology/chemistry lab for use in experiments as human guinea pigs.

4 You are jogging down an alleyway and turn a corner to see a man lying across your path with a gangrenous foot. In a split second you realise that if you carry on running you will stamp on the rotting foot.

5 An evil genius has kidnapped you and has vowed to destroy millions of people in China with an earthquake created by his secret underground atomic bomb. He says that he will stop the earthquake from happening if you agree to have your little finger chopped off.

Most of us have, at some time or other, experienced morality as a feeling of obligation or duty which impels us to act or not act in a certain way. It is irrelevant to the argument whether we actually acted on this feeling of obligation; it is only important that we have felt it. We may use the term 'conscience' to describe the sense of what is right and what is wrong as revealed by such feelings. One way of making sense of the power that our conscience holds over us is to consider morality as something outside of us: as an objective moral law that we are bound to follow. In order to see this, take for example the belief that killing innocent people is wrong. In believing this, I don't regard it as simply a personal opinion. I don't just think it would be a bad thing *for me* to kill the innocent. Rather, what it means to claim that killing innocents is wrong is that it would be wrong for all people and at all times. But, how am I able to make a judgement about what is wrong for all people? A good explanation of this is that there exists a law which I recognise as applying to all and not just to me. Both Newman and Rashdall argue that our experiences of the objective, impersonal status of morality, our experience of it as something that applies to everyone equally, points to the conclusion that there must be a moral law set up by a being existing independently of us, and that being is God.

Newman

An Essay in Aid of a Grammar of Assent[166]

Here is how we might formally express a moral argument for the existence of God.

1 We experience morality as something that is binding and objective (e.g. through our feelings of conscience and duty).
2 The best explanation for our experience of objective and binding moral obligations is that there exists an objective moral law.
3 If there is an objective moral law there must be a moral being capable of creating it.
4 Only God has the power and goodness to create an objective moral law.
5 Therefore God, the moral law-maker, exists.

'It is impossible to think of a command without also thinking of a commander. The analogy with positive law makes this plain,' claimed the Welsh theologian Huw Parri Owen (1926–1996).[167]

Philosophers like H.P. Owen argue that the existence of moral laws implies the existence of a moral law-maker. The assumption here is that it is possible to draw an analogy between ordinary laws of state, which are constructed by legislators, and the alleged 'moral laws' which must also have been constructed. A moral argument such as this can be seen as a special kind of teleological argument. Like some teleological arguments it draws an analogy (between ordinary laws and the moral law), it is based on particular and unusual experiences of the world (our universal experience of morality), and it argues to the best explanation of these experiences (God).

It is also possible to construct another theoretical moral argument based on anthropological evidence, but arriving at the same conclusion.

1 Every human society has had the same basic moral code[168] (e.g. do not kill innocents; tell the truth; respect taboos; keep promises; help your kinfolk).
2 The best explanation for why all societies have the same basic code is that there is an objective moral law.
3 If there is an objective moral law there must be a moral being capable of creating it.
4 Only God has the power and goodness to create an objective moral law.
5 Therefore God, the moral law-maker, exists.

Some criticisms of theoretical moral arguments for God's existence

The moral arguments outlined above are based on the premise that we all have similar experiences of morality through the voice of our consciences; that what we regard as right and wrong is the same for us all; and that moral obligation is understood to be equally binding on everyone; and therefore that it is objective. However, all these related claims can be questioned. First of all, it may be pointed out that sociopaths appear to lack the empathy underpinning conscience. And moral views certainly do appear to vary from person to person, as is evidenced by the passionate disagreements people have over moral issues. Philosophers have also pointed out that people from different cultures appear to have very different notions of what is right and wrong. The observation that different cultures and individuals have different moral opinions is also the basis for the belief that morality may be no more than a matter of 'personal opinion' and for the belief that it is wrong to judge people from one culture by the standards of another. Such attitudes suggest not only that not everyone feels the same way about what actions count as right and wrong, but also that not everyone experiences moral attitudes as universally binding. What is right for me may not be right for you. This suggests that morality may be relative, and therefore neither universal nor objective, and so the first premise of the moral argument is undermined. Philosophers may also take a more extreme position and regard morality simply as a piece of social indoctrination. If it is one way in which society controls us (by making us internalise socially useful behaviours), then it hardly needs explanation by reference to any divine being. Indeed, nihilists claim that moral values may even be a foolish illusion which the sensible person will avoid.

Such moral relativism (the idea that moral values vary from person to person or culture to culture) and nihilism (the rejection of all values), however, do have their problems. For one thing they seem to reduce moral disagreement to a mere difference over personal tastes. Let's say Duncan believes capital punishment to be morally permissible, but Denise disagrees. Now, without appeal to external moral criteria, their argument would appear to work at the same level as that over whether strawberry ice cream is the nicest flavour. Just as the only rational reaction to the latter disagreement would seem to be to agree to differ in one's tastes, so the only rational reaction to a disagreement over the moral issue of the permissibility of capital punishment ought to be to throw up one's hands and agree to differ in one's attitudes. But surely, the objection goes, when Duncan and Denise disagree about a moral issue there is more at stake than a difference of personal taste. In a moral dispute we tend to think of the person we disagree with as actually being mistaken about something substantive.

Moreover, if morality is just a strongly held, but subjective, belief then we cannot justifiably condemn the practices and actions of others. So a society that strongly believes in the right to eradicate a particular ethnic group is as justified in holding its belief as we are justified in condemning their belief: we are both right. To people who hold genocide to be morally wrong, this is an unacceptable position. For a morally committed atheist, it may be better to accept the possibility that morality is objective (and hence allow the moral argument to get off the ground), than to embrace moral relativism or its more sinister nihilist cousin.[169]

Without referring to God, how would you explain the existence of strong moral feelings in humans?

Even if we do agree with the initial premise that morality feels binding or objective we might be able to find a naturalistic explanation for this, i.e. explain it without reference to a 'super-natural' or god-given moral law. Many philosophers (including Bentham, Mill, Hume and Aristotle) believe they are able to explain morality without any reference to God, but also without reducing morality to mere subjective, or social, beliefs. From outside the arena of moral philosophy sociologists and psychologists feel equally able to explain the intense moral feelings that we experience without requiring God as an explanation. For example, we may explain the existence of a moral conscience through education, social conditioning, our genetic disposition as social animals, or the development of subconscious guilt and desires in our childhood.

We have noted that the moral argument is a form of teleological argument, and has a similar structure in that it is based on an analogy. Now we may try to undermine the analogy of the moral law-maker, in the same way that Hume undermined the analogy of the designer, and ask whether there are other similarities between the moral law and laws of state that rattle the analogy. For example: are there moral solicitors? Is the moral legislation subject to review and change? Was there a point at which particular moral laws came into existence? Why should we conclude that there is only one moral legislator, God? After all, laws of state rely on the contributions of many people – politicians, the judiciary, civil servants – for their formation. If the analogy holds this far then we could argue that a collection of benevolent gods constructed the moral law, a move that takes us far from the monotheism that the moral argument is traditionally used to support. So, if a moral argument is to succeed in demonstrating God's existence it must avoid relying too heavily on a comparison with the laws of state.

The anthropological version of the argument rests on the claim that there are universal moral practices common to all cultures. But the evidence of anthropology makes this questionable. For example, if we compare the ethical beliefs of the Netherlands in the late twentieth century with those of Spain in the sixteenth century we find many more differences than similarities: beliefs about the position of women, about people from different cultures and ethnicities, about people with differing religious persuasion, about social justice and welfare, about the treatment of animals . . . the list goes on. And these are two countries, separated by only a few hundred years and a few hundred miles. A comparison of cultures across time and space would suggest that there is no moral law that is common to all societies. Even those few basic practices that societies may have in common can be explained as necessary for the very existence of society (groups that permit excessive lying and killing tend not to survive!).

Finally an atheist may legitimately raise the question of whether God is good. If God is not wholly good, then why should we obey the moral law that he has constructed? There are two pieces of evidence that may count against God being wholly good: first the existence of pain and suffering, secondly the record of questionable commands issued by God. It seems then that the theist who wishes to construct a moral argument for God's existence needs, at the same time, to resolve the problem of evil (i.e. explain why God can be wholly good and yet allow such horror in his creation), and to grasp the first option of the Euthyphro Dilemma (i.e. explain how God's commands to perform acts of genocide or infanticide are morally good commands).

Kant's moral argument for God's existence

In Chapter 2 we saw the contribution Kant made to the attacks on the traditional theoretical arguments for God's existence: he categorised and labelled them, then offered criticisms of each in turn. Although Kant was a devout Christian he argued that God was a being beyond the limits of our intellect and our experience, and as such it was not possible to prove his existence through theoretical arguments.

However, Kant did think it was possible to show that there are strong *practical* reasons for believing in God, even if these reasons do not amount to a proof. The reasons that Kant gives, namely that only God can give meaning to our moral actions, form a practical moral argument for God's existence.

It is morally necessary to assume the existence of God.

Critique of Practical Reason Bk 2, Ch. 2, Section 5

Kant

In order to understand Kant's moral argument for God's existence we need first to outline his ethical theory. For Kant a moral action is an *autonomous* action, that is to say, one that is truly free. This assertion has far-reaching consequences. It means that an action done from desire, or fear, or any self-interested motive cannot be a moral act. This is because actions based upon emotional motives of desire, fear and self-interest are not freely and dispassionately chosen. Actions driven by our emotions are, in a sense, imposed upon us. If I give money to a man on the street because I feel terrible compassion for his plight, then this action is not autonomous because I did not choose my compassion. Compassion is an emotion that comes upon me whether I like it or not. At the same time, Kant argues, if I rescue someone from a burning house because I have been ordered to, then this is not an autonomous action either, since I didn't choose the order. So in neither case can these be moral acts. Significantly this means that acts done because we have been told to do them by God are not autonomous, and so Kant rejects Divine Command Ethics as a moral theory.

So what is a genuinely autonomous act according to Kant? Like Plato and Aristotle, Kant believed that autonomy, i.e. genuine freedom of will, lies in the exercise of *reason*, as only reason is free from the fluctuations of personal circumstances and desires. When we put to one side our own personal prejudices, our emotions and desires, then we can properly exercise our reason, and this will determine the rules by which we should act. Kant argues that we are all rational beings, and so long as we put our self-interest to one side we can all use our reason to work out rules that will be valid for everyone. These rules, which are applicable to everyone, form our moral duties. So it might be in my own best interests to avoid paying taxes, but it is reasonable for everyone to pay taxes including me. Everyone is able to follow this rule, so it is my duty to pay taxes. To repeat: reason determines those universal rules that apply to all of us and which we are bound by as our duties.

There is a further element to Kant's moral theory that we need to bear in mind. A rule can only apply to us, and can only be our duty, if it's within our power to obey it. For example, if Butch Cassidy is drowning in the Rio Grande, and the Sundance Kid can't swim, then Sundance does not have a duty to dive into the river to rescue Butch. Kant's assertion that we only have a duty to do what we are physically capable of doing is neatly summed up in the phrase 'ought implies can'.

To assure one's happiness is a duty.[170]

Kant

From a Kantian position it is possible to derive many duties: to keep promises, to help others, to tell the truth, etc. But we also have a duty to be moral. However, in his *Critique of Practical Reason*, Kant claims that our most important duty is to strive for the *summum bonum*: the highest good. The highest good consists of fulfilling our moral duties whilst being rewarded by happiness. But it is not at all obvious that we will be able to fulfil our duty to reach the highest good: indeed there are many examples of people who have led morally exemplary lives, only to suffer and be miserable. The possibility that we may do our moral duty throughout our lives, yet fail to be happy, troubles Kant. There is a problem here: we have a duty to reach the highest good (so 'ought implies can'), yet we *can't* reach the highest good in this life. Kant resolves this contradiction by introducing God into the equation. He realises that only if we postulate the existence of God can we be assured of happiness, and hence assured of being able to fulfil our duty to the *summum bonum* if not in this life then the next. We can summarise Kant's moral argument as follows.

1 Morality is based on duty, i.e. what we ought to do.
2 A duty to do X implies an ability to do X ('ought' implies 'can').
3 The most important duty that humans have is the duty to reach the highest good (the *summum bonum*, that is a life of morality which is rewarded by happiness).
4 If it is our duty to reach the *summum bonum* we must be able to reach it ('ought' implies 'can').
5 Only a benevolent and omnipotent God can guarantee that we reach the *summum bonum* (i.e. in heaven).
6 Therefore, if morality (i.e. our duty to be moral) is to have any sort of meaning, God must exist.

We said above that this type of argument is a practical argument rather than a theoretical one. Kant does not believe he has proved God's existence, as he thinks proof here is impossible. However, what he does think his moral argument shows is that presupposing the existence of God makes morality meaningful. Without God, morality becomes practically impossible as I am unable to fulfil all my duties, namely my duty to strive for a life of moral fulfilment combined with happiness. Only in heaven is happiness guaranteed. So by postulating the existence of God, and the possibility of an after-life, we are giving ourselves strong practical reasons for being moral: our belief in God will make our lives, and our moral duties, more worthwhile.

Some criticisms of Kant's moral argument

The introduction of happiness into Kant's austere moral theory seems odd. To begin with it seems as if Kant has smuggled a 'moral carrot' (i.e. the prospect of reward in the after-life) into his ethics, and one that undermines his project of keeping moral motives pure. Kant maintained from the beginning that motives related to personal incentives or interest cannot be moral, yet here he is introducing the tempting reward of the happiness we shall receive in heaven if we uphold the moral law in this life. Moreover, it is not clear why happiness becomes a necessary part of the highest good. In Kant's original sketch of his ethics, it is our reverence for the moral law alone that motivates us to do our duty.[171] Rewards, such as happiness, don't enter into it.

Kant's moral argument for God's existence only works within a Kantian ethical framework. It is because we have a duty to be moral, and a duty to strive for the highest good, that Kant feels it necessary to postulate God's existence. If morality were not based on motives of duty, but on some other foundation, then we would not think it necessary to believe in God. The theory most diametrically opposed to Kant's, i.e. a theory that sees all motives as irrelevant to morality, is utilitarianism. To the utilitarian it is only the results of an action, and whether they serve to increase or decrease the welfare of those affected by the action, that matters. Motives, including acting from duty, are irrelevant. As John Stuart Mill (1806–1873) wrote:

He who saves a fellow creature from drowning does what is morally right, whether his motive be duty or the hope of being paid for his trouble.[172]

Let us say that we were able to accept utilitarianism as a successful explanation of morality, and were able to act morally solely because we care for the welfare of others. In this case then we don't need to postulate God in order to make morality meaningful to us: it is meaningful whether or not we go to heaven and are happy. To a utilitarian it is enough to raise the happiness of others, and to see them try to raise our happiness.

It is virtuous activities that determine our happiness.

Aristotle *Ethics*[173]

There is another competing moral theory that, like utilitarianism, would also undermine Kant's moral argument if it were true. Virtue Ethics, which has its origins in Plato and Aristotle, suggests that moral action is grounded in our own best interests. If we are to be truly happy, in other words if we are fully to flourish as human beings, then we must shape our character in order to be virtuous. Virtues are the skills we need to achieve what we want in life, and both Plato and Aristotle include amongst these virtues the extensive moral skills that enable us to live successfully with others. By honing all these skills, and developing a balanced and expert response to life, we achieve happiness. Kant's idea that happiness can only be guaranteed by God has no place in this view of morality. Aristotle recognises that happiness can't be guaranteed,[174] but that doesn't make a virtuous and moral life pointless. What is important to Aristotle is that happiness, the highest good, is a real possibility open to all of us within this life.

Kant may have overstated his case when he claimed that the highest good must be guaranteed in order for it to be our duty to strive for it. Kant's principle, remember, is that 'ought implies can', not 'ought implies success'. So we can strive for things that are out of reach, and which we will never be able to attain: but the possibility that they are attainable means that we are still able to strive for them. It may be our duty to be perfect citizens, just because it is possible for each of us to be a perfect citizen, and we can universalise this. Of course it can't be guaranteed that we will ever be perfect citizens, but the fact that it is a possibility, that we 'can' do it, means we 'ought' to do it. The same may go for the highest good. If it is possible that we may reach the highest good, that we may fulfil all our duties and be happy in this life, then it becomes our duty to strive for the highest good. God may guarantee the highest good, but we don't need God to make it a possibility and hence to make it a duty. So Kant's argument fails even by his own principle that 'ought implies can'.

Finally we can question whether, even if we accept all the premises leading up to the conclusion, Kant's argument requires God (i.e. the almighty, all-loving creator) as a postulate. Would anything else be able to guarantee our happiness in a future life? As Brian Davies suggests:

Why cannot a top-ranking angel do the job? Why not a pantheon of angels? Why not a pantheon of very clever, Kantian-minded angels?[175]

We have seen in our analysis of the theoretical arguments, the arguments that claim to prove the existence of God, that they do not unquestionably demonstrate that God exists, in the required theistic sense. But even here, with Kant's practical argument, we can question whether God is needed to make our moral beliefs worthwhile. Davies' point is a valid one: all that is required to ensure the meaningfulness of our moral duties is that there is some benevolent being/s powerful enough to bring me happiness in the after-life. For C. Stephen Evans the failure of the moral arguments to prove the existence of a theistic God isn't a problem.[176] He suggests that very few contemporary philosophers now think that it is possible to prove the existence of God, containing all the relevant attributes, with a single argument. As belief in God is so complex it is better to think of each type of argument, the teleological, cosmological, moral etc. as providing a cumulative case for God's existence. Each may be taken to reveal further facets of God to someone who explores these arguments and is persuaded by them.

But we suggested throughout Chapter 2 that the arguments for God's existence are most likely to be successful for those who already believe in God. So if the arguments are only useful to the believer as a means of exploring their faith, and the arguments are not attempts to persuade the non-believer, then where does belief come from? We shall explore this issue in our next chapter.

ACTIVITY Read through Kant's moral argument again. For each criticism identify which aspect of the argument it is aimed at (whether it be an attack on a particular premise or on the structure of the argument).

Key points: Chapter 3

What you need to know about the **challenges to believing in God**:

1 The concept of God raises a number of challenges for the believer. For example, can an omnipotent God create beings (humans) that possess freedom of will? If we are genuinely free then this suggests God does not have power over us, so he is not truly omnipotent. Aquinas proposes that God's powers are limited by logic, and he cannot do what is logically impossible. God's omniscience also raises problems for our freedom, for if he knows how we are going to act tomorrow then are these actions really free?
2 Belief in miracles lies at the heart of Christian belief: e.g. the resurrection of Jesus. But it is difficult to frame the concept of 'miracle' in a coherent way: if a miracle breaks a law of nature,

then was the law really a law? If God exists out of time, how can he intervene in the world through miracles? Hume argues that the belief in miracles rests on the testimony of others. As such, this belief is never rational, because what we're told about miracles contradicts everything else that we know about the workings of the world.

3 The greatest challenge raised by the belief in God is the problem of evil. How can an all-powerful, all-knowing and benevolent God create a universe in which so much suffering exists? To some atheists, like J.L. Mackie, this problem demonstrates that an omnipotent, omniscient and benevolent Creator does not exist.

4 Various solutions, known as *theodicies*, have been proposed to the problem of evil. Perhaps Augustine is right and God is striving for a beautiful universe in which there is a balance of light and dark, good and evil; perhaps evil enables people to act in a good or saintly way, as Swinburne suggests; perhaps humans become stronger and better people through their struggle to overcome and cope with evil, as Hick and Irenaeus propose. Underpinning many solutions to the problem of evil is the freewill defence. Humans were given the freedom to choose between good and evil, and our decision to choose evil is our responsibility, not God's.

5 God is often seen to be the source of morality. But the construction of a moral theory based on Christianity is a tricky one, and there is no agreed Christian Ethics. A popular claim is that morality is determined by God's commands, and this Divine Command Ethics raises the Euthyphro Dilemma. Originally posed by Plato, the dilemma questions whether God's commands are good because they stem from God (in which case God's commands to commit acts of genocide would count as good), or because they conform with some other moral authority (in which case we should follow this moral authority and not God).

6 Morality is sometimes seen as evidence for God's existence. It is said that our moral conscience can tell what is right and wrong, and that we experience morality as something binding and absolute. These feelings imply that there is a moral law, which must in turn entail the existence of a moral law-maker, namely God. However, not everyone experiences morality in this way, and even if they did there are plausible alternatives which may account for these feelings (our evolution as social beings, our conditioning as children). Kant offers his own version of a moral argument, but this stands or falls with his own particular ethical theory, and in any case is not a 'proof' of God's existence, but is an account of what makes moral obligations meaningful.

Faith and belief in God

Faith, evidence and reason

The difference between those believers who have religious faith and those sceptics who don't is brought out nicely in the following joke:

A mountain climber slips over a precipice and clings to a rope over a thousand-foot drop. In fear and despair, he looks to the heavens and cries, "Is there anyone up there who can help me?" A voice from above booms, "You will be saved if you show your faith by letting go of the rope." . . . The man looks down, then up, and shouts "Is there anyone else up there who can help me?"[177]

To sceptics, religious faith seems impossible because it lacks suitable foundations: namely tangible evidence; to believers, religious faith becomes significant because of the lack of conclusive evidence for their belief.

The challenge of evidentialism

Now that you have examined the arguments for believing in God, and the challenges to holding onto this belief, you may decide that there are no *reasonable* grounds for believing in the existence of God. The proofs may strike you as inconclusive, and the challenges (such as the problem of evil) as irresolvable. From a philosopher's point of view the lack of rational foundations for belief in God is problematic. After all, reason has always held pride of place within Western philosophy as the method for interrogating and judging philosophical issues. But the question we face in this chapter is whether reason should be the key to determining questions about God, and whether there are other grounds for belief in God.

Read through the assertions 1–10 and answer the following questions for each one.
- **a)** Do you believe it or not?
- **b)** Is your belief (or disbelief) reasonable? Why/why not?
- **c)** What evidence do you have for believing/disbelieving it?
- **d)** Does the evidence guarantee the truth of your belief beyond any reasonable doubt?

1 The sun will rise tomorrow.
2 England will win the next world cup.
3 You are awake now.
4 The personality we have is determined by the month in which we are born.
5 After we die we will be judged for the rights and wrongs we have performed in this life.
6 Your parents dislike you.
7 The astronaut Neil Armstrong was the first man on the Moon.
8 J.F. Kennedy was shot by Lee Harvey Oswald.
9 Intelligent life exists beyond the Earth.
10 Suicide bombing is morally wrong.

Depending on your answers, this exercise might show that many of your beliefs are not 'guaranteed' by evidence. In other words, there is a gap between what you believe (e.g. that your parents dislike you) and the evidence supporting that belief (e.g. that your parents don't let you do whatever you want to do, and they don't give you enough money to do it). We can refer to the gap that exists between the supporting evidence and the belief as an 'epistemic gap' (*episteme* in ancient Greek means 'knowledge'). It seems possible that an epistemic gap exists between many of our beliefs and the supporting evidence. However, this is not to say that these beliefs are therefore unjustified or baseless. Indeed, it is precisely the level of evidence that usually allows us to refer to our beliefs as justified or not.

It is wrong always, everywhere, and for anyone, to believe anything upon insufficient evidence.[178]

Clifford

For some atheists there is simply not enough evidence to justify a belief in God. So anyone who does believe in God is being irrational. This conclusion (that belief in God is irrational) is based on the assumption of EVIDENTIALISM: namely the view that believing in anything without sufficient evidence is irrational. Evidentialism is the position that W.K. Clifford takes in his 'Ethics of Belief' published in 1877, although he doesn't actually use that term. In this article Clifford argues that even for the most trivial of matters we should only believe that for which we have sufficient evidence. For Clifford we have almost a moral obligation to be this rigorous, because tolerating credulity and superstition (belief without evidence) will ultimately damage society.

But in actual fact do all 'wise men', as David Hume says,[179] proportion their belief to the evidence? Moreover when it comes to those beliefs that really matter, that really have an impact on our lives, *should* we proportion our belief to the evidence?

ACTIVITY   Revisit the previous activity.

a) Rate, on a scale of 1 to 5, how strongly or weakly you believe/disbelieve each of the claims. (1 = strongly believe, 5 = weakly believe)

b) Now rate on a scale of 1 to 5 how much evidence you have for each of the claims. (1 = conclusive evidence, 5 = no evidence)

c) Is there a straightforward relationship between the level of evidence and the strength of belief? Or do you hold some beliefs strongly despite the lack of evidence?

Natural theology, through the many arguments for God's existence, attempts to meet evidentialism on its own terms by showing that there is evidence for the existence of God, and that belief in God's existence is therefore rational and reasonable. All of the *a posteriori* arguments for the existence of God (teleological, cosmological, moral, experiential) draw our attention to evidence of God's existence in this world. Our observation of design and purpose, our experience of visions, moral conscience and the very existence of the universe all count as evidence for God. However, we know that many philosophers (e.g. Bertrand Russell, Antony Flew, Anthony Kenny, J.L. Mackie) would disagree and would claim that these arguments fail to provide sufficient evidence for God's existence. As Kenny says:

To me it seems that if belief in the existence of God cannot be rationally justified, there can be no good reasons for adopting any of the traditional monotheistic religions.[180]

Now even many theists accept that no single one of these arguments is sufficient, but they need to be taken as a group to build up a cumulative case for God's existence.[181] But to a non-theist, natural theology provides no evidence, or at best only equivocal evidence, for God's existence, and so the most reasonable position to take is an AGNOSTIC one (i.e. remaining uncommitted about the existence or non-existence of God) or an atheistic one (i.e. holding that God does not exist).

But it is not only atheistic thinkers who reject natural theology (and evidentialism) as a possible route to belief in God. Many ordinary believers, and many Christian philosophers, have held that belief in God's existence is not grounded on reason, or on evidence. We saw in Chapter 1 (page 10) how Pascal urges us to consider 'The God of Abraham, God of Isaac, God of Jacob, not of the philosophers and scholars' and perhaps this is where philosophers like David Hume, Bertrand Russell, etc., have been going wrong. They've assessed God's existence as they might approach any other rationally determinable question. But the God to whom Pascal is referring is a God whose existence does not need proving or justifying. The God of Abraham is a God who is present everyday throughout the lives of those who believe in him. Perhaps we need to recognise that those who believe in the God of Abraham do so because of their faith, not because of any rational argument.

Read through the following uses of the word 'faith'. Do they have anything in common? How would you go about defining faith?

1 Laryssa had faith that the marriage would work out in the end, although her husband was away working on the oilrigs for nine months out of every year.

2 Lassie remained faith-ful to her owner throughout her life. Even after her old mistress had died, Lassie would sit faithfully by the grave.

3 'I've got to have faith,' said Craig, as his demo tape was rejected once again by a record label.

4 The crowd had faith in Tim's ability to win the championship, despite his failure to have ever reached the final.

5 Dr Frankenstein looked at the misshapen body that spasmed on the floor in front of him but he had faith in his calculations, and resolved to try once more to animate the dead.

The response of fideism

The Son of God died: it is by all means to be believed because it is absurd. And he was buried, and rose again: the fact is certain because it is impossible.[182]

Tertullian

To many religious believers, faith and reason complement each other: with faith playing the lead role, but with reason becoming a useful resource when exploring belief in God. However, there is a strong religious tradition of rejecting reason outright when it comes to belief in God, and this is known as FIDEISM. Within fideism, faith, rather than evidence or reasoned argument, is the true foundation of belief in the existence of God. To the fideist, reason is neither relevant to nor essential for belief in God, and is in fact positively damaging to our belief. The fideist may reject reason because it leads to arrogance, to a belief that God isn't necessary for moral and spiritual direction, and that human reason alone can be a guide. Fideists such as Pascal acknowledge that there is an absence of evidence for God's existence: this is the epistemic gap we referred to above. Faced with this gap, however, rather than reject belief in God the fideist requires that we take a 'leap of faith'.

It is possible to distinguish between two forms of fideism: extreme and moderate. Both the extreme and moderate forms of fideism accept that belief in God is not rational, and does not need to be rational. Moderate fideism sees reason as a barrier to knowledge of God, and views natural theology as irrelevant to faith. However, extreme fideists, like Tertullian (AD 155–222), would not only reject natural theology but also take a deliberately anti-intellectual stance, claiming that belief in God is, and ought to be, irrational. Extreme fideism, and its hostility to philosophy, may be summed up in the words of Tertullian *credo quia absurdum est*: 'I believe [in God's existence] because it is absurd'.

In the rest of this chapter we look at four different approaches to faith: first, that faith is about the acceptance of certain truths, in the absence of evidence; secondly, that faith is a BASIC BELIEF, requiring no evidence at all; thirdly that faith is a decision, an act of will, that we make about God's existence in the absence of evidence either for or against it; and finally that faith is an attitude to God and the world, unrelated to reason, truth, or belief. The first three approaches may broadly be termed 'propositional' analyses of faith, because of the connection they make between faith and believing certain things to be true about the world (e.g. that God exists). The fourth approach may be categorised as a 'non-propositional' analysis, because it does not associate faith with truth, but rather with an attitude of trust.

Faith as the acceptance of revealed truths: Aquinas

Aquinas

There is a twofold mode of truth in what we profess about God. Some truths about God exceed all the ability of human reason . . . But there are some truths which natural reason also is able to reach. Such as that God exists.

Summa Contra Gentiles, Bk 1

Aquinas clearly distinguishes between two ways in which believers come to know God, or grasp truths about God. Firstly believers can attain knowledge of God through their own intellectual efforts, and through their experience of the world: this is termed natural theology. All the arguments we have looked at, both deductive and inductive, are a part of natural theology. Secondly there is 'revealed theology' which includes the kind of knowledge that can only be gained by divine intervention, or revelation, and it can never be known through the exercise of human reason alone. In the Christian tradition these revealed truths have been recorded in the Bible, and perhaps also in the experiences of saints and visionaries.

Aquinas believes that it is possible to come to conclusions about some aspects of God by reason. His five ways of proving God's existence show that we can have what he terms 'scientific knowledge' of God's existence. By this he means we can use empirical or *a posteriori* evidence to establish it. But Aquinas acknowledges that most people do not have the time, energy or intellectual capacity to construct such proofs for themselves. This is why 'the provision of the way of faith, which gives all easy access to salvation at any time, is beneficial to man' (Aquinas, *De Veritate*, question 14, article 10).

Faith was held by Aquinas to be the acceptance of revealed truths that were beyond human reason, but were fundamental to the Christian faith. For example, only faith can reveal the truth of the proposition that 'God is the father, the son and the Holy Ghost' or the proposition that 'the bread of communion is the body of Christ'. So revelation gives us a body of truths, and faith enables us to accept this body of truths without evidence. Aquinas' position on faith has been embraced by the Catholic Church, so that in 1870 the Vatican Council pronounced that faith is 'a supernatural virtue whereby, inspired and assisted by the Grace of God, we believe that the things revealed are true'.

On Aquinas' view, faith is the obedient acceptance of revealed truths as encapsulated in the Bible and the creed of the Church. Faith begins with the intellect rather than the heart, it is based on truths as expressed in propositions, rather than on a sense of trust. In philosophical terms, Aquinas' analysis of faith makes it a kind of propositional belief, i.e. belief *that* various propositions are true.

Aquinas does acknowledge that our beliefs that stem from faith are experienced as certainly true, despite lacking the evidence to support them. So for Aquinas faith shares certain features with both 'scientific knowledge' and 'opinion'. Faith, like scientific knowledge, is both firm and free from doubt. But faith, like mere opinion, lacks absolute proof or demonstration. But the truths that are revealed by God are above those of reason, and all that is required for faith is intellectual assent to these truths: an ability to say, for example, 'yes, I do believe that God is the creator'.

In summary, then, for Aquinas:

- faith means assenting to revealed truths
- faith is a form of propositional belief ('belief that . . . ')
- faith is like scientific knowledge in that it is certain
- faith is unlike scientific knowledge in that it lacks evidence.

ACTIVITY Read through the following assertions, made in the context of Christianity.

1 Jesus is the son of God.
2 The Earth was created around 6,000 years ago.
3 It is wrong to work on the Sabbath day.
4 God is wholly loving and good.
5 The Bible is the true word of God.
6 Jesus was crucified and on the third day rose again.
7 God created the universe.
8 Non-believers are going to be tormented in hell for all eternity.
9 God is the origin of the moral law.
10 Jesus is a descendant of King David.

a) Which of these assertions can be known to be true by reason, and which can only be known to be true by revelation?
b) Would Aquinas agree with each of your decisions?

Faith as a basic belief: Plantinga

more difficult

One of the most sustained defences of natural theology in recent years has come from the American philosopher Alvin Plantinga (1932–). We have already seen above (page 131) Plantinga's use of carefully reasoned argument in his reformulation of the ontological argument, and his own version of the freewill defence against the problem of evil. Despite his rigorous analytic approach to the philosophy of religion, Plantinga does not think that belief in the existence of God needs to rest on reason. Because Plantinga claims that belief in God is justifiable independently of reason, his theory may be categorised as a form of moderate fideism. Clearly he rejects extreme fideism (the view that reason gets in the way of belief in God), as he is himself committed to using rational argument to demonstrate the truth of claims about God.

What then is Plantinga's account of religious belief? He refers to his theory as REFORMED EPISTEMOLOGY: 'reformed', after the Protestant Reformation thinkers of the sixteenth century, particularly John Calvin (1509–1564), whose thinking Plantinga revived; and 'EPISTEMOLOGY' because Plantinga is examining the justification for belief and knowledge claims about God. Plantinga's reformed epistemology includes an attack on the 'evidentialist' claims of Clifford and others who maintain that we should only hold beliefs based on sufficient evidence. As a direct response to Clifford (see the quote on page 158 above), Plantinga argues that:

Plantinga

It is entirely right, rational, reasonable, and proper to believe in God without any evidence or argument at all.[183]

Plantinga's argument is that there must be beliefs that we begin with, and from which we infer other beliefs and build up a picture of the world. Such 'basic beliefs' may lack evidence, but nonetheless it is still reasonable and proper to believe they are true. So Clifford is wrong when he says we must never believe anything without sufficient evidence: we must begin with some building blocks, i.e. those beliefs we hold to be basic.

Figure 4.1 *Basic beliefs act as the foundations for our other beliefs*

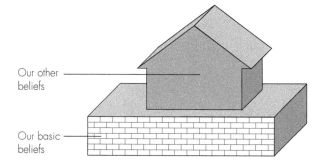

Our other beliefs

Our basic beliefs

Plantinga goes on to argue that in fact most evidentialists do recognise that there are such basic beliefs. This is because evidentialism is based on the epistemological theory known as 'classical foundationalism'. Classical foundationalism claims that our knowledge about the world should be traced back to solid foundations. These foundations are our basic beliefs, which Plantinga describes as 'the starting points for thought'.[184] These basic beliefs do not involve any inference from other beliefs; they are all directly and straightforwardly available to us. Examples of types of beliefs that a foundationalist (and hence an evidentialist) is willing to accept as properly basic include: beliefs that are self-evident to us, beliefs that are incorrigible (e.g. when I feel pain I know I'm in pain) and beliefs based on my present sense data. Plantinga summarises the foundationalist claim as follows:

F: I am entitled to believe something without evidence if and only if it is self-evident, incorrigible or certain to me in some way.

So according to the foundationalist (as described by Plantinga) if a belief meets criterion F then that belief is basic.

experimenting with ideas

a) Which of the following beliefs do you hold?

b) Which do you think are basic (in the foundationalist sense)?

1 It seems to me as if I am currently reading a book on the philosophy of religion.

2 $2 + 2 = 4$.

3 I have a brain.

4 The world did not just come into existence five minutes ago.

5 Other humans are not robots – they have an inner life similar to mine.

6 I am entitled to believe in something without evidence if and only if it is self-evident, incorrigible or certain to me in some way.

7 Bombing civilians is morally wrong.

8 There definitely isn't a God.

9 There is a God.

10 Some people have a 'sixth sense' capable of seeing into the future.

The question is whether the belief that God exists is a properly basic belief. According to an evidentialist/ foundationalist such as Clifford, it is not a basic belief because it fails to meet criterion F. In other words, God's existence is not self-evident, nor is it incorrigible, nor is it plain to our senses. Because God's existence is not a basic belief, the foundationalist maintains that the only way of rationally believing in God is to provide evidence or arguments for his existence. These are the arguments we examined in Chapter 2, which many thinkers have found inconclusive.

However, Plantinga does not accept the foundationalist's assertion that the only way rationally to believe in God is to provide arguments or evidence for his existence. His claim is that belief in God is a basic belief in no need of evidence or proof and that classical foundationalism fails to give an adequate account of basic beliefs. In mounting his attack on foundationalism he asks us to consider the following question: is F itself self-evident or incorrigible or certain in some way to me? No it clearly isn't. In which case it fails its own criterion and believing it to be true is irrational. So foundationalism has shown that it is irrational to believe in foundationalism!

Plantinga gives further grounds for rejecting the foundationalist account of what is properly basic. He says there are many examples of beliefs that are properly basic, and which it is rational to hold, but which fail the criterion given in F. For example, I believe that I had a spicy beanburger at lunchtime. Now this belief is not based on data that is immediately available to me (because I am no longer masticating chunks of spicy burger) but is instead based on my memory of this culinary wonder. Plantinga says that we are entitled to, and we in fact do, treat our recent memories as basic beliefs, despite their failure to meet criterion F. There are other beliefs that also fail criterion F, but which we treat as properly basic, such as our belief that we weren't born yesterday and that other people have inner lives like our own.

So Plantinga rejects the foundationalist account of basic belief on two counts: first it is incoherent, and secondly it excludes many beliefs that are properly basic. Because evidentialism is based on foundationalism it too must fail, and Plantinga concludes that Clifford and others have no grounds for claiming religious belief to be irrational, and they have no grounds for denying religious belief to be a basic belief.

For Plantinga belief in God is a properly basic belief after all. Because belief in God is genuinely a basic belief, believers don't have to give reasons for why they believe it. Nor do they have to give arguments of the sort we looked at in Chapter 2 for their belief. Belief in God's existence is just obvious to the person who holds the belief, like it is obvious that our friends have inner lives like us, and it is obvious that we weren't literally born yesterday. It also means belief in God is a place to start from, rather than a place we need to arrive at: belief in God's existence gives grounds for other beliefs, such as how we should live, and what the purpose of life is.

▶ criticism ◀   Does this mean that Plantinga will permit just about anything to count as a basic belief? Consider Charlie Brown's belief that there is a Great Pumpkin that returns every Halloween to scare naughty children. Is Charlie Brown entitled to hold this as a basic belief? What about belief in voodoo, or magic, or invisible pixies? If these could count as basic beliefs on a par with belief in God, then many people would question Plantinga's account of basic belief.

▶ criticism ◀   We would expect Plantinga's reformed epistemology to have some rigorous criteria to determine what is, and what is not, a properly basic belief. But having dismissed the foundationalist account of basic belief, Plantinga is very vague about precisely what the criterion is for a basic belief.[185] In his most influential paper on this topic ('Religious Belief as Properly Basic') he says that the best way of determining what would count as a basic belief and what would not is to assemble groups of beliefs that we all agree are basic and see what they have in common.

However, in later papers[186] Plantinga does offer some criteria for basic belief; most importantly the belief needs to be 'warranted'. Plantinga gives four conditions under which a belief has warrant:

1 it is the product of a properly functioning mind (i.e. someone who has no mental health problems);
2 it is the product of a mind functioning in an appropriate environment (i.e. it isn't the product of a deceptive environment, like illusions or mirages or hallucinogenic drugs);
3 it is part of those mental processes aimed at producing further true beliefs (i.e. it isn't a product of some subconscious process of wish fulfilment, or memory distortion);
4 it is successful in producing further true beliefs.

Plantinga would argue that belief in the Great Pumpkin isn't a basic belief because it is groundless and it doesn't meet these four criteria. However, for Plantinga the belief in God does meet all these criteria and people do have good grounds for this belief. Plantinga cites some of John Calvin's grounds for belief in God, which include: our sense that the universe has been created; a sense that God is speaking to us when we read the Bible; the pang of guilt when we commit an immoral act. Plantinga acknowledges that strictly speaking it is these beliefs (God has created all this, God is speaking to us, God disapproves of what I've done) that are properly basic, rather than the belief that God exists. But each of these basic beliefs self-evidently entails the belief that God does exist (just as my belief that you stood on my toe self-evidently entails the belief that you exist).

ACTIVITY   Read through the beliefs given in the activity above (on page 165). Which of them would count as basic beliefs according to Plantinga?

Faith as an act of will: Pascal, James and Tennant

Modern theories of faith have emphasised the gap between the evidence for our belief in religion and the certainty of our belief in it. The gap between ourselves and God can only be crossed by an act of sheer will, and there have been many philosophers who have identified this act of will with the concept of faith itself. This analysis of faith is sometimes termed the 'voluntarist' theory of faith. Søren Kierkegaard

(1813–1855) expressed in an incredibly vivid way the feeling that God was absent from his creation, and that we could not experience God in the same way that we can experience the world: there is an epistemic distance between God and his creation. In other words there is not enough evidence to provide a rational justification for a belief in God, and this epistemic gap can only be crossed by a leap of faith.

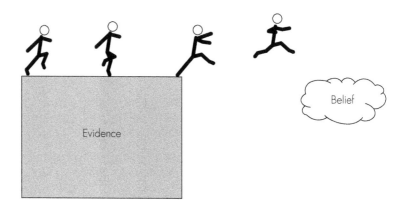

■ **Figure 4.2** *The leap of faith*

Look back at the evidence for each of your beliefs listed in the activity on pages 157–158 above.

Ask yourself how much of an epistemic leap you need to make between your evidence and your belief.

Rank each on a scale of 1–5, as follows.

1 **A small step**	2 **A large stride**	3 **A jump**	4 **A leap**	5 **A huge leap**
The evidence supports your belief as far as it's possible to	There is a reasonable amount of evidence for your belief	There is evidence both in favour of and against your belief	The evidence for your belief is disputed or controversial	There's no evidence for your belief

One thinker who understood that faith in God begins with an act of will was the seventeenth-century philosopher and mathematician Blaise Pascal. Pascal put his theory in the form of a wager:

Pascal

Let us weigh the gain and loss in wagering that God is (exists). Let us estimate these two chances. If you gain, you gain all, if you lose, you lose nothing. Wager, then, without hesitation, that He is.[187]

For Pascal this is a decision that we cannot avoid: either we choose to believe in God or we don't. Each of these beliefs has certain consequences, and we can weigh up these consequences to help us determine which belief will bring us the most happiness. We can represent the options given by Pascal in the form of a table showing the costs and benefits of each choice:

	God really does exist	**God really does not exist**
I believe that God exists	*Eternal life*	*Wasted a few Sundays*
I don't believe that God exists	*Eternal damnation*	*Gained a few Sundays*

The way Pascal has framed these two choices (to believe in God or not) makes it pretty clear which option would bring us the most happiness. Not believing in God brings some benefits if we're right, but a huge cost if we're wrong, whereas believing in God brings us a huge benefit if we're right, and a small cost if we're wrong. So to Pascal it makes much more sense to choose to have faith in God. This is not to say that we can suddenly decide to believe in God, because of the reward heaven brings. Rather Pascal sees his wager as a sensible first step towards true faith, especially for those who 'do not know the road'.[188] By taking this first step we act, and through our actions (going to church, praying, following the life of Christ) we will develop the habits and attitudes that are the hallmarks of true faith.

ACTIVITY

1 Would you decide to believe in God on the basis of Pascal's wager?

2 Do you think it's appropriate for someone to believe in God because of the rewards it will bring them?

3 Are there any other costs to believing in God (if God doesn't exist)?

4 Are there any other rewards to not believing in God (if God does exist)?

▶ criticism ◀ The way that Pascal has put it, using the metaphor of a wager, belief in God appears to be a kind of life-insurance policy. So we are being encouraged to develop our faith because of the rewards it will bring us (and the punishment we will avoid). It may well be that God does not mind how we come to believe in him, just as long as we do so, in which case Pascal's wager is as good a place as any to start. But if God judges the morality of our belief, and the process by which we came to believe, then we may be in trouble. For example, William James suggests that God would take pleasure in denying the reward of heaven to those who had followed such a cynical and calculated scheme as Pascal's.

Pascal gives an account of how faith develops after someone has made the wager and has gambled on God. For example, Pascal speaks of behaving like a believer, taking holy water, going to Catholic Mass, and this will lead you to God. Somehow Pascal seems to assume that faith will develop by habituation: that by going through the motions, and acting in the same way as other believers, belief in God will emerge. But his account of the path to belief doesn't capture the depth of the personal relationships that believers (including Pascal) feel that they have with God. And this personal relationship doesn't necessarily arise from making a rational decision to go to church regularly: as Pascal himself acknowledges 'it is the heart which perceives God and not reason. That is what faith is: God perceived by the heart, not by reason.'[189]

The American philosopher William James (1842–1910) was not a Christian, but his analysis of religious belief is still illuminating for believers. James disputed Pascal's claim that faith can result from an act of sheer will-power where there is no previous inclination to believe. James felt that the idea that we could switch beliefs at will was a preposterous idea, as this is not how our belief system works: new beliefs are adaptations of, or are connected with, previously held beliefs. In a lecture entitled 'The Will to Believe', James gives a much more sophisticated psychological account of what it means to decide voluntarily to believe in God, but he does defend the view that belief is rational even in the absence of sufficient evidence.

experimenting with ideas

Which of the following decisions would you postpone making until you had more evidence?

Describe what for you would count as sufficient evidence in each situation.

1 You have been in a loving relationship with your partner for ten years. They are the first and only person you have ever really been in love with. They ask you to marry them but you are unsure the marriage will be a success. Do you say yes?

2 The government is cracking down on crime and brings in laws that require everyone to be monitored by CCTV in their own home, 24 hours a day. More and more people are arrested and disappear as a result of this constant monitoring. You hear of a group of people dedicated to resisting this type of monitoring. When you get the chance do you join this resistance movement?

3 You're driving down through France at night when your car breaks down in the middle of nowhere. Eventually a car pulls up. The man in it asks where you're heading. Do you hitch a ride with him?

4 You're in a train carriage when two men in masks walk in, armed with knives and metal bars. They demand that everyone hands over their wallets, mobile phones, jewellery, etc. All the passengers are looking at each other, aware that if they all resist at once the masked men don't stand a chance. Do you stand up and resist the robbery?

5 In your old age, doctors discover that you have an incurable illness that eventually leads to sudden and constant pain and an agonising death. The law now allows for voluntary euthanasia. Do you decide to die?

For James there are certain situations in our life where we must make a decision, and where it is rational to make a decision, even though we have insufficient evidence. He argues that these types of decision are only rational under specific conditions. First the situation has to be one where the evidence is indeterminate between two beliefs; in other words, where the evidence is ambiguous, or equal on both sides (or completely lacking on both sides). Secondly, the situation has to be one where we face what James terms a 'genuine option'. James' concept of a genuine option arises from his analysis of the choices we face throughout our lives:

1 They may be *living* options or *dead* options. A living option is one where the choices available to me are ones that are real possibilities for me – choices that I could genuinely take. A dead option is one where the choices although not physically impossible are not ones that I would take.

2 They may be *forced* options or *avoidable* options. A forced option is one where I have to make a choice one way or another, I can't opt out. An avoidable option is one where, even though it may seem I have to make a choice, I can find a way round making a decision, or I can get away without choosing at all.

3 They may be *momentous* or *trivial* options. A momentous option is one that is unique, it may be the only time in life you get to make such a decision, or it may be a decision from which there is no turning back. A trivial option is one that you can reverse, or one that happens regularly throughout life.

A 'genuine option', according to James, is one that is living, forced and momentous. So for James it is sometimes rational to believe in God even though there is insufficient evidence for his existence, where the choice to believe is a genuine option.

Read through the decisions you faced in the activity above.
Which decisions would James say it was rational to take, even
though there was insufficient evidence?

James argues that Pascal's wager doesn't represent a genuine
option, because Pascal has presented his wager from within a very
specific religious perspective that assumes eternal damnation to be
the cost of not believing in God. To someone who does not
believe in the possibility of hell, Pascal's wager isn't a genuine
option. This is because it is not a forced option (someone can
always remain agnostic about belief in God), nor is it a living
option (someone who is immersed in a different religion could
not accept the assumptions on which Pascal's argument is based).
However, James does acknowledge that, where a person is open
to the possibility that a Catholic interpretation of Christianity is
the correct one, Pascal's wager may indeed clinch the deal and
enable that person to make the leap of faith.

James goes on to say that sometimes we may face a 'genuine
option' and lack evidence, but we make a decision anyway, and
subsequently the evidence reveals itself to us as a consequence
of taking that course of action. So faith (i.e. a decision to
believe made in the absence of evidence) has enabled us to
unearth the evidence we required. Let us consider an example
to help us understand what James means. It may be that if we
are to experience the good will of strangers we must first have
faith in their honesty. It is only by believing that they are
honest, and not treating them suspiciously, that they are able to
reveal themselves as truly honest. Similarly, with religion: there
is no conclusive evidence for God either way, but we have to
make a decision as to whether or not to believe and whether or
not to change our lives accordingly. For James, that is what
faith is: seizing the opportunity and taking a risk; if a man
ignores his advice then he 'might cut himself off forever from
his only chance of making the gods' acquaintance'.[190]

Although James avoids some of the criticisms aimed at
Pascal (e.g. he acknowledges that our relationship with God is
a personal one) there are still some problems with his account
of belief in God.

▶ criticism ◀ James assumes that there is no evidence for or against God's
existence. This absence of evidence is what makes faith an act
of will rather than an act of reason. But to many believers this
is not the case. For example, we have seen in Chapter 2 how
Aquinas attempted to demonstrate God's existence (in five
ways) on the basis of the evidence we find around us in the
world. We have also seen that to Plantinga whether there is
evidence or not for God's existence is actually immaterial, and
that belief in God is something immediate and basic.

▶ criticism ◀ James seems to imply that faith brings something that doesn't exist into existence, such as the honesty of a stranger, or the existence of God. But the point is that either the stranger is honest or she isn't, either God exists or he doesn't. Whether or not we have faith won't make any difference to the reality of these things. The most James can offer is to say that reality is revealed (rather than brought about) by faith.

▶ criticism ◀ Finally both James and Pascal ignore, or fail to capture, what is ordinarily meant by 'faith' to those believers who possess it. Those people with living faith see God as acting on them, and in their lives. The task of the believer is not to encourage others to make a gamble, but to make them see that God is already in their lives, whether they like it or not.

There is one final philosopher we should consider in this section, F.R. Tennant (1866–1958). Tennant, like Pascal and James, considers faith in God to be an act of will, and to help us see it in this way he uses an analogy. The analogy is that of scientific discovery, and the journey towards it. Tennant describes how every journey of discovery or development of a new theory, involves not only the process of theorising, but also an act of will that carries the operation through to completion. This act of will actually enables the new theory to be verified, or the new discovery to be made. When it comes to religious belief, then, Tennant's thought is that faith is an act of will that helps us to discover religious reality. In this it is rather different from James' view that faith actually helps bring it about.

How does the analogy between religious faith and scientific discovery work? Let us look at the similarities that Tennant thinks they have.

First there is the construction of the hypothesis. In science this is the attempt to explain the structure of the universe; in religion this is the attempt to explain the meaning and purpose of the universe. Secondly there is the act of will, which is an act of faith, that fuels the whole project of investigating the hypothesis. Such faith is the motive driving our exploration of the unknown, both in religious and non-religious contexts. Thirdly there is the potential verification of the hypothesis. In scientific terms this would be confirming instances and observations. In the religious analogy this 'verification' would be the transformation of the believer's life, the change in their behaviour and beliefs.

▶ criticism ◀ There are many limitations to Tennant's analogy, in particular the claim that we can 'verify' the religious hypothesis by seeing how it has transformed the believer's life. Scientific verification is public and objective, in other words anyone can check on the results. Tennant's 'religious verification' is private and subjective, it cannot be checked by other people, but relies on the believer confirming that the transformation in their life *is* due to their faith, and not to any other change in circumstances. The fact that gaining faith makes someone feel differently is not evidence that there is a real God who is the object of their faith.

▶ criticism ◀ Tennant's theory also fails to capture the way in which believers experience faith: for them religious faith is not 'like a scientific hypothesis that's been verified (except weaker)'. As John Hick says, for a believer, faith is more like a religious experience, a direct awareness of God.[191] Ludwig Wittgenstein (1889–1951) said that to compare religion to science is a blunder of enormous magnitude, and philosophers who do so reveal that they don't understand what the living faith of believers really is. We shall return to this point in the next chapter, on pages 202–203.

Faith as an attitude

So far we have been examining the view that faith is intimately connected to the belief that God exists. Aquinas, Plantinga and James etc. all view religious faith as a special kind of belief; special because it lacks evidence or because it doesn't need any evidence. These interpretations offer 'propositional' accounts of religious faith, the belief that the proposition 'God exists' is true; they also tell us how faith enables us to assent to this proposition in the absence of evidence. But this account of faith seems distant from the understanding of faith that most believers have (in perhaps the same way that we saw in Chapter 1 how the 'God of the philosophers' is remote from the God of the Bible). The final account of faith that we look at makes more of an effort to understand the attitudes to faith that ordinary believers possess. This account focuses on the existential concern of what living faith is like, and is more about an attitude to God rather than about the belief that God exists.

The Protestant Reformation of the sixteenth century, driven by the reformers Martin Luther and John Calvin, marked a switch away from a relationship with God mediated through the Church, towards an emphasis on the direct personal relationship believers can have with God. In this new Protestant tradition, faith was not about assenting to certain propositions (as Aquinas claimed), but instead was a way of experiencing and being in a relationship with God. To understand the difference between this new understanding of faith and the 'propositional' interpretation that we have so far been looking at, we shall draw on the distinction between two kinds of belief: 'believing that' and 'believing in'.

Let us examine the first kind of belief. 'Believing that . . .' entails believing certain propositions to be true. Take the example:

I believe Aretha Franklin is the greatest soul singer ever.

Now what this means is:

I believe *that* the proposition 'Aretha Franklin is the greatest soul singer ever' is true.

Most of the time when philosophers are talking about belief they are talking about this kind of propositional belief, i.e. belief about the truth (or falsity) of propositions. On this view, religious beliefs are simply beliefs about special kinds of propositions: propositions about certain supernatural facts, such as that Christ rose from the dead, or that God loves us.

There is another way in which we use the word 'belief', and that is when we say that we 'believe in' something. H.H. Price (1899–1985) raised the question of whether all statements about 'believing in something' could be reduced to, or translated into, statements about 'believing that' something was the case.[192]

experimenting with ideas

1 'Translate' each of the following statements from a 'believe in' statement to a 'believe that' statement. For example 'I believe in invisible pixies' can be translated as 'I believe that invisible pixies exist.'

2 Which of your translations has resulted in a change in meaning of the original statements? Which of your translations have preserved the meaning of the original?

a) I believe in miracles.
b) I believe in the Loch Ness Monster.
c) I believe in lifelong learning.
d) I don't believe in aliens.
e) I believe in most conspiracy theories.
f) I believe in the survival of the fittest.
g) I believe in doctors.
h) I don't believe in Robin Hood.
i) I don't believe in ice cold baths.
j) I believe in equality of opportunity.

In the activity you might have found that there are difficulties in rendering all 'belief in' statements as 'belief that' statements, without changing the meaning of the sentence. Price argues that there are two different senses of 'belief in'. The first sense is a factual sense, and sentences that use 'belief in' in this way can be translated into 'belief that' without any real loss of meaning. So when someone says they believe in ghosts or UFOs what they really mean is that they believe that ghosts or UFOs exist. It may even be the case that when some philosophers talk about 'believing in God' what they really mean is 'believing that God exists' or 'believing that the proposition "God exists" is true'.[193]

However, there is another sense of 'belief in', which Price calls the evaluative sense, that cannot be translated into 'belief that'. So people say they believe in an institution (e.g. the government) or a theory (e.g. evolution) or a course of action (e.g. seeing dentists). Price argues that this sense of 'belief in' captures an attitude of trust, commitment and belief in the *value* of the institution, theory, course of action, etc. We also talk about believing *in* a specific person, and this is being used in the evaluative sense too. For example, the statement 'Gary believes in David Beckham' might mean that in his heart Gary trusts and values Beckham and feels he will play for the English football team in the best possible way. However, it clearly does not mean that he believes that David Beckham exists. So when we talk about belief in a person we are talking about a particular kind of attitude we have to that person, and the question of their existence doesn't even come into it; it is assumed. To believe in someone means to trust them, to commit to them, to rely on them, and to have confidence in them.

Belief in God means trusting God, accepting God, accepting his purposes, committing one's life to him and living in his presence.[194]

Plantinga

Price says that it is the evaluative sense of 'belief in' that people use when they say 'I believe in God';[195] and this means more than simply 'I believe that God exists.' To someone with religious faith, someone who believes in God, the existence of God is a given. God is a given because, to the believer, God is part of their way of seeing the world, the 'mental spectacles' they wear which help them make sense of the world, and within which their other beliefs have meaning and a place (compare this thought with R.M. Hare's concept of 'bliks' discussed below on pages 197–198).

On this account then, religious faith, or belief in God, goes far beyond discussions about God's existence, and instead encompasses an attitude towards a being, God, who is already present in the believer's life. So religious faith also describes the experience believers have of God, and the spectrum of emotions that accompany this experience. For John Hick, belief in God is an awareness of God, which means 'to see oneself as a created, dependent creature, receiving life and well-being from a higher source . . . the only appropriate attitude is one of grateful worship and obedience'.[196]

We have examined a number of different accounts of religious faith. These accounts differ in how they align themselves against argument, evidence, scientific method and other tools of reason. What all the accounts have in common, however, is that faith is central to the believer and provides grounds for worshipping God that are independent of rational argument or evidential support. You have seen, in Chapter 2, the serious difficulties that the rational arguments for God's existence face, and you may have wondered how any believer could base their belief on such potentially shaky foundations. But perhaps now we should consider these arguments in a different light. Perhaps we should see the arguments of religious thinkers such as Anselm, Aquinas, Descartes, Kant, Paley and so on, not as 'proofs' of God's existence (in the sense of a scientific or a mathematical demonstration) but as explorations of faith, a faith that these philosophers already have, but also a faith they wish to examine further so that they might better understand their God.

It's worth recalling here Wittgenstein's comment that mistaking religion for a kind of pseudo-science, based on questionable evidence, is a blunder so big as to miss the whole point of religious belief. If he is right (and we return to this in Chapter 5), it may well be a mistake to consider arguments for God's existence as flawed proofs. As both Anselm and Augustine said: *Credo ut intelligam*, 'I believe so that I might understand.' In other words, reason is not used to prove God's existence beyond any intellectual doubt. Rather faith comes first, and reason is then used in order to help explore that faith. The arguments for the existence of God become an expression *of* belief, rather than a foundation *for* belief.

Key points: Chapter 4

What you need to know about **faith and belief in God**:

1 The claim that all our beliefs must be grounded in sufficient evidence is known as evidentialism. For some atheists there is simply not enough evidence to justify a belief in God's existence. To a believer it is possible to take a 'leap of faith' to cross the gap between the evidence and the belief in God. However, there is an issue as to whether belief in God needs to be based on evidence, or other rational foundations at all: isn't faith enough? An extreme version of this, known as fideism, proposes that reason is actually a barrier to belief in God.

2 Aquinas understands 'faith' to be the firm acceptance of revealed truths (for example, as given in the Bible) in the absence of evidence. For Aquinas faith and reason go hand in hand, in the form of both revealed and natural theology. Aquinas thinks that faith is necessary to supplement reason. Reason can only take us so far in our understanding of God, and many of us do not have the necessary time or intellect to engage with natural theology.

3 Alvin Plantinga sees belief in God as a basic belief. He rejects the claims of evidentialism and points out that many of our fundamental beliefs do not rest, and do not need to rest, on sufficient evidence. These basic beliefs are building blocks for our other beliefs, and the belief in God counts as a properly basic belief. This makes irrelevant the criticism that there isn't enough evidence to believe in God.

4 Other philosophers have seen belief in God as a choice we make. Pascal describes our choice to believe in God or not as a gamble that we have to take. For Pascal the decision to believe in God brings far greater potential rewards than the decision not to believe in God. William James also views this decision as unavoidable: in the absence of sufficient evidence we must choose whether or not to believe in God. James believes that there are times when it is only by having faith and making a commitment to believe in something, that we discover whether or not we were justified in our choice.

5 A distinction needs to be made between propositional and non-propositional types of belief. Sometimes when people say 'I believe in God' they mean 'I believe that God exists': this kind of 'belief that . . . ' is the propositional sense of 'belief'. However, perhaps faith is best understood as 'belief in God' in a non-propositional sense. In this sense, God's existence is assumed, and what 'belief in God' means is having a particular attitude towards God: trusting in God, relying on God, having confidence in God.

Talking about God

Introduction

The challenges of religious language

The French monk, and writer, François Rabelais once described how two fictional scholars conducted a philosophical argument using only grotesque signs and obscene gestures to convey their meaning. As one of the philosophers explained: 'these matters are so difficult that human words would not be adequate to expound them to my satisfaction'.[197]

But, for most of us, words and language are indispensable to communicating complex ideas; indeed, it would be very hard to imagine how the ideas discussed in this book could be effectively communicated by any other means, such as through images, dance, or mime. Language is essential for, and some would say identical with, complex thinking, and as philosophers tend to indulge in complex thought they naturally use language to do so. However, over the last hundred years or so philosophers have become ever more interested in the nature of language so that now the philosophy of language has become one of the most important areas of philosophical inquiry. The philosophy of language addresses such questions as:

■ What do words or concepts *mean*?
■ How do propositions *refer* to the world?
■ What is the *relationship* between language and thought?

Some philosophers have argued that such questions are the most important of all on the grounds that we need first to have answers to these before we can pursue any further philosophical questions. Until we understand how the medium through which we engage in philosophy works, how can we hope to do philosophy properly? Some philosophers of language also claim that many, if not all, philosophical problems arise simply because of the way in which we misuse, and so become confused by, language. According to this view, philosophical problems aren't genuine problems about the world at all, they are simply problems in the way we express ourselves. We have already seen how this approach to philosophy can work. For example, Bertrand Russell argued that a proper examination of the meanings of the words involved can reveal what is wrong with the ontological argument. The trick of proving God exists is foiled once we see how the proof misuses the term 'existence' by treating it as a predicate (see above, pages 40–42).

In this chapter we are going to look at the nature of religious language. The questions we need to deal with are:

- What special features does religious language have?
- Are religious concepts meaningful?
- Are religious propositions meaningful?

To answer these questions we need to look at examples of religious language and assess the different theories of meaning that philosophers have put forward.

The nature of religious language

The philosophy of religious language looks at the meaning of both religious concepts (such as God, omnipotence, Father) and at religious propositions. A proposition is an assertion or statement about the world, what in an English lesson might be called an 'indicative' sentence. We all express our beliefs in the form of propositions; here are some examples:

The world is round.
I am a student.
The grass is always greener on the other side.
We should treat others as we would like to be treated.

Now, on the surface, religious propositions appear very much like other kinds of proposition. They appear to be giving us information about the world, telling us what the world is like or what is true of it. In other words they appear to be FACTUALLY SIGNIFICANT. However, compare the following religious propositions with some ordinary propositions:

God is the Father, the Son and the Holy Ghost.	Jeremy Jones is a father, a son and a teacher.
God is transcendent.	Jeremy Jones is trendy.
The Lord spoke unto Moses about the liberation of the Israelites.	Jeremy Jones spoke to Mischa about the incident in the library.
Our Father, who art in Heaven, hallowed be thy name.	Jeremy Jones, who lives in Hendon, has an unusual middle name.

On the face of it, both sets of propositions are very similar. However, on closer inspection, it becomes evident that propositions like those on the left, religious propositions, reveal themselves to have features that make them rather different from those of ordinary language. For example:

- Religious propositions are often contradictory or paradoxical. To say that 'God is the Father and the Son and the Holy Ghost' is to say that he is at once *one* and *three*: a claim that is rather puzzling. We can understand how Jeremy Jones might be a father and a son, because there exist separate persons, Jeremy's son and Jeremy's father, who explain these relations. It is hard to understand how God could be a father and son to himself. The claim that 'God is omnipotent' appears to be contradictory, as we saw in Chapter 3, because an omnipotent being both can and cannot give itself a task which it could not perform. Does this mean that such claims are incoherent or meaningless?
- The word that is most central to religious language, 'God', refers to a being that lies beyond human experience. Many theologians have held that 'God' is a concept beyond our understanding, and that our language is woefully inadequate when it comes to talking of God. For example, the early Christian mystic Pseudo-Dionysius said this of our attempts to talk about God: 'the inscrutable One is out of reach of every rational process. Nor can any words come up to the inexpressible Good . . . Mind beyond mind, word beyond speech, it is gathered up by no discourse, by no intuition, by no name.'[198] Do all our attempts to talk meaningfully about God fail, because of his transcendent nature?
- Religious language is also peculiar in that it often describes God in human terms. In Genesis, for example, we are told that God walked in the Garden of Eden. Does this mean that God has legs? God also spoke to Moses on Mount Sinai. Does this mean he has a tongue and lips? How are we to make sense of such talk if God is a being who is outside of space and time?
- Finally, there are peculiarities in the uses made of religious language, for example during religious ceremony or prayer. Are we supposed to interpret prayer as a literal request for help, like dialling 999 for the fire-brigade? Or are we supposed to find in it another layer of meaning, perhaps a form of worship, an expression of faith, or an act of devotion?

Our task, then, is to determine whether and how religious language can be meaningful. To do this we will examine various theories of meaning and what they say about the nature of religious language.

Theories of meaning

Before turning to the theories of meaning themselves, it may be instructive to think a little about what meaning is or what we mean by 'meaning'.

How many different meanings does 'mean' have? What do the following examples of 'mean' mean?

1 I *mean* to send you a get well card.
2 Dark clouds *mean* rain.
3 He had a *mean* look on his face.
4 When your boy/girlfriend says 'I think we need a break' what they really *mean* is 'I've fallen in love with someone else.'
5 I *mean* the world to Julia.
6 Do you know what I *mean*?
7 The *mean* rainfall in Morecombe is 10 centimetres.
8 I'll report you to the police next time you slash my tires – I *mean* it!

In each of these propositions the word 'mean' is used in a different way, and there are other ways too. Ogden and Richards in the *Meaning of Meaning*[199] identified sixteen different meanings of the word 'meaning', which shows how ambiguous the meaning of the word can be. But superficial ambiguity isn't the only problem with 'meaning'. It seems that, although we may be able to use words happily enough, and can even explain what most words mean, it is much harder to say what it is for a word to have a meaning in the first place.

A useful starting point in giving a theory of meaning is to try to establish which sentences are meaningful and which aren't. If we can establish whatever it is that all meaningful sentences have in common and meaningless sentences lack, then we should have a good idea of what makes them meaningful and so we will be well on the road to building a theory of meaning. Now obviously sentences with made-up or crazy words will not be meaningful. For example,

'Twas brillig, and the slithy toves did gyre and gimble in the wabe.[200]

clearly makes no sense. For even though some of the words are English, and these allow us to recognise the grammatical structure of the sentence, we don't know what *toves* are or what it is to *gimble*, and so cannot make proper sense of what is being said. This suggests that the constituent parts of any sentence must be recognisable words for the sentence to be meaningful.

However, any old collection of English words is not necessarily going to make a meaningful sentence. Consider the following, for example:

With happily six the and swim.

This is clearly not meaningful because the words used aren't put together in a meaningful way. This suggests that meaningfulness requires at least two conditions: that the words used are themselves meaningful, and also that they are combined in ways that follow certain rules. But what rules are these? The example we've just looked at suggests one answer: the words must be combined in ways that follow the rules of *grammar*. For one obvious thing that is wrong with the sentence above is that it is not grammatical.

However, to be meaningful a sentence needs more than to be composed of proper words arranged grammatically. To see this, consider the following (originally composed by Noam Chomsky):

Colourless green ideas sleep furiously.

Can ideas sleep? Can something be colourless and green? Probably not. So, although this sentence is grammatical, and uses real English words that you'd find in any dictionary, it is still empty of significance, because nothing clear is being communicated in this sentence.

So it seems we have identified three features that meaningful sentences must have: they must use real words, they must be arranged grammatically, and they must be trying to communicate something. So we have here the beginnings of a theory of meaning, that is to say, we have begun to consider what the criteria are by which we can determine whether a sentence or use of language is meaningful or not. However, our theory remains rather vague at this stage. In particular our third condition would need to be unpacked and examined in a good deal more detail before it became at all interesting. What exactly does it mean to 'try to communicate something'? How can we decide whether or not a sentence does this effectively?

Each of the following sentences uses proper words and is grammatically correct. However, it may still be that not all of them are meaningful. Read through each sentence in turn and for each decide whether it is **a)** meaningful **b)** apparently meaningful (but actually meaningless) or **c)** obviously meaningless.

1 It is morally wrong to believe in something without sufficient evidence.
2 It is possible to doubt everything; it is even possible to doubt whether you are doubting.

3 There is life after death.
4 Birth is one of the miracles of nature.
5 I love you.
6 One, two, three, jump!
7 What came before time?
8 God loves the world like a father loves his children.
9 Respect!
10 The universe and everything in it doubled in size last night whilst we were asleep.
11 There are invisible pixies that live in my fridge who disappear without trace as soon as I open the door.
12 Jesus is the Way, the Truth and the Light.
13 It is possible for an infinitely powerful being to create a stone so large that they cannot move it.
14 The universe is expanding.
15 Bondi beach contains more than 1 billion particles of sand.
16 The history of all hitherto existing societies is the history of class struggle.
17 There are two mistakes in the the sentence written here.
18 It is possible to know the unknowable.
19 The sunset over Victoria Falls is the most beautiful sight on earth.
20 I am who I am.

Now make a note of all the sentences that you thought were meaningful. You may find it helpful to draw up a table as follows and list some of the features that meaningful and meaningless sentences appear to have.

A sentence is meaningful if:	A sentence is meaningless if:

What do the meaningful sentences have in common? What is it about them that makes them meaningful? Write down some criteria for what makes a sentence meaningful.

In completing this exercise it is hoped you will have come up with your own criteria for a meaningful sentence. You may have decided that *all* the sentences were meaningful, in which case you probably reckon that a) being grammatical and b) using genuine words are sufficient conditions for meaningfulness. Perhaps you added additional criteria to these, such as c) not being paradoxical or contradictory. Alternatively you may have thought that only the sentences that you could do something with, that you could see a practical use for in your daily life, were meaningful.

In the rest of this final chapter we shall examine various theories of meaning. After you have read about a theory of meaning, you may find it helpful to come back to this exercise and apply that theory of meaning to the above sentences, just to see which are 'ruled in' as meaningful, and which are ruled out.

Cognitivism and non-cognitivism

There are many different theories concerning what makes a sentence meaningful, and they broadly fall into two types: COGNITIVE and NON-COGNITIVE theories.

Some philosophers (most notably the young Ludwig Wittgenstein and A.J. Ayer) have argued that sentences are only meaningful if they are connected in some identifiable way to the world. Such sentences describe the world either truly or falsely. For example,

Socrates was executed in 399 BC.

is meaningful because it tries to tell us something about the world. It is irrelevant for this theory of meaning whether a sentence is actually true; false sentences are still meaningful because they still 'paint a picture' of the world. A theory that says that sentences are meaningful because they refer to the world (either truly or falsely) is known as a cognitivist theory of meaning.

However, many other philosophers have argued against this view. They believe that statements can be meaningful even though they do not refer to the world, and even though they cannot be shown to be true or false. The many different theories which take this approach can be thought of as 'non-cognitive', and they tend to emphasise the complexity of language, and the context within which language use takes place.

In the rest of this chapter we look in some detail at examples of cognitive and non-cognitive theories of meaning, and how they apply to religious language. First we examine some cognitive theories of meaning, including VERIFICATIONISM and FALSIFICATIONISM; we then go on to look at some non-cognitive theories of religious language, including those of Wittgenstein and his followers, and those that take a more metaphorical interpretation of religious language.

Verificationism and falsificationism

A.J. Ayer and the verificationist theory of meaning

A.J. Ayer (1910–1989) was a British philosopher who was very much under the influence of Ludwig Wittgenstein's early philosophy and of a group of Austrian philosophers known as the Vienna Circle. These philosophers (often known as *Logical Positivists*) were angered by what they took to be the gibberish that many philosophers, particularly in the nineteenth century, had a tendency to spout. They argued that language was only meaningful if it confined itself to discussing what fell within human experience. Once our language steps beyond the realms of what we can experience then it ventures into nonsense.

Ayer was greatly affected by this idea and when he was in his mid-twenties he wrote a book called *Language, Truth and Logic* that popularised Logical Positivism in Britain and America. In this book he used the ideas of the Vienna Circle and applied them to all aspects of philosophy. He defended what is known as the *verification principle*, which is a kind of test that a sentence must pass if it is to count as genuinely meaningful. The verification principle states that:

A sentence is meaningful if and only if:
either (a) it is a tautology, i.e. true by definition;
or   (b) it can – in principle – be proved to be true or false, i.e. it is verifiable.

The principle proposes that in order to say something is meaningful we must know what would make what we say true. If a proposition isn't a tautology, and there is no empirical way of discovering its truth, then it is meaningless. Ayer's point is that meaningful propositions must make claims about the world; they must say that the world is *this way* or *that way*. So, if upon reading a proposition we are unsure what the world would be like if it were true as opposed to false, in other words, if we did not know what would count as verifying it, then the proposition doesn't appear to be making a claim about the world after all. It is factually insignificant and meaningless.

So, for example, the claim that it snowed in London on Christmas Day 2000 is clearly meaningful because it could be verified by contemporary observations from London on that day. Similarly, the proposition that Jesus was put to death by crucifixion is meaningful, because we could verify it by examining the historical records. Note, however, that there are claims which are meaningful according to the verification principle, even though we cannot verify them in practice. For example, it is meaningful to say that there is life on the planet Neptune, even though at present we have no means of verifying this claim. For Ayer, such claims are meaningful because we could *in principle* verify them. In other words, we know the kinds of things we would need to do – send a sophisticated space probe to Neptune, for example – to determine whether they are true. So the verification principle isn't saying that we can *as a matter of fact* verify all meaningful propositions, just that we could do so *in principle*.

ACTIVITY   Refer to the list of propositions in the previous activity.

1 Re-categorise each proposition according to Ayer's verification principle.
2 Are there any propositions that Ayer would say were meaningless, but which to you are obviously meaningful?
3 What implications does this have for Ayer's theory?

The verification principle is also useful in identifying statements that look as if they are meaningful but are in fact word games, grammatical errors or simply incoherent. John Hick gives two useful examples of sentences that appear at first sight to be meaningful and about the world but which cannot be verified, and so must be nonsense according to the verificationist.[201]

The universe doubled in size last night.
There is an invisible, intangible, odourless, tasteless and silent rabbit in this room.

According to Ayer's verification principle both these sentences would be meaningless because neither of them can be verified. They *appear* to be making claims about the world, but when you look at them closely you see that whether they are true or false (i.e. whether the world is the way they say it is) makes no difference to our experience. There is no possible experiment we could perform which could establish their truth or falsehood and so they are not factually significant.

▶ criticism ◀   What of generalisations such as 'at sea level water boils at 100 degrees centigrade'? The problem with the truth of general claims like this is that they can never be conclusively proved, not even in principle, since we can't boil all the water in the universe to confirm that it always boils at 100 degrees. This category of propositions looks as though it could represent a serious difficulty for the verification principle, as most scientific claims are of this general sort and yet Ayer regarded science as the paradigm case of a body of meaningful claims. Note also that much of science deals with entities which are not directly observable, for example sub-atomic particles such as protons and quarks. So how can we verify their existence, and the truth of propositions which refer to them?

Ayer gets round these problems by differentiating between a *strong* and a *weak* version of verification, with scientific theories fulfilling the weaker conditions.

- The *strong* version states that a statement is meaningful if we can verify it by observation – and therefore establish its truth/falsity for *certain*.
- The *weak* version states that a statement is meaningful if there are some observations that can establish the *probable* truth of the statement.

So Ayer's weaker version of the verification principle is saying that a proposition counts as meaningful just if we know what observations would count towards or against the likelihood of its being true.

One of the most significant consequences of Ayer's theory is that it appears to make all claims about religion and about God meaningless.[202] This is because many religious claims are about something transcendent; that is to say, about objects which lie beyond human experience, for example God, heaven, or life after death. But talk about what lies outside experience is, according to the verification principle, meaningless. Statements such as 'God loves the world', or 'God is the Father, the Son and the Holy Ghost', appear to be telling us something about someone. But when we look at such statements from the point of view of verificationism it becomes clear that there are no possible ways of checking whether they are true or false. There are no experiments we could carry out or observations we could make to prove them, and so such statements are not factually significant. Importantly, then, Ayer does not regard the claim that God exists as false, but rather as meaningless. Equally the claims of the atheist that God does not exist are also meaningless, as they too fail the verification principle's test. For Ayer we just cannot meaningfully talk about God.

Criticisms of Ayer

There are, however, some serious difficulties facing Ayer's verification principle. The first criticism is that the principle seems far too strong since it not only outlaws religious language from the realm of the meaningful, but it also makes much of what humans speak and write about meaningless as well, including art, beauty and our inner feelings and sensations. After all, how can we prove that the Mona Lisa is beautiful? The verification principle makes poetic and metaphorical language meaningless: e.g. I cannot verify that my love is a rose. Moreover, it makes all ethical judgements simply a matter of personal feeling and it makes most philosophical speculation nonsense. This need not be a problem, but it certainly suggests that Ayer's notion of meaning is very different from the one we operate with in everyday life.

But perhaps Ayer's prescriptive account of meaning should trouble us. The philosopher Stewart Sutherland described Ayer's theory as 'conceptually restrictive and intellectually imperialistic in its character'.[203] Sutherland goes on to compare the prescriptions of Ayer (on what we can and can't talk about) with George Orwell's invented language 'Newspeak' described in his novel *1984*. Newspeak is an artificial language that is developed by a totalitarian government with the specific intention of limiting what can be said by people. The ultimate goal of Newspeak is to enable people to speak about practical matters, and things that are permitted by the government, but to prevent people from talking about, or even thinking about, anything that might encourage heretical behaviour. This is a terrifying thought, as all human creativity, philosophy, religion, literature, theorising, would be impossible within Newspeak. Rather like, Sutherland says, the effects of Ayer's verification principle, which would also rule out as 'non-sense' these areas of human activity, and eventually diminish human thought.

A second criticism is that the principle of verification is itself meaningless according to its own criterion. The principle claims that 'for any proposition to be meaningful it must either be verifiable or true by definition'. So if this claim is *itself* meaningful it must either be true by definition or verifiable. However, it is clearly not true by definition. We cannot recognise its truth simply by examining the meanings of the terms it uses. But neither does it appear to be verifiable, as it is hard to see in what way the world (if the principle were true) would differ from the world if it were false. So if the verification principle is neither verifiable nor true by definition it must itself be meaningless!

John Hick and eschatological verification

A further significant criticism of Ayer comes from the Christian philosopher John Hick, who argued that religious statements can in fact be verified and therefore that they are factually significant and so meaningful, even according to the verification principle. There are three main aspects to Hick's approach: first his definition of 'verification', which is different from Ayer's; secondly his parable of the celestial city, showing that verification of religious statements is possible and reasonably straightforward; thirdly his account of personal identity after death, showing that resurrection is possible. Let us deal with each aspect in turn.

Hick agrees with Ayer that only statements that are factually significant are meaningful, and that FACTUAL SIGNIFICANCE is judged by whether the truth or falsity of an assertion makes a difference to our experience of the world. For example, whether the statement 'There is an invisible, odourless, intangible rabbit in this room' is true or false makes no difference to our experience. Hence it is not factually significant; it tells us nothing about the world and is not meaningful. Like Ayer, Hick proposes that the factual significance of an assertion is best assessed by whether it can be verified. Hick goes onto say that verifiability should be judged by whether it is possible to remove the grounds for rational doubt about the truth of the claim in question. For example, claiming that there is a family of foxes living at the bottom of the garden can be verified if you keep finding mutilated squirrels on the lawn, if you have seen a red furry tail sticking out from a hole under the shed, and if your night-vision goggles reveal frolicking fox cubs. Such evidence would effectively remove any serious doubts about the matter.

Now, Hick accepts that religious propositions cannot be falsified. They cannot be falsified because, if there is no God, then after we die we'll just be dead and we won't be able to say 'ah-ha – there is no God, those theists got it wrong!' But Hick's argument is that although religious statements may never be falsified they *can* be verified, in the sense that rational doubt can be removed about their truth. For Hick it is the potential verifiability of religious statements that makes them meaningful. To illustrate how such verification is possible he offers his celebrated parable of the Celestial City:

Two men are travelling together along a road. One of them believes that it leads to the Celestial City, the other that it leads nowhere; but since this is the only road there is, both must travel it . . . During the journey they meet with moments of refreshment and delight, and with moments of hardship and danger. All the time one of them thinks of his journey as a pilgrimage to the Celestial City. He interprets the pleasant parts of the journey as encouragements and the obstacles as trials of his purpose . . . The other, however, believes none of this . . . Since he has no choice in the matter he enjoys the good and endures the bad . . . When they do turn the last corner it will be apparent that one of them has been right all the time and the other wrong.[204]

This parable points to the possibility of what Hick calls 'eschatological verification', that is to say, verification after our death in the next life (ESCHATOLOGY concerns what happens at the end of things, for instance at the Last Judgement). Hick is arguing that many religious statements, particularly in

Christianity, rest on the claim that there is an after-life, and they are meaningful because they can be verified in the after-life. I can verify whether there is a heaven or not if, after I die, I find myself in heaven. For Hick such experience would remove grounds for rational doubt about the existence of heaven.

Hick recognises that the possibility of eschatological verification relies on the possibility of me retaining my personal identity through the processes of death, but there are certain difficulties with this idea. One important difficulty is that we all know that when people die their bodies quickly decompose. How, if the body of which you are made has dissipated, can you possibly be thought to have survived? If someone subsequently appears in heaven, in what sense can it be said to be the same person? If I am resurrected how can this new body be thought of as still me?

To answer such questions, Hick presents three separate 'thought experiments' which try to show that a person appearing in an after-life can meaningfully be considered as the same person as someone who had lived and died in this life.

1 First Hick asks us to imagine a person, X, disappearing in America, while at the very same moment someone else, who is the exact double of X (same physical features, the same memory, etc.) appears in Australia. If this happened would you consider the person appearing in Australia to be the same as X? Hick thinks that we would.
2 Now imagine that person X, instead of disappearing, dies in America, and at the very same moment their double appears in Australia. Wouldn't we still say they were the same person? Hick thinks that if we accept that it is the same person in the first scenario, we would have to accept that it is the same in this scenario.
3 Finally, imagine that person X dies in America, and their double now appears, not in Australia, but in heaven. Again Hick thinks that if we accept that it is the same person in scenarios 1 and 2, that we must accept it is the same in this scenario too. And if we accept that it is the same person, then we are accepting that it makes sense to talk about surviving one's death and preserving one's personal identity.

What these thought experiments are supposed to show is that resurrection is at least logically possible. And if we are resurrected in heaven, we (or at least some of us) will be in no doubt that it is heaven that we are in. For Hick there are two factors that will remove all rational doubt that we are in heaven: firstly our final understanding of the purpose and destiny given to us by God; and secondly our encountering our saviour Jesus Christ. Note that Hick says that only some of us may be able to verify this, namely those who already believe in God. But, nonetheless, if it is logically possible that at least someone will be able to verify (remove rational doubt from) the claim that 'God exists', then this claim is meaningful.

Criticisms of Hick

One line of criticism against Hick is to question the conclusions he draws from his thought experiments. Each scenario, it may be urged, really produces a duplicate person in a new location, and so is not really the self-same person who disappeared or died. To see this, consider altering the scenarios slightly, such that in each case the original person remains alongside the double appearing in Australia or heaven. In such cases we would be inclined to think the double a different person from the original. However, this alteration to the scenario has not changed the status of the double itself, and so the double cannot be the same as the original. God could certainly create a duplicate of me in heaven on my death, but a duplicate of me is not me. Our intuitions appear to suggest that, for my personal identity to survive the process of death, there would have to be some form of bodily continuity. Simply rebuilding a perfect copy is not resurrecting the self-same person.

A second difficulty concerns whether we truly can verify through our post-mortem experience the various religious claims in question. Consider the most obvious claims that God and heaven exist. In order to verify that we are now in heaven, or are now experiencing God, we need to first recognise that this vision in front of us is heaven (or God). But we saw when we examined the arguments from religious experience (above, page 91) that it may not be possible to recognise something we have never seen before and that lies beyond our understanding. So if, as some philosophers say, God is beyond our comprehension, then perhaps it won't be possible to recognise, and hence verify, that this is God or heaven we see before us.

Antony Flew and falsificationism

In his famous 1955 lecture 'Theology and Falsification' Antony Flew outlined his own attack on the meaning of religious propositions. Like Ayer, Flew believed that propositions are only meaningful if they are factually significant, in other words if they make a genuine claim about the world. However, unlike Ayer, he argues that it is not the possibility of verification, but the possibility of falsification, that shows that a statement is meaningful.

Flew argues that religious statements are not falsifiable, that is to say, they cannot be proved wrong, and this is why they tell us nothing about the world. He borrows a parable from John Wisdom written in 1944 and alters it to make his case. Wisdom asks us to imagine two people arriving at a run-down garden. One person notices the flowers and the organisation of the plants and takes this as evidence that someone has been caring for the garden. The other person notices the weeds and the disorder and concludes that no one has been tending the garden. Wisdom's point is that although two people can be presented with exactly the same empirical evidence – it is the same garden that both are experiencing – their responses need not be the same. This shows that empirical observation or evidence does not, by itself, determine the very different conclusions that people draw about the world. How we interpret the evidence presented to us is, at least in part, influenced by our attitudes towards it. The atheist may focus on the disorder of the universe and interpret this as evidence of the absence of any divine plan. Meanwhile, the theist attends to the order and beauty of things and sees this as evidence of the work of a divine intelligence.

In Flew's reworking of Wisdom's gardener parable, the two people spend some days in the garden. Since they do not observe any gardener visiting to tend the plants, the sceptic reckons there must be no gardener. However, her companion, rather than give up the belief that there's a gardener, concludes that the gardener must come at night. So the two of them stay up all night keeping vigil, hoping to spot the mysterious gardener, but none appears. Again the sceptic takes this as evidence that there is no gardener, but the believer stubbornly responds that the gardener must be invisible. So they put up an electric fence around the garden and guard it with sniffer-dogs, but still they find no evidence of a gardener sneaking in to tend the land. Despite this the believer continues to maintain that there is a gardener, but now claims he is not only invisible, but also odourless and intangible, which accounts for why they have so far been unable to find direct evidence of his activity. Eventually the sceptic despairs and asks the believer 'how does your claim that there is an invisible, odourless, intangible gardener differ from the claim that there's no gardener at all?' Because the believer holds onto the belief that there is a gardener, despite the failure to apprehend him, the believer has shown that no evidence at all will make them surrender their belief. Each time their effort to find the gardener fails the believer simply modifies their belief so that it isn't falsified. Thus their belief is effectively unfalsifiable.

In Flew's and Wisdom's parables what do the following represent:

a) the garden
b) the flowers
c) the weeds
d) the differences in belief between the two people in the garden.

Flew is arguing that a statement, such as 'there is a gardener', is only meaningful if it is about the world, i.e. if it is factually significant. But it is only factually significant if the person making the claim can imagine being wrong, in other words if there is a possibility of their statement being falsified. This is because someone who refuses to give up their belief, no matter what is discovered about the world, is not really talking about the world at all. When presented with evidence showing that their statement is false, they add to and qualify it so that the new evidence no longer refutes it. In other words, they move the goal posts to accommodate the new evidence.

An example of how this happens with religious belief might be the Biblical story about the creation. Traditionally, Christians believed it to be literally true that God created the universe in six days, and that he created humans out of earth. Modern cosmology and evolutionary theory have cast serious doubts on such claims, and most theists nowadays have qualified their belief in God, so that it can accommodate such scientific advances. So, instead of saying that the fact that humans have evolved from other life forms shows that God doesn't really exist, they have modified their beliefs. God, it is now urged, created humans through a process of evolution. But such manoeuvrings don't impress Flew. If one repeatedly qualifies one's belief in the light of the new evidence to avoid having to give it up, then one's belief suffers what Flew calls 'death by a thousand qualifications'. The statement is unfalsifiable and therefore it is not factually significant and therefore is not meaningful.

Let's look at another example. Imagine you have a friend who is convinced that Jennifer Lopez has romantic feelings for him. More than this, he claims that Jennifer Lopez loves him. So his claim is:

Jennifer Lopez loves me.

In questioning this claim you point out that Ms Lopez' agent called your friend recently, and told him to stop sending flowers, love poems and personal effects. The agent made it very clear that Ms Lopez was not interested. But your friend explains to you that the agent was merely protecting his client from the damaging effects of her passion. Eventually Ms Lopez herself calls to tell your friend that if his pestering doesn't stop she will call her lawyers. He tells you that she is just playing hard-to-get. His original claim is now qualified as follows:

Jennifer Lopez loves me (but she is playing hard-to-get).

You explain patiently that she doesn't even know him; that she has never even seen him; and that she is known to be in love with someone else. However, your friend claims that this is because she has to keep her love for him a secret in order to avoid a scandal in the tabloid newspapers. You realise that he's made a further adjustment to his claim:

Jennifer Lopez loves me (but she is playing hard-to-get and it is a deeply secret love).

Even when the court order arrives forcing your friend to keep at least 2 miles away from Ms Lopez, your friend explains to you that her entourage don't want her to become romantically involved with someone so young.

Jennifer Lopez loves me (but she is playing hard-to-get, it is a deeply secret love, and her entourage is conspiring to prevent us from getting together).

Eventually you ask him if there is anything that anyone could say or do, anything that could happen, that would demonstrate to him that Jennifer Lopez doesn't love him. He confesses that nothing could come between him and J-Lo, that her love for him is forever, and even if she doesn't yet realise it, deep down she will always be in love with him.

Ian McEwan's novel *Enduring Love* ends on a similar, and sinister, one-sided declaration of love. A stalker, who has finally been imprisoned, continues to write passionate letters to his victim, finding in his prison cell all sorts of signs that his victim returns this love. His thousandth letter ends as follows: 'Thank you for loving me, thank you for accepting me, thank you for recognising what I am doing for our love. Send me a new message soon.' The 'message' that the deluded man is referring to is simply the sun rising over the prison.

Antony Flew would argue that these claims to enduring love are empirically empty because for the person who makes them they cannot be falsified by any evidence. If the evidence merely leads to an adjustment (or qualification) in the claim, so that it remains immune to falsification, then the belief is not sensitive to the facts. For Flew the consistent failure of someone to alter their belief in accordance with new information that's made available to them, suggests that the belief isn't actually about the world at all. And if it is not about facts (i.e. it's not factually significant) then for Flew the belief is meaningless.

Flew is particularly interested in religious claims, and argues that believers hold on to them no matter what. Flew uses the example of the belief that God loves us like a father loves his children. If we point out to the theist that no father would let his children suffer what humans suffer, they typically respond by qualifying their statement and saying that God's love is a mysterious love. So, Flew asks, how much suffering and evil must there be before the theist will admit that either God doesn't exist, or he doesn't love us? Flew is probably right when he says that nothing will count as evidence against this belief (in other words, that no amount of suffering will ever lead them to give up belief in God). After all, in one of the most important books of the Old Testament, Job, who has lost everything (his family, livelihood, friends, health) and who is sitting on a dungheap wondering what on earth he's done to deserve this (nothing, actually), still asserts that 'I know my redeemer liveth.'[205]

For Flew, if nothing counts against the belief, if it is unfalsifiable, then the statement about God's love is not factually significant. The theist may qualify their belief in God's love, but they won't ever give it up no matter what horrors humans suffer, and so it is unfalsifiable and meaningless. If the believer does accept that the suffering of humanity could, in principle, establish that God doesn't love us, then Flew claims they should give up their belief now, since the amount of suffering clearly suggests that no loving God exists.

Imagine the following people are having a conversation, and construct a dialogue that might take place between them:

Person A has an unshakeable belief that they will never give up no matter what the evidence	Person B wishes to provide evidence that shows person A they are wrong
1 The Prime Minister believes that a certain country in the Middle East has weapons of mass destruction.	1 The United Nations chief weapons inspector is carrying out thorough inspections and finds nothing.
2 Someone from the Flat-Earth Society sincerely believes that the Earth is flat and there is a conspiracy to 'prove' it is round.	2 A specialist in astronomy and geography is out to disband the Flat-Earth Society.
3 A child believes that there are monsters under their bed.	3 A mother is trying to reassure her child to help him get to sleep.
4 A fanatical England football supporter believes that the England team play the best football in the world.	4 A football historian wants to show this fan that all the evidence of past tournaments show the England team are simply average.
5 A student is convinced that all her lecturers are out to ruin her life, no matter how helpful they might appear.	5 A counselling tutor is trying to help this student, so that she might rejoin her classes.
6 A believer is convinced that God loves the world.	6 An atheist is convinced that a loving God does not exist, because of the amount of suffering in the world.

Criticisms of Flew

There are many examples of statements that we would all consider to be meaningful, but which cannot be falsified. For example, universal statements that make claims about the future, such as 'all men are mortal'. What would you have to do in order to falsify this statement? It cannot be falsified because, no matter how long someone has lived for, we could never be sure that they wouldn't die the next day. Furthermore, as with Ayer's theory, many other types of statements – spiritual statements, statements about beauty or morality – also fall outside Flew's account of meaning; they are meaningless because they cannot be falsified. We cannot falsify the claim that it is wrong to eat meat, or that the Mona Lisa is beautiful. We should be suspicious of a theory of meaning which strays too far from the common consensus.

Further criticisms come from the replies given to Flew's lecture 'Theology and falsification' by R.M. Hare and Basil Mitchell. Let us take Hare's response first. Hare gives his own parable to help us to understand the strange nature of religious statements, which we can call the parable of the paranoid student:

A certain lunatic is convinced that all dons want to murder him. His friends introduce him to all the mildest and most respectable dons that they can find, and after each of them has retired, they say, 'You see, he doesn't really want to murder you; he spoke to you in a most cordial manner; surely you are convinced now?' But the lunatic replies 'Yes, but that was only his diabolical cunning; he's really plotting against me the whole time, like the rest of them; I know it I tell you.' However many kindly dons are produced, the reaction is still the same.[206]

Like the person who believes in the invisible gardener, the paranoid student cannot imagine being wrong, his statement 'my teachers are out to get me' is unfalsifiable. And yet, Hare argues that this belief remains very meaningful. After all, it has a profound influence on how the student approaches the world, how he forms other beliefs and how he lives his life. It is true that it operates so centrally within his belief system that it cannot be falsified, and all evidence is twisted to fit with this fundamental belief; but the very centrality of the belief means that it is deeply meaningful, contrary to the position that Flew takes.

So Hare argues that it is possible to assent to a proposition which is not falsifiable but which is nonetheless meaningful. And such beliefs are not confined to the unusual case of paranoia. According to Hare we are all in some ways like the

© 1986 Universal Press Syndicate

WATTERSON   5-6

Figure 5.1
The paranoid six-year-old

student: we *all* have fundamental beliefs or principles on which we base our actions and which we will never give up. These thoughts and principles often form the very basis for our other beliefs, and they are both unverifiable and unfalsifiable. For example, most of us believe that all events have a cause. Imagine that a sceptic tried to falsify this belief. They might point to events for which no cause could be observed, such as the unexpected disappearance of your cat, or the sudden appearance of a puncture in your bicycle tyre. We can suppose that you had spent months trying to find out how or why your cat disappeared, or hours looking for the offending object that had penetrated your tyre, but had found nothing. Would you accept such failure as evidence that these events just happened without any reason or cause? Probably not. What you would try to do instead is hold on to your belief that everything has a cause, and explain your failure to find any in these cases as related to the fact that you didn't search long or hard enough. If you had had the time, perhaps you would indeed have found the cause. And no matter how many events the sceptic might describe that appear to lack a cause, you may well respond in the same way: refusing to give up your belief that all events have causes despite the mounting number of events cited where no cause is forthcoming.

Hare thinks that beliefs like this are perfectly meaningful, even though unfalsifiable. He invented the word 'blik' to refer to such fundamental thoughts and principles and argued that many religious beliefs fall into this category. For example, when believers say that 'God exists' they are expressing a *blik*: it is a belief that figures in the way they understand the world, and in terms of which they interpret their whole lives. They may never be prepared to give it up, but the very fundamentality of the belief ensures that it remains important to them, and distinctly meaningful. So if *bliks* have meaning it is an error to suppose, as Flew does, that all our meaningful beliefs are falsifiable.

► criticism ◄ Basil Mitchell criticises Flew, but from a different angle to Hare. He disagrees with the view that religious beliefs are unfalsifiable and he tells another parable to make his point, this time about a resistance leader.[207]

Imagine your country has been invaded and a resistance movement develops to overthrow the occupiers. One night you meet a man claiming to be a resistance leader, and he convinces you to put your trust in him and the movement. Over the months you sometimes see the man act for the resistance, but sometimes you also see him act against the movement. This troubles you, you worry that he might be a traitor, but your trust in him eventually overcomes your concerns and you continue to believe in him. Your belief that 'the stranger is on your side' is one that you don't give up, even though you see many things that suggest you are wrong.

Mitchell argues that this belief in the resistance leader is meaningful, even though you refuse to give it up. He does not think that it is a *blik*, however, because there are many occasions in which you do doubt your own belief. This doubt shows that your belief is falsifiable, i.e. that you can imagine circumstances under which you would give up your belief. Mitchell's parable reflects the doubts that religious believers sometimes have when they encounter great suffering in their lives (see 'The challenge of evil' in Chapter 3 above). These 'trials of faith' show that Flew is wrong to think that believers simply shrug off evidence that goes against their beliefs. Some believers, after all, do lose their faith in the face of terrible and apparently senseless episodes in their lives. Mitchell also thinks, like John Hick, that one day (in the parable when the war is over, or for the religious believer after we die) the truth will be revealed. So for Mitchell a belief that 'God exists' is both falsifiable (there are trials of faith) and verifiable (after we die), and therefore religious statements are meaningful. So Mitchell's parable of the resistance leader can be used to undermine both Flew's falsificationist account of meaning, and Ayer's verificationist account.

Wittgenstein's theory of meaning

Ludwig Wittgenstein (1889–1951) was one of the most significant philosophers of the last century. Wittgenstein put forward two distinct theories of meaning, one when he was young and the other later in his career. Wittgenstein in both his early and later phases believed that the heart of philosophy lay in the study of language and that by studying language we could clear up many of the disputes of philosophers and perhaps even make philosophy no longer necessary. The early Wittgenstein adopted a 'picture theory' of meaning, arguing that language is a way of representing facts. So a sentence like 'The cat is on the mat', is meaningful because it represents or pictures some state of affairs in the world. Wittgenstein argued that when we attempt to use language to do anything other than to say things about the world we stray into the realm of nonsense. This picture theory of meaning was an influence on the Vienna Circle and A.J. Ayer, and is closely allied to the cognitivist claim that meaningful sentences must be factually significant.

However, the later Wittgenstein was one of the foremost critics of this simplistic view of meaning. He attacked the Logical Positivists and his own early work, arguing that it utterly failed to capture the complexity of language. For Ayer and the Logical Positivists the only meaningful statements were ones about science or about the world we see, or ones that were true by definition. But Wittgenstein realised that our language was so much richer and more varied than this, and it was a ridiculous mistake for philosophers to rule out the rest of language because it couldn't be true or false. For example, when we talk about beauty, or love, or poetry, or religion, or art, or the meaning of life we seem to understand one another – yet Ayer tells us that we are talking nonsense. So Wittgenstein searched for a new way of understanding the nature of meaning.

ACTIVITY   Construct as many different sentences as you can that contain the word 'down'.
How many different meanings of the word 'down' have you used?

From this simple exercise you can immediately see that words don't have a single meaning. There are many, many different meanings of the word 'down', over twenty if you include slang and colloquial uses. The later Wittgenstein argued that there was no such thing as *the* meaning of a word or sentence, since there are many different ways in which language can be meaningful. He rejected the idea that a single theory of meaning was possible. Presuming that words must have some specific meaning, he argued, is the source of many philosophical difficulties. What we need to do is to be alive to the vagueness of words, to the great variety of different meanings they can have, and to the many ways they can be used.

Go back to the many ways in which the word 'down' can be used: in the context of rambling (the South Down Way); of upholstery (down as in duck feathers); of giving directions (you go down the road); of dog training (a command for a dog to grovel); of crosswords (down clues); of emotions (feeling down); of dancing (get on down); of drinking (down in one); and there are many, many more. And the nature of meaning itself is as varied as the meanings or uses of words. Understanding the meaning of a word is not a matter of catching hold of some abstract idea which is *the* meaning, but is a practical matter of being able to use the word appropriately in a variety of contexts. So you know the meaning of the word 'down' just because you can use it, but this doesn't mean that there is one thing, the word's *meaning*, which you have in your head.

The meaning of a word is its use in the language.[208]

Wittgenstein

So Wittgenstein's later theory of meaning denied that the meaning of language could be reduced to how it pictured the world. This may be one function of language, but it is certainly not the only one. Language can be used to do so many more things than this, and Wittgenstein cites the following as some examples of the multiplicity of language use: to give orders, to describe an object, to report an event, to make up a story, to tell a joke, to ask, thank, curse, greet, pray, etc.[209] All these uses are legitimate. So if we wish to know the meaning of a word we should look for how it is used, according to Wittgenstein, and this idea is sometimes condensed into the phrase 'meaning is use'.

The term 'language-game' is meant to bring into prominence the fact that the speaking of language is part of an activity.[210]

Wittgenstein

The different uses of language are activities that take place in different social contexts, which Wittgenstein famously termed LANGUAGE GAMES. He did not mean 'game' in a flippant or competitive sense, but in the sense that language use is an activity governed by certain rules, and these rules vary from context to context. For example, the rules governing the use of the word 'experience' in science are very different from those governing this word in a religious context. But Wittgenstein argued that it was a mistake to think that one use of a word was better than or more fundamental than another.

ACTIVITY
1 How many different types of language games can you think of?
2 Can you describe how some of the rules of these language games differ?

Remember what Ayer and Flew claimed: that for a statement to be meaningful it must refer to the world. But Wittgenstein is now suggesting that statements are meaningful so long as they are understood by other language users in a specific context. He therefore thinks (unlike Ayer) that morality, art, poetry, etc. are all meaningful; they are all language games. Now, when it comes to religious statements and concepts, according to Wittgenstein's approach, they are meaningful because they form part of a religious language game. Believers are users of this language, they are immersed in the practice of following its rules, and if we consider meaning to be equated with use then such a language is meaningful to whoever is able to use the language appropriately, that is to say, to 'players' of the game.

So, to understand religious statements, we need to be a part of the religious language game; as Wittgenstein said, we need to be immersed in the religious 'Form of Life'. If we are not immersed in that particular way of living, if we don't share those beliefs, or use those concepts in a familiar and regular way, then we cannot understand religious statements. This is the problem with philosophers like Ayer and Flew. They think that there is only one way language can be meaningful, namely if it is factually significant; so when religious language fails to be factually significant they accuse it of being meaningless. But the error is to think that meaning lies only in factual significance, i.e. in statements that describe the world. The mistake made by Ayer and Flew is to treat statements from one language game (expressions of religious faith), as if they came from another (descriptions of the world): to treat religious talk as if it were scientific talk.

Wittgenstein

Suppose someone were a believer and said: 'I believe in a Last Judgement', and I said: 'Well, I'm not so sure. Possibly.' You would say that there is an enormous gulf between us. If he said 'There is a German aeroplane overhead', and I said 'Possibly, I'm not so sure' you'd say we were fairly near.[211]

For Wittgenstein, science and religion are two different language games; they are not in competition with one another, and neither can help solve the problems of the other. For Wittgenstein it might be appropriate to take a cognitive approach to the meaning of scientific statements, in the way Ayer and Flew suggest, by demanding that they be verifiable or falsifiable. But a non-cognitive approach, one that doesn't attach meaning to truth or falsity, is more appropriate when looking at the meaning of religious statements.

When a believer says 'the Creator exists' they are not using 'exists' in the same way as when a scientist says 'duck-billed platypuses exist'. For when a believer is talking about the Creator they are also being reverential; they are expressing their faith and their understanding of the purpose of life. Although 'the Creator exists' looks very similar to a statement like 'the chairs exist', it is a much richer and more resonant phrase, it is an expression of 'belief in' and not simply a description of 'belief that' (see above, page 176). Atheists just don't get it, and they can't get it unless they become involved in a religious way of life.

▶ criticism ◀ However, there are problems with Wittgenstein's theory. The most fundamental problem arises because a meaningful statement (within a religious language game) no longer has to be connected to the world, it no longer has to be true or false. So we can imagine a group of religious language users who can talk meaningfully about the existence of goblins, elves and pixies so long as they have a consistent set of rules governing their concepts. The fact that there aren't any such creatures is irrelevant to the meaningfulness of the language game. This view about the nature of language, that it doesn't refer to the world, is termed anti-realism. However, being anti-realist about religious language doesn't sit well with what most believers think they are doing when they talk, for example, of God or the after-life. Making religious statements seems to involve making claims about what does and doesn't exist in reality. So there is a problem in supposing, as Wittgenstein does, that religion is nothing other than a game played in words and deeds by a community of people. The religious language game includes a set of substantive metaphysical claims, regarding the existence of God, heaven, Jesus, the after-life, the creation, etc. So many believers would disagree with Wittgenstein's point that religion is different from science. For believers, the Creator is real, and not simply another piece in a complicated language game.

We shall now look at two religious philosophers, Ian Crombie and Richard Braithwaite, who were influenced by Wittgenstein's analysis of meaning as use.

Braithwaite and Crombie on the uses of religious language

Like Wittgenstein Braithwaite rejected a simplistic cognitivist theory of meaning in favour of a non-cognitivist approach that claimed religious statements had a very definite meaning that is determined by their use. Braithwaite proposed that religious statements are used by believers to express a commitment to a certain way of life, in other words to a certain morality.[212]

Although Braithwaite's essay is called 'An empiricist's view' his analysis of religious language differs from that of other empiricists, such as Ayer and the Vienna Circle. EMPIRICISM is a type of philosophy that considers observation and experience to be the foundation of all our concepts. And as we have seen, for Ayer, statements must refer to something empirically verifiable if they are to be meaningful. However, Braithwaite argues that we must consider the empirical *use* of a statement, as well as its verifiability, when looking at its meaning. Braithwaite believes that empiricism, through observing how religious statements are used, can uncover their meaning.

His basic argument is that religious statements are used in the same way as moral statements. According to Braithwaite when we look at how moral statements are used we find they are expressions of an attitude towards life, and a commitment to a certain way of behaving. So when I say 'killing animals is wrong' what I mean is that I will never kill an animal, and will discourage other people from doing so. Religious statements are also expressions of a commitment to a certain way of life, and Braithwaite identifies the statement 'God is love' as meaning 'I will act in a selfless, agapeistic, way' (for more on agapeistic ethics, see above, pages 143–144).

Braithwaite recognises that there might be a number of religions which recommend similar ways of living, but this does not make them identical. What differentiates one religion from another is not just the actions of its believers, but also the set of stories in which it is embedded. These background stories, such as the Flood and Noah's Ark, or the exodus from Egypt by the Hebrews, also distinguish religious statements from moral statements (as moral statements are not embedded in such stories).

▶ criticism ◀ However, Braithwaite's account of the meaning of religious propositions doesn't really capture what believers think they are saying when they talk about God, Jesus, etc. Most believers do not simply think of their beliefs as a type of morality embedded in a set of myths. Nor do believers think that when they say that 'God is love' they are using this statement to prescribe a course of action. Most believers would hold that they are talking in a literal way about the universe, and referring to a literal God, a literal Creation, a literal Resurrection, etc. In some way it belittles religious language to reduce it to the 'intention to carry out a certain behaviour policy', as Braithwaite claims.[213]

more difficult

Another philosopher who was influenced by Wittgenstein's approach to meaning was Ian Crombie. Crombie's aim is rather narrower than Braithwaite's and it is simply to defend religious language against the critic's claim that it is meaningless. The central claim being made by the critic is that the word at the heart of all religious language use, i.e. 'God', does not refer to anything. Crombie aims to show how the word 'God' can remain mysterious and incomprehensible, yet can also be shown to be meaningful.[214]

'God' is a proper name in that it identifies an individual being, namely God. However, it does not behave in our language in the same way as other proper names. With normal proper names, such as 'Kylie', people can point to the person that the word refers to, interact with them, shake their hand, etc. However, with the name 'God' we cannot do any of these things, as God is a transcendent being who is beyond our comprehension and experience. Crombie says that the word 'God' is an 'improper' proper name. The critic of religious language maintains that, because this central concept, God, does not refer to anything, talking about God is simply meaningless.

Crombie aims to show that we can refer to God, whilst at the same time preserving the mystery of God's nature. He argues that we must be prepared to understand religious terms in a negative way. Here Crombie is drawing on a well-established theological tradition that runs back to St Augustine and to the Jewish philosopher Moses Maimonides (1135–1204). This approach is known as the *via negativa* (a Latin phrase meaning 'the negative way/path'). This tradition holds that we cannot understand or make substantial claims about who God is, since he is so totally beyond our experience. As Maimonides says: 'When our tongues desire to declare His greatness by descriptive terms, all eloquence becomes impotence and imbecility.' However, although we cannot make any positive assertions about God's essence, we can begin to describe him by talking about what he is *not*. In other words we can assert that God is not limited, not finite, not dependent, not MATERIAL, not temporal; he is the opposite of those things. In Figure 5.2 God is the area that

■ **Figure 5.2 *God can be defined by what he is NOT***

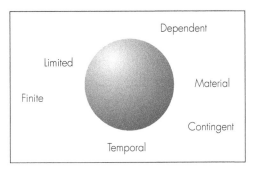

remains once we have determined what he is not: he is defined by his opposites.

Crombie takes an approach similar to the *via negativa* in that he suggest that we can define the 'reference range of God' negatively.[215] The words which we use to refer to God ('infinite', 'necessary', 'atemporal', etc.) are all paired to other words ('finite', 'contingent', 'temporal', etc.), and we come to understand what the word 'God' refers to by grasping what it does not refer to. Crombie says, for example, that part of the meaning of the word 'God' comes from our recognition that the world is contingent, and this helps us to refer to a non-contingent being (i.e. God), who is not part of the world. By describing what God is not, we can sketch what God is; Crombie claims that the word 'God' refers to this negative range of concepts (infinite, unlimited, immaterial, etc.).

So Crombie believes that he has answered those critics who assert that religious language is meaningless. He claims to have shown that the concept central to religious language, 'God', does stand for something and hence is meaningful. However, he also points out that this argument is unnecessary for someone who does believe in God, as they have a much more natural answer to the question 'what is God?': it is the 'name of the Being who is worthy to be adored'.[216]

ACTIVITY   For each of the philosophers you have read about in this chapter (Ayer, Hick, Flew, Wittgenstein, etc.) answer the following questions.

1 Do you think they are an atheist or a believer?
2 What memorable parable or phrase sums up their theory?
3 Do they think meaning is related to factual significance?
4 Do they think that religious propositions are factually significant?
5 Do they think that religious statements are meaningful?

Religious language as myth, symbol and analogy

We have now looked at two cognitivist theories of meaning (verificationism and falsificationism), i.e. ones that judge the meaningfulness of a statement by whether it can be shown to be true or false. These two theories were very much a response to the logical positivist movement in the early twentieth century, which equated knowledge with observation and linked philosophy with science. We have also examined some theories of meaning that reject this simple account of religious language. Wittgenstein, Braithwaite and Crombie take a non-cognitivist approach to the meaning of religious statements, rejecting the idea that meaning has to be connected to truth or falsity, and arguing that it is connected to the social context of communication, and the use of language within that context.

The theories that we are now going to look at take a more sympathetic approach to the meaning of religious statements. These theories presume that religious language is meaningful and instead focus on *how* religious language is best interpreted. The interpretations that we examine are: the symbolic interpretation, the mythic interpretation, and the interpretation of religious expressions as analogies.

Religious language as symbolic

Paul Tillich (1886–1965) believes that religious language is best understood as symbolic and not taken as a set of literal assertions about the world. Tillich makes a clear distinction between a sign (such as a set of traffic lights) and a symbol (such as a national flag). Both signs and symbols 'point beyond themselves' and refer to the world, and both can be words or objects or actions.[217] Although they have these two things in common they are nonetheless significantly different.

Signs are arbitrary representations of something, and they have no connection to that thing. So the red light on traffic lights is a sign for 'stop' and the green light is a sign for 'go', but there is no real connection between 'red' and 'stop' or 'green' and 'go', and any colour might have been chosen (purple and blue might have gone nicely with amber). On the other hand, symbols might begin as being arbitrarily chosen, but they gradually become associated with the thing they represent. Words, actions, objects, events may all be interpreted symbolically. For example, when people see the United States flag, which is a symbol for the USA, they associate it so closely with the country that it evokes passionate feelings, leading some to salute it and others to burn it. This association Tillich thinks of as the sign's coming to participate or share in the reality of what it represents.

experimenting with ideas

Find out what the following religious symbols mean to Christian believers. What might they be associated with?

1 Father
2 A Crucifix
3 Lamb
4 Making the sign of the cross
5 Kneeling in church
6 The colour blue on the dress of Mary
7 The use of water in baptism
8 Rosary beads
9 The Last Judgement
10 The Resurrection

For Tillich, belief in God can only be truly expressed through the use of symbolic language. As he says, 'the language of faith is the language of symbols' and in this way 'it points beyond itself whilst participating in that to which it points'.[218] So, for Tillich, a statement like 'Jesus is the Lamb of God' is best understood as having a symbolic meaning: 'lamb' is a symbol of sacrifice and represents Jesus' sacrifice for our sins. Other examples of religious symbols (including words, objects or actions, etc.) have various associations with humility, worship, love, sacrifice and the other central features of the Christian faith. In particular, for Tillich, religious symbols point towards the Holy, or what Rudolf Otto called 'the numinous' (see page 87).

Tillich believes that God is the 'object of ultimate concern', the being whom we strive to understand, and religious faith is being in a 'state of ultimate concern' for God. Now these expressions of faith, and of concern, cannot be expressed in ordinary, literal language. Tillich claims that symbols and symbolic language, especially as they are used in religion, enable us to 'open up' deeper levels of reality that would otherwise remain closed to us. If we were just stuck with literal language then we would not understand the religious or spiritual world around us. Through the use of symbolic language we are able to express the special nature and qualities of faith and religious belief.

J.H. Randall, who also believes that religious language is best interpreted as symbolic, argues that religious symbols serve four important functions.[219] It is these functions that make religious symbols so powerful.

The first function Randall identifies is a motivational one, as religious symbols (such as the cross) fire up the emotions and inspire people into action. So, for example, Shakespeare's Henry V urges his troops into battle ending his speech with the words 'Cry – God for Harry, England and St George'.[220] The second function is a social one, and arises from the fact that people have a common understanding of religious symbols, and this binds them together, enables co-operative action and strengthens social bonds. In many a Hollywood film (e.g. *McCabe & Mrs Miller*) the construction of a church, and the final placement of a cross on the spire, is a symbolic act that brings the community together. The third function of religious symbols is one of communication. The literal use of language, which A.J. Ayer seemed to wish we all used, cannot express the religious faith and experiences of believers, or capture the things they believe. However, a symbolic use of language can communicate some of these qualities. In William Blake's utopian poem 'Jerusalem', the building of Jerusalem in England is a symbol of hope and potential salvation from the 'dark satanic mills' of the industrial revolution. The fourth function of religious symbols is one that we have already seen Tillich ascribe to: that religious symbols can clarify and disclose our experience of the divine. In the same way that an artist or poet can reveal hidden depths to our world, so a prophet or a saint can use religious symbols to 'teach us how to find the Divine; they show us visions of God'.[221]

▶ criticism ◀ There are problems with Tillich's claims that symbols somehow 'participate' in the thing that they symbolise. He is vague about what he means by 'participate' and how a symbol might share in the reality and power of the thing it symbolises. For example, how does a flag (the example of a symbol most frequently used by Tillich) participate in the power and dignity of a nation?

Tillich could mean that a flag carries powerful connotations, and that the presentation of a flag (let's say at an anti-war rally) brings to people the same flood of emotions (positive or negative) as they would have when thinking about a whole nation. In this sense, in its capacity to strongly influence people's thoughts and actions, a symbol may be said to have the power of the thing it symbolises.

▶ criticism ◀ There is a further problem with the symbolic interpretation of religious language, which is that it suggests that religious claims are not literally true. Controversially, Randall like Wittgenstein veers towards anti-realism when it comes to God. In other words he does not believe that the concept 'God' actually refers to anything in the real world. Randall is happy to treat 'God' symbolically, as representing our ultimate concern, our ideals, and our values. Moreover, for both Tillich and Randall, religious statements like 'God is good' are to be interpreted symbolically, not literally (e.g. as a statement about the moral goodness of God). But John Hick wonders which aspect of this statement is the symbolic part: is it the whole proposition 'God is good' or is it the idea of 'God's goodness'?[222] To a believer it seems important that God is in fact good, and not that God's goodness symbolises something else. If religious language is only symbolic then it would seem to deprive it of substance, and the words of prophets and saints (to use Randall's phrase) would teach us very little about who God is or how to follow a Christian way of life.

Religious language as myth

Some theologians have chosen to interpret religious statements and religious texts as myths. There are many examples of religious myths, from those of the ancient Egyptians to the gods of the Greeks, Romans and Vikings, but even in monotheistic religions like Christianity we can find many mythic stories. There are three senses in which the word 'myth' could be applied to religious texts and religious statements:

1 The myth could be a story or a fable that is not true, but which has some other value. For example, Braithwaite argued that religious stories are inspirational to us, and they provide us with the motivation to lead a moral life.
2 The myth could be a literary device that enables us to talk about things that are 'ineffable', i.e. beyond language. So myths help us to speak of spiritual and supernatural events in natural terms.
3 The myth could be a method of interpreting 'ultimate reality' in the sense that Tillich described above. So myths have symbolic meaning in the sense that they open up new levels of reality or, as Randall argues, their purpose is to bind communities together, urge us to action, etc.

One advantage of interpreting religious language as 'mythological' is that Biblical stories, which seem strange or absurd to the scientifically-minded modern believer, become more palatable. So a believer might read the Bible and enjoy it as a powerful piece of literature, which, although not historically true, is an excellent source of spiritual and moral guidance.

There is a further advantage of not taking a literal view of religious language. If a revelatory text like the Bible is supposed to be taken as recording historical or scientific occurrences and predictions, then many of its claims can be shown to be false. For example, it is possible to use the Bible to calculate the age of the universe, and it is reckoned to be a few thousand years. But the scientific consensus now reckons the universe to be billions (possibly 13 billion) of years old. However, if we interpret the Bible in a mythological sense then the stories of the Old and New testament cannot be 'proved wrong' by scientific or historical evidence. Taking a mythological view of religious language also side-steps the criticisms of Flew and Ayer, namely that religious language is not factually significant (because it can't be verified or falsified) and is therefore meaningless. These attacks become irrelevant if it is conceded that religious statements are myths. This is because we don't expect myths to be factually significant: their power lies in their metaphorical or symbolic meaning.

And as they still went on and talked, behold, a chariot of fire and horses of fire separated the two of them. And Elijah went up by a whirlwind into heaven.

2 Kings 2:11

Then I saw an angel coming down from heaven . . . And he seized the dragon, that ancient serpent, who is the Devil and Satan, and bound him for a thousand years.

Revelation 20:1–3

Chariots of fire and heavenly whirlwinds, angels, dragons and Satan, these are images worthy of Tolkien, but the Bible is full of such objects and descriptions. For Rudolf Bultmann (1884–1976), believers can no longer take these things literally. Bultmann was one of the foremost advocates of the view that the Bible should be interpreted as myth.[223] He argued that it is only by reading the Bible as a mythological text that modern believers are able to square their scientific understanding of the world with the miraculous events of the Bible. It was clear to Bultmann that the Bible was written in a pre-scientific era when myths were everywhere and were an acceptable method of conveying meaning. For example, the cosmology of the Bible (literally consisting of three levels: hell down below, heaven in the skies above and Earth somewhere in the middle) can only be understood as a mythical cosmology, given what we now know about the Earth, the solar system, the stars, etc. But now that our worldview has changed we must strip the Bible of its myths (DEMYTHOLOGISE it in Bultmann's terms) so that it may speak clearly to us again. Demythologising for Bultmann doesn't mean editing out the myths, but reinterpreting them in order to reveal their personal meaning to Christians today.

The real point of myth is not to give an objective world picture; what is expressed in it, rather, is how we human beings understand ourselves in the world.[224]

Bultmann

One example given by Bultmann of a Biblical myth that needs demythologising is Luke's account of the birth of Jesus in a stable. By stripping away the mythic trappings of this story it is possible to reveal the simple message that God can be found in even the most humble and excluded parts of the world. Another example is the resurrection of Jesus. Bultmann claimed that the myth of a heavenly redeemer who was killed and then resurrected was popular all over the

Middle East in the first century AD. The gospel writers then attached this myth onto a historical figure, Jesus of Nazareth, who was executed in Palestine by the Romans. For the writers of the New Testament, such as John and Paul, Jesus' resurrection was a story to be told in order to impress upon people the imminence of the apocalyptic Last Judgement. However, the Last Judgement, it turned out, was not so imminent and this meaning of the resurrection story has become irrelevant, as Christians are no longer waiting for the Last Judgement. So for Bultmann the myth of the resurrection now needs to be reinterpreted (demythologised) for a modern age, in order to get at its true meaning, namely the reinvention of an individual when they are baptised and become a Christian.

ACTIVITY

Bultmann holds that in an age of hi-tech gadgets, which are the product of the success of science, it is difficult to take the miracles and stories of the Bible literally.

1 Write down a list of those Biblical stories and miracles that you think are best understood as myths.
2 For each of these myths, what relevance or meaning could they have for the modern believer?
3 Are there any stories of miracles in the Bible that you think even a 'scientifically minded' Christian would hold to be literally true?

▶ criticism ◀

A fundamental difficulty with interpreting religious stories as myths is that (as with the symbolic interpretation) it undermines their status as true accounts of actual events. But it is precisely the fact that believers take them to be true which gives weight and meaning to their faith. If God did not literally create the world in six days; if Mary was not really a virgin when she gave birth to Jesus; and if Jesus did not really rise from the dead on the third day; if, in other words, these are just reassuring stories, then what is the point of being a Christian? It is precisely because God is thought to be *literally* the creator of the universe that he deserves our worship, and it is precisely because of the historical facts of the miracles of the virgin birth and Christ's resurrection that the truth of Christ's divinity is revealed to us and so gives us reason to believe. Many would argue that it is a necessary condition of being a Christian that you believe that Christ is literally the son of God. Perhaps if you don't really believe this, if you think it is some sort of myth, then you are not really a Christian at all.

► criticism ◄ Alvin Plantinga argues that to claim that 'God exists' is to make an existential assertion, i.e. an assertion about the existence of a special kind of being. It is not to talk symbolically, or mythologically, or to adopt a certain attitude or behavioural policy (as Braithwaite maintains). Plantinga maintains that when a Christian speaks of the existence of God they are claiming 'first, that there exists a *person* of a certain sort – a being who acts, holds beliefs, and has aims and purposes. This person, secondly, is immaterial . . . is perfect in goodness, knowledge, and power, and is such that the world depends on him for its existence.'[225] It seems as if a theory of meaning that is capable of capturing what a believer is saying when they talk about God must be able to incorporate Plantinga's claim. In other words, it must be capable of treating religious concepts, such as 'God', as if they refer to something real.

Religious language as analogy

The unusual properties of religious language that we've been discussing in this chapter were first discussed by scholastic philosophers of the Middle Ages, and the greatest of these, St Thomas Aquinas, offered an influential and enduring analysis of religious language. The problem, as Aquinas saw it, is that when we talk about God, and the attributes of God, we are not using words in the same way as when we talk about humans and their properties. For example, when the author of Psalm 31 described God as his 'rock' and his 'fortress',[226] he did not imagine God to be constructed from impenetrable materials. And when we read in Exodus that 'The Lord is a great warrior: Almighty is his name'[227] this does not mean that God is triumphant in warfare over other gods (which is the meaning that the ancient Greeks might have intended when referring to Zeus as a great warrior).

Despite the difficulties of knowing anything about God, Aquinas is still confident that we can talk about God in a positive and literal way.[228] He is not a follower of the *via negativa* (i.e. the claim that God can only be spoken of by saying what he is not), although he does accept that the words we use to describe God only do so in an imperfect way. He is also opposed to the idea that we can only speak of God in a non-literal way (e.g. through metaphors like 'rock' and 'lion'). The question for Aquinas is how it is possible to talk about God in a substantial way, when God is beyond experience, and our language cannot describe what is beyond experience.

Aquinas' solution to the problem of talking about God rests on his identification of three distinct ways of using words:

1 Univocal use: if I use a word univocally in two sentences then it has the same meaning in both those sentences. For example, in the statements 'There's a rat in the kitchen' and 'You look like a drowned rat' the word 'rat' has the same meaning, and is being used univocally.

2 Equivocal use: if I use a word equivocally in two sentences then it has different meanings in both those sentences. For example, in the sentences 'He was feeling a bit down after his disappointing exam result' and 'She told her sister to climb down from the electric pylon' the word 'down' has different meanings, so in these cases it is being used equivocally.

3 Analogical use: if I use a word analogically in two sentences then there is a similarity between the meanings of the two words. For example, if I say that 'Lassie was faithful to her owner' and 'The people were faithful to their leader' then I am applying the word faithful to the dog in a way that is analogous (similar) to the faithfulness of the people. In other words there is a resemblance between the behaviour (and perhaps thoughts) of a dog and a human. Aquinas refers to this resemblance as 'proportion', because there is a sense in which the faithfulness of the dog is proportioned to the faithfulness of a human being. The proportion of faithfulness in the dog is less than that in the human, because it is a less complex creature.

experimenting with ideas

For the second sentence of each pair, identify whether the word in **bold** is being used in a univocal, an equivocal, or an analogical way as the same word in the first sentence of the pair.

1 a) His eyes stayed focused on the window across the street.
   b) The eyes are a **window** to the soul.
2 a) The guards fought the thieves in order to protect the crown.
   b) The king fought a bloody war in order to protect his **crown**.
3 a) The artist drew a blank white square on the canvas.
   b) The detective drew a **blank** when interviewing the first suspect.
4 a) The fresh air had brought a healthy glow to her cheeks.
   b) He had a very **healthy** appetite for a two year old.
5 a) Nottingham Castle was a stronghold for the oppressed.
   b) God is a **stronghold** for the oppressed (Psalms 9:9).

Aquinas goes on to analyse whether the words that we use to describe God are being used univocally, equivocally or analogically. He says that when we say 'God is good' we cannot be using the word in the same way that we use it when we are talking about humans. God is so different from any other being that it is impossible to ascribe to him the same properties that we ascribe to humans or other creatures. So we cannot use words like 'good', 'wise' or 'compassionate', univocally of both God and human beings. However, this does not mean that we are therefore using these terms in a completely different (equivocal) way when we talk about God. Aquinas believes that there is a resemblance between the meaning of the words that we use to describe God, and of the words we use to describe his creation (and the creatures that inhabit it).

So Aquinas rejects the view that words applied to God are identical to those applied to everyday beings, i.e. the univocal use. He also rejects the view that the words we use to talk about God (like goodness) bear no relation to the words we use to talk about humans i.e. the equivocal use. Instead Aquinas argues that when we talk about God we are generally using words analogically. This means that there is a resemblance between the meaning of 'faithfulness', 'wisdom', 'goodness', etc. when applied to God and the meanings of these terms when ascribed to humans. But it is only a resemblance, and our words cannot come close to accurately describing God, such is the extent of the difference between God's perfections (which are unified and indivisible from one another) and our own flawed virtues (which do not come altogether as a single package).

This failure of words accurately to describe God arises because words 'apply primarily to creatures, not God'.[229] So we are taking a tool (language) which has been developed to do one particular task, namely to talk about the world around us, and we are using this tool to do a task for which it isn't equipped, namely to talk about God. For example, we are comfortable using the word 'love' to describe the fiery, finite and jealous emotion that humans feel for each other. But the same word hardly conveys at all the power and depth of God's love, which is held to be infinite, all embracing and an inseparable part of his essence. However, we can see that there is a sort of resemblance between God's love and our own feeble love, and so for Aquinas the word 'love' can be used to talk about God in a literal sense. The words we use to describe human thoughts, feelings and actions are the only ones we have available to us when it comes to talking about God. We just have to remember that, with religious language, we are using these words in an analogical way.

► criticism ◄

But there is a difficulty with claiming that we can talk about God, even in an analogical way. In Stanislaw Lem's novel *Solaris*, human beings have discovered a planet, called Solaris, covered by an ocean which seems to be alive, which moves and extends its 'tendrils' out into the atmosphere, and which might even have a mind. For decades scientists investigate the behaviour of this living planet, and countless theories are proposed as to what Solaris is: a psychic ocean; a dying organism; an introverted hermit; an inorganic fluid; the cradle of a new god . . . Because Solaris is beyond anything that humans have experienced, the scientists are only able to express their theories through the language of analogy: by finding correspondences between the apparently purposeful activities of the planet and the purposeful activities that we already know about and understand, namely human or animal behaviour. But ultimately the scientists cannot explain or predict the purpose or meaning of the planet's behaviour. As Lem puts it:

Transposed into any human language, the values and meanings involved lose all substance; they cannot be brought intact through the barrier.[230]

The inner workings and consciousness of Solaris lie completely beyond human understanding and words. Because Solaris remains inexplicable and incomprehensible to humans, the analogical language we use to describe it becomes meaningless: the scientists can never know whether Solaris is 'like' a human in any respect. The problem that Lem's scientists face on Solaris is the same as that faced by believers in the real world: how can we be sure whether our analogical descriptions of God (as good, or wise, or loving) actually refer to any property of God. If God is so utterly different from humans, then even analogical language might fail to describe him in any significant way. Perhaps, as St Paul said, we shall have to wait until we meet God in order to know exactly what we're talking about when we speak of 'God'.

For now we see through a glass, darkly, but then face to face; now I know in part; but then shall I know even as also I am known.

Paul, 1 Corinthians 13:12

Philosophy and religion revisited

Throughout this book you may have felt the tension between three groups of people with an interest in religious belief: philosophers who are atheists, such as David Hume and Antony Flew; philosophers who are believers, such as St Thomas Aquinas and Alvin Plantinga; and non-philosophers who are believers: those ordinary folk who happen to believe in God.

From the point of view of religious philosophers, it might seem as if the criticisms and alleged 'insights' of atheistic philosophers are beside the point. The atheists make demands that have no real bearing on the belief in God. These demands include: water-tight proofs of God's existence; evidence for every religious belief; a complete justification for why there is suffering in the world; an account of how we can talk meaningfully about a being who is beyond experience. When Pascal left behind that accusatory note after his death, telling us that his God was the God of Isaac, Jacob and Abraham not the God of the philosophers, he was echoing the thoughts of many religious philosophers before and since. Atheistic philosophers just don't get it: they don't understand what it is to really believe in *God*. Wittgenstein made a remark along the same lines: to be able to really understand what someone is saying you have to immerse yourself in their way of life. And this is something that few atheist philosophers appear to have an interest in, or the capability of, doing.

From the point of view of some atheist and agnostic philosophers, the philosophy of religion is an obstinately evasive subject: it's like eating jelly with a fork. Religious philosophers use all the tools and methodologies of Western philosophy (construction of arguments, conceptual analysis, clarification of questions, etc.) but only up to a point. To the atheist philosopher it seems as if the moment the beliefs of the religious philosopher are under threat they resort to some non-philosophical, non-rational trick which preserves their belief in God. For example, they offer various proofs of God's existence, and then when it is shown that these don't work, they claim that actually these are not like other sorts of proofs, because they are not supposed to persuade non-believers of the truth of the conclusion. Other tricks include: redefining and qualifying their beliefs in response to any piece of evidence that could knock down their old beliefs; or playing around with the idea of meaning, even to the extent that some 'anti-realist' theologians claim that when they assert 'God exists' what they really mean isn't that there's a thing, God, who exists, but something else entirely! In other words it seems to the atheists that religious philosophers are breaking Plato's cardinal rule of philosophy, which is to follow the argument wherever it leads.[231] Religious philosophers follow the argument where it leads, so long as it leads to the place where they want it to go. As soon as it doesn't go there, rational argument is thrown out of the window and it's all 'faith, faith, faith'.

Finally from the point of view of the ordinary believer, the approaches of both types of philosopher (atheist and believer) are simply wrong-headed. Philosophy has little bearing on the thoughts, actions and lives of most believers around the world. When ordinary believers do come across philosophical questions ('Can God make a stone so large that he can't move it?', 'What caused God?', 'What does "God" mean?') they may well shake their heads, and wonder in bewilderment why anyone would want to waste their time thinking about such ridiculous and obscure questions. For the ordinary believer, God is someone who is woven into every part of their lives, like breathing or thinking or feeling, and there's no more to it than that.

Perhaps we must finish with two more sobering remarks, one from a believer (Blaise Pascal) and one from an atheist (Steven Pinker), about our capacity to discover and understand metaphysical and religious truths.

Reason's last step is the recognition that there are an infinite number of things which are beyond it. It is merely feeble if it does not go as far as to realize that. If natural things are beyond it, what are we to say about supernatural things?[232]

Pascal

Maybe philosophical problems are hard not because they are divine or irreducible or meaningless . . . but because the mind of Homo Sapiens lacks the cognitive equipment to solve them. We are organisms, not angels, and our minds are organs, not pipelines to the truth.[233]

Pinker

Key points: Chapter 5

What you need to know about **religious language**:

1 Religious language contains some puzzling features, many of which arise from the concept of 'God'. Words used to describe God, like 'omnipotence' or 'omniscience', seem to be ill-defined or even paradoxical. God is sometimes referred to in human terms, as speaking with us, or walking with us. Moreover, if God is beyond experience, and beyond words, then how is it possible to talk meaningfully about God? Many philosophers have offered distinct theories of meaning, which determine more precisely what is meaningful and what is nonsense.

2 The verificationist theory of meaning claims that only those sentences that can be shown to be true (or false) count as meaningful. These sentences make genuine claims about the world: they are 'factually significant'. According to A.J. Ayer, discussions about God are not meaningful, because they cannot be verified. However, according to John Hick, they can be verified if they are true, but only after we die. Antony Flew shifts the focus of meaning to falsifiability. Flew argues that what someone says is factually significant (and meaningful) only if they can imagine being wrong. If they can't imagine being wrong, and if they keep qualifying their original statement when presented with situations that falsify that claim, then they are not talking about the world at all. Hare and Mitchell undermined Flew's position, by describing situations when certain claims would be meaningful, even though they could not be falsified.

3 Wittgenstein eventually rejected the idea that all uses of language were governed by the same rules of meaning (e.g. that they must make statements capable of verification). Wittgenstein held that language use is complex, and that different rules operate in different areas of life. It is a mistake to think that the rules governing one part of life (e.g. science) must also apply to another part of life (e.g. religion). Yet this is what people like Ayer seem to be doing, and for Wittgenstein this is simply a mistake. Wittgenstein argued that if we wish to know the meaning of a word we must look to how it is used in a particular 'language game'. So if we wish to know the meaning of religious terms, we must fully understand the religious context in which they are being used.

4 Other philosophers have proposed that religious language is best understood not in a literal way, but as symbolic or mythological. Treating religious language as symbolic means that we are able to dig deeper into its significance: as motivating people; as bringing people together; as a poetic

representation of faith and belief; as a way of disclosing our experience of the divine. Rudolf Bultmann argued that we have to treat the language of the Bible as mythological. He claimed that these myths have none of the power and meaning that they once had, because our scientific worldview has transformed the way that we think about the universe. For Bultmann we must 'demythologise' the stories of the Bible, and reinterpret them in a way that makes sense to believers today.

5 Aquinas recognised that words could be used in different ways: univocally (when they share the same meaning in different sentences); equivocally (when the same word has a different meaning in different sentences); and analogically (when there is a connection or resemblance between the same word in different sentences). When we talk about God, Aquinas says that we are using our words analogically. Terms like 'good' or 'wise' were originally intended to describe human beings, but we can use them in an analogous way to talk about God. So when we talk about God we are talking literally about God, but our words really don't come close to describing God's true essence.

Glossary

A POSTERIORI A Latin term that describes a belief that can only be known via experience of the world: for example that 'snow is white' or that 'the Atlantic is smaller than the Pacific'. *A posteriori* beliefs are contrasted with **a priori** beliefs.

A PRIORI A Latin term that usually describes a belief (or knowledge) that is known prior to or independently from experience. For example, that '1,000,000 + 1 = 1,000,001' can be known independently of counting a million apples, adding another one, and then recounting them. *A priori* beliefs are contrasted with **a posteriori** beliefs, which are ones derived from experience.

AGAPE The ancient Greek word for thoughtful or selfless love, sometimes translated as 'charity'. Some theologians, such as Fletcher, have seen *agape* as the basis for a Christian Ethics.

AGNOSTIC/AGNOSTICISM This is the position that we do not have enough grounds either to believe in God, or to disbelieve in God. It may be a personal claim ('I am undecided about God's existence'), or it may be global claim ('It is impossible to know whether or not there is a God').

ANALOGICAL According to Aquinas, a word is used analogically in two sentences when there is an imperfect likeness in the meaning of the two words: 'imperfect' because the two things are different, but 'likeness' because the two things have something in common. Aquinas believed that we could only talk about God analogically.

ANALYTIC A term that describes the manner in which a proposition is true. An analytic truth is a proposition that is true in virtue of the meanings of the words alone. In other words an analytic truth is one that is true by definition, for example 'A bachelor is an unmarried man.'

ANTHROPIC PRINCIPLE Confusingly, the Anthropic Principle isn't a single principle, but has been advocated by thinkers both to support and undermine the belief in God. Both sides acknowledge that the existence of self-conscious life – i.e. of humans – in the universe seems to be astonishingly improbable and requires an explanation. (Anthropic stems from the Greek word for 'human being'.) Believers (such as Tennant) have framed the Anthropic Principle so that it seems impossible to believe that humans could come to exist by chance; hence there must be a guiding hand behind the development of the universe. Non-believers (such as Brandon Carter) have developed the Anthropic Principle to show that humans should not be surprised that the universe has led to our existence, because if it hadn't led to our existence we wouldn't have been around to be surprised.

ANTI-REALISM An anti-realist claims that particular aspects of the world have no real existence beyond human minds and language. For example, an anti-realist about numbers would claim that numbers are the products of human minds and language and have no existence outside of these spheres. An anti-realist about God would claim that although talk of God is perfectly meaningful, and may be very important, 'God' has no existence beyond human minds and language. See also **realism**.

ARGUMENT FROM ANALOGY See **induction**.

ARGUMENT FROM DESIGN See **teleological arguments**.

ATEMPORAL Outside of time. It is generally agreed that God is eternal, but some **theologians** maintain that this means that God exists outside of time: he has no past, present or future.

ATHEISM/ATHEIST In the tradition of Western philosophy, atheism generally refers to the belief that there is no God in a Christian (or Jewish, or Islamic) sense. In contrast to **theism**.

BASIC BELIEF According to Plantinga, a belief is basic if it provides the foundations for other beliefs, and does not need further evidence to justify it. Plantinga proposes that belief in God is a properly basic belief, and so does not need any evidence to justify it.

BENEVOLENCE   The desire and disposition to do good for others. Christian philosophers maintain that God has the property of benevolence.

COGNITIVISM/NON-COGNITIVISM (COGNITIVE/NON-COGNITIVE)   Cognitivism is a position in the philosophy of language which holds that judgements or statements must be true or false if they are to mean anything. Cognitivist perspectives on religious language include **verificationism** and **falsificationism**. Non-cognitivism is the position that statements can be meaningful, even if they don't refer to the world and the concepts of 'truth' and 'falsehood' don't apply to them. Examples of non-cognitivist perspectives on religious language come from Wittgenstein, and from the interpretation of religious language as mythical or symbolic.

CONCLUSION   A belief or statement that an argument tries to prove.

CONTINGENT   See **Necessary**.

COSMOLOGICAL   Cosmology is the study of the universe as whole. Cosmological arguments for the existence of God operate by claiming that there must be some ultimate cause or reason for the existence of the universe. This explanation cannot be found within the universe and so must be found in some supernatural being, namely God.

DEDUCTION   A deductive argument is one where the truth of the **conclusion** is guaranteed by the proof of the premises. This is in contrast to an **inductive** argument. **Ontological** arguments are deductive proofs of God's existence.

DEMYTHOLOGISE   A term used by Rudolf Bultmann to refer to the stripping away (or re-interpreting) of the myths of the Bible, in order to uncover their true meaning to modern believers.

DETERMINISM   See **freewill**.

EMPIRICISM   An **epistemological** position which holds that our beliefs, and knowledge, must be based on experience. David Hume was one philosopher who rigorously applied his empiricist approach to questions in the philosophy of religion.

EPISTEMOLOGY/EPISTEMOLOGICAL   The theory of knowledge. The study of what and how humans know. See also **reformed epistemology**.

ESCHATOLOGY/ESCHATOLOGICAL   In Christian terms, this is the area of theology concerned with death, the after-life, the Last Judgement and generally with what happens at the end of things.

EUTHYPHRO DILEMMA   In the philosophy of religion this dilemma raises the question 'in what way are God's commands good?' and offers two problematic options. The first option is that whatever God commands is good, in which case his commands to commit genocide (Deuteronomy 3:2) or infanticide (Genesis 22:2), for example, are good. The second option is that God's commands are good because they conform to some external moral law, in which case we should pay attention to this moral law, rather than God.

EVIDENTIALISM   The position that our beliefs must be grounded in sufficient evidence. Atheist philosophers often maintain that a belief in God lacks evidence, and hence is unjustifiable. Plantinga argues that even evidentialism recognises beliefs which do not need evidence (he calls them **basic beliefs**), but which support our other beliefs.

EVIL   Extreme kinds of moral wrongdoing. Philosophers usually distinguish between moral evil, which is the suffering caused by humans, and natural evil, which is the suffering brought about by natural events such as earthquakes. The existence of evil in the universe presents a challenge to believers known as the **problem of evil**.

FACTUAL SIGNIFICANCE   A statement has factual significance if it tells us something about the real world. Some theories of meaning (such as **verificationism**) maintain that a sentence is only meaningful if it is factually significant.

FALLACY   This refers to an argument which has gone wrong: either because a mistake has been made, rendering the argument invalid; or because the argument has a form, or structure, which is always invalid (e.g. the **fallacy of composition**).

FALLACY OF COMPOSITION   The mistake of arguing that, because every member of the group has a property in common, the group taken as a whole must also have that property.

For example, just because every human has a mother doesn't imply that the human species has a mother. Hume thinks that this fallacy applies to the **cosmological** argument: just because every event has a cause, it doesn't mean that the whole chain needs a cause.

FALSIFICATIONISM   A philosophical belief about the nature of meaning. Closely related to **verificationism**, falsificationism claims that for a proposition to be meaningful we must be able to grasp what would count as proving the proposition false (i.e. what would falsify it).

FIDEISM   The position that belief in God is based on faith and not on reason. In its most extreme form it sees reason as a barrier to belief in God, and something that should be avoided when arriving at that belief.

FIRST CAUSE   The cosmological argument proposes that the universal chain of causes and effects must have begun with something that was uncaused, or rather which was the cause of itself. Believers like Aquinas maintain that this First Cause is God.

FREEWILL   Also known as metaphysical freedom. The idea of freewill is that the self controls aspects of its own life, e.g. bodily movements like picking up a pencil. Many religious philosophers believe that God granted humans freewill. Freewill can be contrasted with *determinism*, which is the belief that all events in the universe are the necessary consequence of physical laws, and these laws apply to human actions as well. A determinist might claim that humans are like complex pieces of biological machinery with no real freedom of will.

HOLY   The concept of 'holy' is used to encapsulate everything that is special and sacred about God. It can also be used to describe religious objects which share in this sacredness. Rudolf Otto described the overpowering experience of God's holiness as **numinous**.

IMMATERIAL   Not made of matter. According to Descartes this would mean not occupying physical space. God is said to be immaterial in this sense.

IMMUTABLE   Something that can never change. God is said to be immutable, and this is bound up with the idea that God is simple (he is one thing, and his attributes such as **benevolence** and **omnipotence** cannot be separated from one another).

INCORPOREAL   Without a physical body.

INDUCTION/INDUCTIVE   An inductive argument is one where the truth of the conclusion is not fully guaranteed by the truth of the premises. For example: moving from particular examples (every raven I've seen has been black) to a generalisation (all ravens are black). Arguments from analogy are also inductive: they compare two things, and move from what these two things are known to have in common, to draw a conclusion about other (unknown) things they are supposed to have in common. The **cosmological** and **teleological arguments** are inductive arguments for God's existence.

INFINITE REGRESS   A regress is a process of reasoning from effect to cause, or of going backwards in a chain of explanations. An infinite regress is one where the process never stops, where it is repeated endlessly. This is generally considered problematic in a philosophical argument, and a sign that a mistake has been made. However, when criticising the cosmological argument some philosophers have argued that an infinite regress is a more plausible explanation than a **First Cause**.

LANGUAGE GAME   The phrase used by Wittgenstein to convey the idea that language has meaning within a particular social context, and that these contexts are governed by rules (in the same way that different games are governed by different rules). The way in which a sentence is meaningful therefore varies according to the context in which it occurs.

MATERIAL   Made of physical matter. According to Descartes this involved occupying physical space. In contrast, God is thought of by Christian philosophers as **immaterial**.

NATURAL THEOLOGY   Gaining an understanding of God through the use of our reason. This may be through an examination of the world around us (which leads, for example, to the **teleological argument**), or through an analysis of concepts (which leads, for example, to the **ontological** argument). This is in contrast to **revealed theology**.

NECESSARY/CONTINGENT BEINGS   A contingent being is one whose existence depends on something else (e.g. humans are contingent because their existence depends on the existence of parents, of oxygen, of food, etc.).

A necessary being is one that does not depend upon anything else for its existence. There are both **cosmological** and **ontological** arguments that hold God to be a necessary being.

NECESSARY/CONTINGENT TRUTHS   In the most restricted sense, a necessary truth is one where the opposite is logically impossible: for example, 'a triangle has three sides' (a two-sided triangle is logically impossible and cannot be imagined). A contingent truth is one where the opposite is logically possible: for example, it's true that Winston Churchill was once the Prime Minister of the United Kingdom (but it's entirely possible that this may never have happened). It is supposed by some philosophers that the proposition 'God exists' is a necessary truth, because the concept of 'God' already contains the idea of 'a being who must exist'. This claim lies at the heart of some **ontological** arguments.

NON-COGNITIVISM   *See* **Cognitivism**.

NUMINOUS   A term invented by Rudolf Otto to describe the overwhelming experiences of an encounter with God. These experiences combine terror and dread, with awe and wonder.

OMNIPOTENCE/OMNIPOTENT   All-powerful. Along with **benevolence** this is one of the main attributes of God.

OMNIPRESENCE/OMNIPRESENT   Everywhere at once. Like **benevolence** and **omnipotence** this is one of the attributes of God.

OMNISCIENCE/OMNISCIENT   All-knowing. As with **benevolence**, **omnipotence** and **omnipresence** this is one of the attributes of God. However, it is important to remember that these attributes cannot be separated from one another in God, this is because God is simple and **immutable**.

ONTOLOGICAL   Ontology is the study of existence. If you were to write down everything you thought existed (cats, dogs, electrons, aliens, etc.), then this list would form your own personal ontology. If aliens were present on the list then you could be said to be making an ontological commitment to the existence of aliens (in other words you claim they exist). All believers (except **anti-realists**) include God in their ontology. The ontological argument is a particular proof of God's existence, and tries to show that the very meaning of the concept 'God' implies that he must exist.

PHYSICO-THEOLOGICAL   A term used by the philosopher Immanuel Kant to describe an argument for God's existence based on particular features of the world (e.g. order, regularity, design). The phrase didn't catch on, and we now refer to these arguments as **teleological**.

PREDICATE   Many propositions can be divided into a **subject** and a predicate, where the subject is the thing that the sentence is about and the predicate gives us information about the subject. For example, in the sentence 'The balloon was red' the term 'was red' is the predicate, the term 'the balloon' is the subject. Some philosophers argued that in the sentence 'God exists', 'exists' is a predicate applying to 'God'. However, philosophers from Kant onwards have doubted whether existence is a genuine predicate.

PROPOSITION   A proposition is a sentence that makes a claim about the way the world actually is. For example, 'There is a cat on my mat' or 'I am thinking about a dragon'. Other sentences can play different roles, for example, 'Sit down NOW' or 'What are you looking at?' Such sentences (commands, questions, exclamations) do not make specific claims about the way the world is, and hence are not propositions.

PREMISE   A statement or claim used to build or support an argument.

PROBLEM OF EVIL   A problem recognised by both **believers** and **atheists**: how can an all-powerful, all-loving and all-knowing creator have created a world which seems to contain so much unnecessary pain and suffering?

REALISM   The belief that objects of different kinds actually exist (in contrast to **anti-realism**). For example, a realist about numbers would believe that numbers have some sort of existence beyond human minds and human language. A realist about theoretical entities like electrons believes that electrons have an existence independent of human minds and language. Most believers are realists about God.

REDUCTIO AD ABSURDUM   A method of argument by which you prove that your position is reasonable, by showing that the only alternative position is absurd. In order to do this you imagine the alternative position to be true, then you take it to its logical conclusion, and by doing so you reveal it to have ridiculous or absurd consequences. This leaves your position as the strongest. Aquinas uses a *reductio ad absurdum* in his cosmological arguments.

REFORMED EPISTEMOLOGY   A term used by Plantinga, and his followers, to describe the revival of the Protestant approach of the sixteenth-century Reformation to belief about God. Plantinga argues that it is perfectly reasonable to believe that God exists, even though there may not be sufficient evidence for this belief. This is because belief in God is a **basic belief**, and like other basic beliefs it doesn't need sufficient evidence.

REVEALED THEOLOGY   Gaining an understanding of God though the revelations of sacred texts and prophets. This is in contrast to **natural theology**, although to Aquinas the two approaches are compatible with each other.

REVELATION   Information that is revealed, or disclosed, to humans by a supernatural source, such as God or angels. The Bible is a work of revelation, and it forms the basis of **revealed theology**.

SUBJECT   In grammar, the part of a proposition that picks out the main object which is being described or discussed. For example, in 'The red balloon popped' the subject is 'The red balloon'. In the sentence 'God is the greatest conceivable being', God is the subject.

TELEOLOGICAL   Derived from the Greek word *telos* meaning purpose, goal or end. A teleological explanation is a way of accounting for events by reference to their purpose or ultimate goal. For example, you notice a green shoot emerging from an acorn. A teleological explanation will refer to the purpose of this event, or to a future state that needs to be attained: 'because it is trying to grow into a tree', or 'because it is searching for soil and water'. Such a teleological approach may be contrasted with efficient or mechanical explanations, which explain events only by making reference to physical factors leading up to the event. So the green shoot emerges because of certain changes in temperature and the production of enzymes, which lead to the growth of certain cells, which eventually shatters the acorn shell etc.

TELEOLOGICAL ARGUMENTS   Arguments which propose that God exists on the basis of certain teleological features of the universe. For example, observations concerning the ordered nature of the universe, or concerning the apparent design and purpose of the parts of living organisms. Such arguments are also known as arguments from design.

THEISM/THEIST/THEISTIC   Belief in one God, who is a person, who is generally held to be perfect, who is the creator of the universe, and who has a relationship with that universe. This is in contrast to **atheism** (the belief that there is no such God) and **agnosticism** (refusing to commit to either atheism or theism).

THEODICY   The attempt to justify God's actions, and to show why, for example, a perfect God has created an imperfect world. The most common form of theodicy are the responses to the **problem of evil** that explain why God allows such pain and suffering to exist.

THEOLOGY/THEOLOGIANS   The study of God from a religious perspective. This is in contrast to the philosophy of religion, which begins from a philosophical perspective.

VIA NEGATIVA   A Latin term meaning 'the negative way'. It refers to the claim by Maimonides, and others, that we can only come to understand God by knowing what he is not.

VERIFICATIONISM   A philosophical belief about the nature of meaning. Logical Positivism claims that for a proposition to be meaningful it must be (hypothetically) verifiable or true by definition. Other than truths by definition most propositions make a specific claim about the universe – that it is this way or that – for example that 'There is a cat on my mat' or that 'The leaves on my tree are green.' In such cases it is easy for us to imagine how such claims could be verified or not. However, take the claim that 'God loves the world.' How could we verify this claim? What could we look for in the world to see whether that claim is true or not? If it is not clear how the universe would look if that claim were true or not, then it is not clear what that claim is asserting about the universe. Thus Logical Positivists claim that religious propositions are not meaningful.

Notes

■ Chapter 1

1 Graham Greene, *The End of the Affair*, Penguin 1975, pp. 94–95.

2 Fyodor Dostoyevsky, *The Brothers Karamazov*, Bantam 1970, p. 309.

3 Ninian Smart, *Philosophers and Religious Truth*, SCM Press 1964, p. 12.

4 Blaise Pascal, *Pensées*, Penguin 1985, p. 83.

5 Francis Bacon, *Essays*, quoted in David Hume, *The Natural History of Religion*, Oxford University Press 1998, p. 154.

6 Ninian Smart, *Philosophers and Religious Truth*, SCM Press 1964, p. 19.

7 Henry Fielding, *The History of Tom Jones*, Penguin 1984, p. 129.

8 Umberto Eco's novel *The Name of The Rose* (Picador 1984) vividly captures the oppressive intellectual atmosphere of medieval scholasticism (see, e.g. pp. 337–348). For a more immediately accessible version, watch the 1986 film directed by Jean-Jacques Annaud.

9 David Hume, *Dialogues Concerning Natural Religion*, Oxford University Press 1998, p. 43.

10 Maimonides, *The Guide of the Perplexed*, trans. Shlomo Pines, University of Chicago Press 1963, p. 135.

11 For example, see F.C. Copleston, *Aquinas*, Penguin 1965, pp.131–133.

12 Reprinted in C. Taliaferro and P.J. Griffiths, eds, *The Philosophy of Religion*, Blackwell 2003, pp. 146–161.

13 St Augustine, *City of God*, Book 8, Ch. 10, trans. Henry Bettenson, Penguin 1984, pp. 312–313.

14 St Anselm, *Proslogion*, Ch. 2 in Alvin Plantinga, ed., *The Ontological Argument*, Macmillan 1968, p. 4.

15 René Descartes, Meditation 3, *Descartes – Selected Philosophical Writings*, Cambridge University Press 1993, p. 93.

16 Richard Swinburne, *The Coherence of Theism*, Clarendon Press 1977, p. 2.

17 Blaise Pascal, *Pensées*, Penguin 1985, p. 150.

18 J.L. Mackie, 'Evil and Omnipotence' in Basil Mitchell, ed., *The Philosophy of Religion*, Oxford University Press 1971, pp. 101–104.

19 Antony Flew, 'The Presumption of Atheism' reprinted in P.L. Quinn and C. Taliaferro, eds, *A Companion to Philosophy of Religion*, Blackwell 1999, pp. 410–416.

■ Chapter 2

20 Woody Allen, 'Mr Big' in *Complete Prose*, Picador 1997, p. 285.

21 First Vatican Council, 1869–1870, Chapter 2.1.

22 Immanuel Kant, *Critique of Pure Reason*, trans. Norman Kemp Smith, Macmillan 1980, p. 500.

23 In eighteenth-century France, scientists and naturalists attempted to discover whether the Beast of Gevaudan (a creature that had apparently killed 140 people) really existed. For a stylish fictionalised version of their attempts see the film *Brotherhood of the Wolf* directed by Christopher Gans (2001).

24 The philosopher J.N. Findlay argues that this definition is correct as it arises out of a genuinely religious attitude. To a believer the object of worship 'should have an *unsurpassable* supremacy along all avenues [and] tower *infinitely* above all other objects'. (J.N. Findlay 'Can God's Existence be Disproved?' in A. Flew and A. MacIntyre, eds, *New Essays on Philosophical Theology*, Macmillan 1955, p. 51) However, Findlay then goes on to disprove God's existence in order to show the absurdity of the ontological argument!

25 Alvin Plantinga would also add that God is 'worthy of worship'. An imaginary God is not worthy of worship, but the supreme being must be at the very least worthy of worship, and so must exist (Alvin Plantinga, ed., *The Ontological Argument: From St Anselm to Contemporary Philosophers*, Macmillan 1968, p. x).

26 Gaunilo's reply 'On Behalf of the Fool' is reprinted in Plantinga, *The Ontological Argument*, pp. 6–13. Other philosophers have had a lot of fun with the ontological argument. For example D. and M. Haight used it to prove the existence of the greatest conceivable evil being ('An Ontological Argument for the Devil', *The Monist*, no. 54, 1970).

27 F.C. Copleston sees Aquinas' rejection of the ontological argument as evidence of his 'empiricism' (Copleston, *Aquinas*, Penguin 1965, p. 113). Aquinas does offer five alternative proofs of God's existence (see page 48), all of them based on our experience of the effects of God's existence – namely the world we see around us.

28 *Descartes – Selected Philosophical Writings*, Meditations 5, p. 107. For a more detailed expansion and analysis of Descartes' ontological argument, read Clement Dore's article 'Ontological arguments' in Quinn and Taliaferro, *A Companion to Philosophy of Religion*, pp. 323–329.

29 Kant, *Critique of Pure Reason*, pp. 500 ff.

30 This is a position also taken by David Hume in his *Dialogues Concerning Natural Religion* (Oxford University Press 1998, p. 91). For both Hume and Kant a proposition is a NECESSARY TRUTH if, when we reject the predicate, a contradiction results. So 'Bachelors are unmarried men' is necessarily true because, when we reject the predicate, and assert that 'Bachelors are married men' then we have a contradiction. However, for Hume and Kant no statement about existence can be necessary, as it is always possible to deny something exists, without that statement being contradictory. So to say 'God does not exist' is not a contradiction, which means 'God exists' is not a necessary truth.

31 Kant calls propositions that are true by definition, and known to be true a priori, 'analytic' propositions (e.g. all bachelors are unmarried). This is in contrast to what he calls 'synthetic' propositions; these are statements that tell us something new about the world (e.g. some bachelors eat baked beans straight from the tin).

32 The Dutch theologian Johan de Kater (Caterus) made a similar criticism of Descartes' argument, and this was included in the first published edition of the Meditations as 'The First Set of Objections'. See *Descartes – Selected Philosophical Writings*, p. 136.

33 Kant, *Critique of Pure Reason*, p. 504.

34 Bertrand Russell, *Why I am Not a Christian*, Routledge 1996, p. 137.

35 Alvin Plantinga, 'A Valid Ontological Argument?' reprinted in Plantinga, *The Ontological Argument*, pp. 161–171.

36 David Hume, *Dialogues Concerning Natural Religion*, Oxford University Press 1998, p. 91.

37 The ancient Greek word for universe was 'cosmos', hence Kant labelled these types of arguments 'cosmological' (Kant, *Critique of Pure Reason*, p. 508).

38 There is some disagreement between Kant and Hume over this. Hume refers to cosmological arguments as *a priori* because they hinge on the concept of God as a necessary being (Hume, *Dialogues Concerning Natural Religion*, Part 9). However, Kant categorises them firmly as *a posteriori* because the premises depend upon our experience (Kant, *Critique of Pure Reason*, p. 508).

39 St Anselm, *Monologion* III, in *St Anselm, Basic Writings*, trans. S. D. Deane, Open Court Publishing 1994.

40 For a very clear account of the threat Aristotle posed to Christian thought and of the assimilation of Aristotelian philosophy by Aquinas into Christian theology, see Copleston, *Aquinas*, pp. 63–69.

41 Aquinas, *Summa Theologica* 1:2:3. Reprinted in J. Hick, ed., *The Existence of God*, Macmillan 1964, pp. 82–85.

42 Causal cosmological arguments were also proposed by medieval Islamic scholars such as Al-Ghāzālī (1058–1111) and are known as kalām arguments.

43 F.C. Copleston argues that this second interpretation is the one we should take when reading Aquinas (*Aquinas*, p. 122).

44 David Hume, *Dialogues Concerning Natural Religion*, pp. 63–64.

45 J.L. Mackie, *The Miracle of Theism*, extract reprinted in Taliaferro and Griffiths, *Philosophy of Religion*, p. 247.

46 James Sadowsky, 'The Cosmological Argument and the Endless Regress', reprinted in Brian Davies, ed., *Philosophy of Religion: A Guide and Anthology*, Oxford University Press 2000, pp. 239–241.

47 David Hume, *Treatise on Human Nature*, Book 1, Part iii, Section 3, Oxford University Press 1978.

48 Elizabeth Anscombe, 'Hume's Argument Exposed', reprinted in Davies, *Philosophy of Religion*, p. 237.

49 Bertrand Russell and F.C. Copleston, 'The Existence of God – a Debate' in Russell, *Why I am Not a Christian*, p. 141.

50 David Hume, *Dialogues Concerning Natural Religion*, p. 92.

51 This example is taken from Paul Edwards' article 'The Cosmological Argument' in Davies, *Philosophy of Religion*, pp. 207–208.

52 Russell and Copleston, 'The Existence of God – a Debate' in Russell, *Why I am Not a Christian*, p. 140.

53 The Islamic philosopher Avicenna (937–1037) proposed a cosmological argument that takes this form.

54 J.L. Mackie analyses these two parts very succinctly in *The Miracle of Theism*, extract reprinted in Taliaferro and Griffiths, *Philosophy of Religion*, p. 245.

55 *Ibid.*, p. 246.

56 Smart, *Philosophers and Religious Truth*, p. 96.

57 Philosophical pedants might like to note that even this most banal example of a necessary proposition has been questioned, revealing the fuzziness of the concept of 'bachelor'. See Terry Winograd's article 'Moving the Semantic Fulcrum', *Linguistics and Philosophy* 8: 1 (1985), pp. 91–104.

58 Aquinas, *Summa Theologica*, 1:2:1.

59 The VIA NEGATIVA, as it is known, enables us to understand God by realising what God is not: for example, God is not temporal, or limited, or material, or finite. See Copleston, *Aquinas*, pp. 131–133. For a modern use of the *via negativa* see I.M. Crombie, 'The Possibility of Theological Statements' in Basil Mitchell, ed., *The Philosophy of Religion*, Oxford University Press 1971, pp. 39–43.

60 Russell and Copleston, 'The Existence of God – a Debate' in *Why I am Not a Christian*, p. 140.

61 Antony Flew, *An Introduction to Western Philosophy*, Thames & Hudson 1978, p. 206.

62 Terence Penelhum describes cosmological arguments as 'Existential' arguments, and teleological arguments as 'Qualitative' arguments. See 'Divine Necessity' in Mitchell, *The Philosophy of Religion*, pp. 180–181.

63 Kant, *Critique of Pure Reason*, p. 520.

64 Jonathan Barnes analyses this, and other passages from Aristotle's *Parts of Animals*, in *Aristotle*, Oxford University Press 1982, pp. 73–77.

65 Aquinas, 'Is the World Ruled by Providence', extract in Davies, *Philosophy of Religion*, pp. 251–252. Aquinas gives other analogies in this passage, for example between the governance by God of the universe, and the governance by a ruler of a kingdom.

66 Antony Flew, *An Introduction to Western Philosophy*, p. 207.

67 William Paley, *Natural Theology*, extract reprinted in Davies, *Philosophy of Religion*, p. 257

68 *Ibid.*, p. 259.

69 David Hume, *Enquiry Concerning Human Understanding*, Section X, part 1, Oxford University Press 1982, p. 110.

70 Although Hume is usually read as an out-and-out atheist, this over-simplifies his beliefs. For a lively account of Hume's occupation of the 'borderlands between belief and unbelief' see Stewart Sutherland, *Faith and Ambiguity*, SCM Press 1984, pp. 28–41.

71 Hume, *Dialogues Concerning Natural Religion*, pp. 51–52.

72 William Paley, *Natural Theology*, in Davies, *Philosophy of Religion*, p. 254.

73 Hume, *Dialogues Concerning Natural Religion*, p. 49.

74 *Ibid.*, p. 78.

75 *Ibid.*, p. 67.

76 *Ibid.*, p. 114.

77 Robert Hambourger, 'Can Design Arguments be Defended Today?' in Davies, *Philosophy of Religion*, p. 286.

78 Hume, *Dialogues Concerning Natural Religion*, p. 129.

79 Darwin quoted in E.S. De Beer, *Charles Darwin and T. H. Huxley: Autobiographies*, Oxford University Press 1974, p. 50f.

80 Richard Swinburne, *The Existence of God*, Clarendon Press 1979, p. 135.

81 Hume, *Dialogues Concerning Natural Religion*, p. 84ff.

82 F.R. Tennant, quoted in John Hick, ed., *The Existence of God*, Macmillan 1964, p. 128.

83 Paul Davies, *God and the New Physics*, Penguin 1990, p. 179. However, it has been pointed out that the beginning of the Big Bang 'is so poorly understood that it has been aptly compared with the regions of maps of ancient cartographers marked "Here there be dragons" – it can be filled with all sorts of fantasies'. William Craig, 'Theism and Physical Cosmology' in Quinn & Taliaferro, *A Companion to Philosophy of Religion*, p. 420.

84 Paul Davies, *The Accidental Universe*, Cambridge University Press 1982, p. 95.

85 For an interesting speculative account of how intelligent primates like humans might have emerged, see Steven Pinker, 'Revenge of the Nerds', *How the Mind Works*, Penguin 1997.

86 Russell Stannard, *Grounds for Reasonable Belief*, Scottish Academic Press 1989.

87 Brandon Carter, 'Large Number Coincidences and the Anthropic Principle in Cosmology', *Confrontation of Cosmological Theories with Observational Data*, Reidel 1974, pp. 291–298.

88 Mark Twain, 'Was the World Made for Man?' in John Carey, ed., *The Faber Book of Science*, Faber & Faber 1995, p. 250.

89 Richard Swinburne, *The Existence of God*, pp. 249–252.

90 Rudolf Otto, *The Idea of the Holy*, extract in Taliaferro and Griffiths, *Philosophy of Religion*, p. 148.

91 See Keith Yandell, 'Religious Experience', in Quinn and Taliaferro, *A Companion to Philosophy of Religion*, pp. 371–372.

92 See, for example, Bertrand Russell, 'Mysticism', in *Religion and Science*, Oxford University Press 1997.

93 Luke 4:1–13.

94 Bertrand Russell, 'Mysticism'.

95 V.S. Ramachandran and Sandra Blakeslee, 'God and the Limbic System', in *Phantoms in the Brain*, Fourth Estate 1999.

96 Brian Davies, *Introduction to the Philosophy of Religion*, Oxford University Press 1993, p. 125.

97 Rudolf Otto, *The Idea of the Holy*, extract in Taliaferro and Griffiths, *Philosophy of Religion*, p. 148.

98 See Russell and Copleston, 'The Existence of God – a Debate' in *Why I am Not a Christian*, pp. 143–144.

99 A.J. Ayer, *Language, Truth & Logic*, Penguin 1980, p. 152.

100 John Hick, 'Theology and Verification' in Mitchell, *The Philosophy of Religion*, pp. 53–71.

◼ Chapter 3

101 Anthony Burgess, *Earthly Powers*, Penguin 1980, pp. 456–458.

102 George Orwell, *1984*, Penguin 1982, p. 215.

103 J.L. Mackie, 'Evil and Omnipotence' in Mitchell, *The Philosophy of Religion*, pp. 102–104.

104 St Thomas Aquinas, *Summa Contra Gentiles*, 3:101: 2–4.

105 David Hume, *Enquiry Concerning Human Understanding*, Section X, part 1, Oxford University Press 1982, p. 115.

106 Richard Swinburne, ed., *Miracles*, Macmillan 1989, p. 6.

107 Reports state that 30,000 people were killed in Lisbon during the six minutes of this earthquake in 1755. It inspired Voltaire to write a famous philosophical poem 'On the Disaster of Lisbon', and the novel *Candide*, which both questioned the claim that the world was created by a benevolent God.

108 From the musical *Jesus Christ Superstar*. Lyrics by Tim Rice, music by Andrew Lloyd Webber. The original reference can be found in Luke 23:8.

109 See, for example, Ninian Smart, *Philosophers and Religious Truth*, SCM Press 1964, p. 48.

110 For an accessible introduction to the distinction between an everlasting and an atemporal God see Peter Vardy, *The Puzzle of God*, Fount Press 1995, pp. 37–50.

111 Richard Swinburne, 'The Concept of Miracle', in Davies, *Philosophy of Religion*, p. 425.

112 David Hume, *Enquiry Concerning Human Understanding*, Section X, part 1, Oxford University Press 1982, p. 113.

113 Truman Capote, *In Cold Blood*, Penguin 2000, p. 237.

114 See, for example, John Hick, *Evil and the God of Love*, Fontana 1968, p. 18.

115 For a more detailed analysis of pain and suffering in relation to evil see Hick, *ibid.*, pp. 328–372.

116 St Augustine, *Confessions*, Book 7, Ch. 5, Oxford Paperbacks 1998.

117 Capote, *In Cold Blood*, p. 84.

118 St Augustine: 'God is good, yea most mightily better than all his works . . . Where, then, is evil, and whence does it come and how has it crept in?' in *Confessions*, Book 7, Ch. 5. Aquinas: 'If, therefore, God existed there would be no evil discoverable; but there is evil in the world. Therefore God does not exist,' in *Summa Theologica* 1:2:3; see http://www.ccel.org/ccel/aquinas/summa .html

119 Quoted in John Hick, *Evil and the God of Love*, Fontana 1968, p. 5.

120 *Ibid.*, p. 3.

121 Reprinted in Mitchell, *The Philosophy of Religion*, pp. 92–93.

122 Although Mary Baker Eddy, the Christian Scientist, did claim that evil is an illusion in *Science and Health*, Christian Science Publishing 1934, p. 480.

123 Darwin quoted in E.S. De Beer, *Charles Darwin and T. H. Huxley: Autobiographies*, Oxford University Press 1974, p. 52.

124 Hume, *Dialogues Concerning Natural Religion*, p. 105.

125 William Rowe, 'The Problem of Evil and Some Varieties of Atheism' in Taliaferro and Griffiths, *Philosophy of Religion*, pp. 368–373.

126 This term appears to have been invented by Leibniz and is drawn from the ancient Greek words for God (*theos*) and justice (*diku*).

127 Significant theological anti-realists include Don Cuppit and followers of Ludwig Wittgenstein, such as D.Z. Phillips. For a brief introduction to some of the issues around anti-realism see Roger Trigg, 'Realism and Anti-Realism' in Quinn and Taliaferro, *A Companion to the Philosophy of Religion*, pp. 213–220.

128 For a succinct account of a new process theodicy as proposed by David Griffin see John Hick, *Philosophy of Religion*, Prentice Hall 1990, pp. 48–55.

129 Job 1:12 and 2:6.

130 Quoted in Hick, *Evil and the God of Love*, p. 90.

131 *Ibid.*, p. 95.

132 Mackie, 'Evil and Omnipotence' in Mitchell, *The Philosophy of Religion*, p. 96.

133 *Ibid.*, p. 95.

134 Hick, *Evil and the God of Love*, pp. 328–329.

135 Voltaire, *Candide*, Wordsworth Classics 1996, p. 12.

136 Richard Swinburne, 'The Problem of Evil', extracts reprinted in Davies, *Philosophy of Religion*, pp. 610–611.

137 Hick, *Evil and the God of Love*, p. 370.

138 *Ibid.*, pp. 322–323.

139 *Ibid.*, p. 369.

140 Elim Klimov's film, *Come and See* (1985) offers a compelling and graphic account of these atrocities from a child's perspective.

141 Fyodor Dostoyevsky, *The Brothers Karamazov*, Bantam 1970, pp. 295–296.

142 Genesis 3:14–20.

143 Peter Vardy, *The Puzzle of Evil*, Fount Press 1992, pp. 38–39.

144 Antony Flew, 'Divine Omnipotence and Human Freedom' in Flew and MacIntyre, eds, *New Essays in Philosophical Theology*, SCM Press 1955.

145 J.L. Mackie, 'Evil and Omnipotence' in Mitchell, *The Philosophy of Religion*, pp. 100–101.

146 See, for example, Bernard Williams, *Ethics and The Limits of Philosophy*, Fontana 1985, pp. 32–33.

147 Fyodor Dostoyevsky, *The Brothers Karamazov*, Bantam 1970, p. 80.

148 Jean-Paul Sartre, *Existentialism and Humanism*, Methuen 1987, p. 33. Sartre misquotes Dostoyevsky in this passage.

149 Norman Geisler, *Christian Ethics: Options and Issues*, Apollos 1989, p. 17.

150 *Ibid.*

151 John Stott, *Issues Facing Christians Today*, Harper Collins 1990.

152 For example, see Acts 10:9–15.

153 See, for example, Geisler, *Christian Ethics*, p. 280.

154 Emil Brunner, *The Divine Imperative*, Lutterworth 1947, Ch. 9.

155 Jean-Paul Sartre, *Existentialism and Humanism*, p. 31.

156 Søren Kierkegaard, *Fear and Trembling*, trans. Alastair Hannay, Penguin 1985, pp. 83–95.

157 For example, see Book 1, Ch. 7 of Aristotle's *Ethics*, Penguin 1988, pp. 73–76.

158 See *Summa Theologica* 1:2:58.

159 David Hume, *A Treatise on Human Nature* Book 3 Part 1 Section 1, Oxford University Press 1978, final paragraph.

160 John Searle, How to Derive 'Ought' from 'Is', *Philosophical Review*, Jan 1964, 73: 43–58.

161 Jean-Paul Sartre, *Existentialism and Humanism*, p. 28.

162 John Robinson, 'Honest to God', SCM Press 1963, p. 18.

163 Joseph Fletcher, *Situation Ethics*, SCM Press 1966.

164 C. Stephen Evans, 'Moral Arguments' in Quinn and Taliaferro, *A Companion to Philosophy of Religion*, pp. 345–350. See also Hick, *Philosophy of Religion*, p. 28.

165 Extract reprinted in Hick, *The Existence of God*, p. 150.

166 Extract reprinted in Stuart Brown, *Philosophy of Religion*, Routledge 2001, pp. 143–145.

167 H.P. Owen, 'The Moral Argument for Christian Theism', extract in Davies, *Philosophy of Religion*, pp. 646–658.

168 Wallace Matson refers to these minimal conditions of the successful functioning of a social group as 'low morality', in contrast with 'high morality' which is the theoretical justification of these rules, for example by religion or moral philosophy. 'The Expiration of Morality' in E.F. Paul, F.D. Miller and J. Paul, eds, *Cultural Pluralism and Moral Knowledge*, Cambridge University Press 1994, pp. 162–165.

169 For a short introduction to the problems relativism raises for morality see Simon Blackburn, *Being Good*, Oxford University Press 2001, pp. 19–29.

170 Immanuel Kant, 'Groundwork for the Metaphysic of Morals' in H.J. Paton, *The Moral Law*, Hutchinson 1972, p. 64.

171 *Ibid.*, p. 66.

172 John Stuart Mill, *Utilitarianism*, Fontana 1985, p. 270.

173 Aristotle, *Ethics*, Penguin 1988, p. 83.

174 *Ibid.*, p84.

175 Brian Davies, *An Introduction to the Philosophy of Religion*, Oxford University Press 1993, p. 177.

176 C. Stephen Evans, 'Moral Arguments' in Quinn and Taliaferro, *A Companion to Philosophy of Religion*, p. 345.

Chapter 4

177 Steven Pinker, *How The Mind Works*, Penguin 1999, p. 550.

178 W.K. Clifford, 'The Ethics of Belief' reprinted in Taliaferro and Griffiths, *Philosophy of Religion*, p. 199.

179 David Hume, *An Enquiry Concerning Human Understanding*, Section X, part 1, p. 110.

180 Anthony Kenny, *The Five Ways*, Routledge 1969, p. 4.

181 C. Stephen Evans in Quinn and Taliaferro, *A Companion to Philosophy of Religion*, p. 345.

182 Quoted in Quinn and Taliaferro, *A Companion to Philosophy of Religion*, p. 60.

183 Alvin Plantinga, 'Religious Belief as "Properly Basic"' in Taliaferro and Griffiths, *Philosophy of Religion*, p. 201.

184 Alvin Plantinga, 'Reformed Epistemology' in Quinn and Taliaferro, *A Companion to Philosophy of Religion*, p. 384.

185 Alvin Plantinga, 'Religious Belief as "Properly Basic"', pp. 219–220.

186 Alvin Plantinga, 'Reformed Epistemology', pp. 386–388.

187 Blaise Pascal, *Pensées*, Penguin 1985, p. 151.

188 *Ibid.*, p. 152.

189 *Ibid.*, p. 154.

190 William James, *The Will to Believe and Other Essays in Popular Philosophy*, Section X, Dover Publications 1956.

191 John Hick, *Philosophy of Religion*, Prentice Hall 1990, pp. 64–65.

192 H.H. Price, 'Belief In and Belief That' in Mitchell, *The Philosophy of Religion*, pp. 143–167.

193 See, for example, Alvin Plantinga in Davies, *Philosophy of Religion*, p. 44.

194 Alvin Plantinga in Davies, *Philosophy of Religion*, p. 44.

195 H.H. Price, 'Belief In and Belief That', pp. 166.

196 Hick, *Philosophy of Religion*, Prentice Hall 1990, p. 65.

Chapter 5

197 François Rabelais, *The Histories of Gargantua and Pantagruel*, Penguin 1955, p. 231.

198 Pseudo-Dionysius, 'The Divine Names' in *The Complete Works*, trans. Colm Lubheid, SPCK 1987, pp. 49–50.

199 C.K. Ogden and I.A. Richards, *The Meaning of Meaning*, Harcourt 1989.

200 From Lewis Carroll's poem 'The Jabberwocky' in *Through the Looking Glass and What Alice Found There*, Wordsworth 1993, p. 20.

201 John Hick, *Philosophy of Religion*, Prentice Hall 1963, p. 95.

202 A.J. Ayer, *Language, Truth & Logic*, Penguin 1980, pp. 151 ff.

203 S.R. Sutherland, 'Language, Newspeak and Logic' in A. Phillips Griffiths, ed., *A. J. Ayer: Memorial Essays*, Cambridge University Press 1992, p. 78.

204 John Hick, 'Theology and Verification' in Mitchell, *The Philosophy of Religion*, pp. 59–60.

205 Job 19:25.

206 Quoted in Mitchell, *The Philosophy of Religion*, p. 16.

207 *Ibid.*, pp. 18–19.

208 Ludwig Wittgenstein, *Philosophical Investigations* No. 43, Blackwell 1981, p. 20.

209 *Ibid.*, No. 23 pp. 11–12.

210 *Ibid.*, No. 23, p. 11.

211 Ludwig Wittgenstein, *Lectures and Conversations on Aesthetics, Psychology and Religious Belief*, Blackwell 1970, p. 53.

212 R.B. Braithwaite, 'An Empiricist's View of the Nature of Religious Language' in Mitchell, *The Philosophy of Religion*, pp. 72–91.

213 *Ibid.*, p. 89.

214 I.M. Crombie, 'The Possibility of Theological Statements' in Mitchell, *The Philosophy of Religion*, pp. 23–52.

215 *Ibid.*, pp. 48–51.

216 *Ibid.*, p. 52.

217 Paul Tillich, *Dynamics of Faith*, Harper & Row 1958, p. 42.

218 *Ibid.*, p. 45.
219 J.H. Randall, *The Role of Knowledge in Western Religion*, Beacon Press 1958.
220 William Shakespeare, *Henry V*, Act 3, Scene 1.
221 J.H. Randall, *The Role of Knowledge in Western Religion*, pp. 128–129.
222 John Hick, *Philosophy of Religion*, Prentice Hall 1990, p. 87.
223 Rudolf Bultmann, 'New Testament and Mythology: The problem of demythologising the New Testament Proclamation' trans. Schubert M. Ogden, Fortress Press 1984.
224 *Ibid.*, p. 9.
225 Alvin Plantinga, 'Religious Belief as "Properly Basic" ', pp. 45–46.
226 Psalms 31:3.

227 Exodus 15:3.
228 Thomas Aquinas, 'The Words we use for God', from *Summa Theologica*, reprinted in Davies, *Philosophy of Religion*, pp. 156–167.
229 *Ibid.*, p. 164.
230 Stanislaw Lem, *Solaris*, Faber and Faber 1991, p. 172.
231 This well-known Socratic principle is articulated in several dialogues by Plato, although never in this precise form. For example, see *The Republic* 394d (Penguin 2003), *Euthyphro* 14a (in *Last Days of Socrates*, Penguin 2003) and *Sophist* 224e (Dover 2003).
232 Blaise Pascal, *Pensées*, Penguin 1985, p. 85.
233 Steven Pinker, *How The Mind Works*, Penguin 1998, p. 561.

Selected bibliography

Recommended reading

Davies, Brian, *Introduction to the Philosophy of Religion*, OUP 1993
Davies, Brian, ed., *Philosophy of Religion: A Guide and Anthology*, OUP 2000
Hick, John, *Philosophy of Religion*, Prentice Hall 1990
Hick, John, ed., *The Existence of God*, Macmillan 1964 (Anthology)
Mitchell, Basil, ed., *The Philosophy of Religion*, OUP 1971 (Anthology)
Quinn, P. L. and Taliaferro, C., eds, *A Companion to Philosophy of Religion*, Blackwell 1999 (Anthology)
Taliaferro, C. and Griffiths, P.J., eds, *The Philosophy of Religion*, Blackwell 2003 (Anthology)

Further reading for reference purposes

Baggini, Julian, *Atheism: A Very Short Introduction*, OUP 2003
Copleston, F.C., *Aquinas*, Penguin 1965
Hick, John, *Evil and the God of Love*, Fontana 1968
Hume, David, *Dialogues Concerning Natural Religion*, OUP 1998
Mackie, J.L., *The Miracle of Theism*, OUP 1982
Macquarrie and Childress, eds, *A New Dictionary of Christian Ethics*, SCM 1986
Pascal, Blaise, *Pensées*, Penguin 1985
Plantinga, Alvin, ed., *The Ontological Argument: From St Anselm to Contemporary Philosophers*, Macmillan 1968
Swinburne, Richard, *The Existence of God*, Clarendon Press 1979

Index